Smash the Church, Smash the State!

The Early Years of Gay Liberation

Edited by Tommi Avicolli Mecca

City Lights Books
San Francisco, California

Cover collage and design by John Borruso

Unless specifically noted otherwise, copyright to the individual works is held by the authors. Although every effort has been made to trace and contact copyright holders and persons portrayed in photographs included herein, in a few instances this has not been possible. If notified, the publishers will be pleased to rectify any omissions in future editions.

Page 304 constitutes an extension of this copyright page.

Library of Congress Cataloging-in-Publication Data
Smash the church, smash the state! : 40 years of gay liberation / [edited by] Tommi Avicolli Mecca.
    p. cm.
Includes bibliographical references.
ISBN 978-0-87286-497-9
1. Gay liberation movement—United States—History. I. Mecca, Tommi Avicolli.
HQ76.8.U5S63 2009
306.76'60973—dc22
                                        2008036997

Visit our Web site: www.citylights.com

City Lights Books are published at the City Lights Bookstore,
261 Columbus Avenue, San Francisco, CA 94133

Dedicated to Saj Powell, who told me before he died of AIDS that I would survive to write the history of those wonderful, outrageous early days of gay liberation. And to my best friend from those early days: Cei Bell.

Cei Bell in 1985

Saj Powell performing at the 1973 pride march at Independence Mall in Philadelphia.

© Tommi Avicolli Mecca

© Jo Hofmann

Contents

Introduction *ix*
  Tommi Avicolli Mecca

OUT OF THE BARS AND INTO THE STREETS

Militant Foreshadowings *3*
  Susan Stryker

Eighth Grade Epiphany *11*
  Kenneth Laverne Bunch

Kiyoshi Kuromiya: Integrating the Issues *17*
  Liz Highleyman

A Consciousness Raised *22*
  Hal Tarr

Coming Out and into the GLF: Banned No More in Boston *31*
  John Kyper

My Adventures as a Gay Teacher *40*
  Tom Ammiano

Pre-Now *43*
  James C. Roberts

My Memories as a Gay Militant in NYC *48*
  Néstor Latrónico

From the Closets of New Haven to the Collectives of New York GLF *55*
  Jason Serinus

Even Iowa Homos Got the Blues *62*
  Dennis Brumm

There's a Certain Kind of Woman *68*
  Mara Math

A Poem by Fran Winant *74*

TUNING IN

No Girl in My Soup   79
  Thom Nickels

Coming Out as a Reluctant Activist in a Gay Maoist Cell
who Mostly Just Wanted to Get Laid   85
  Mark Freeman

Our Passion Shook the World   93
  Martha Shelley

Sylvester: A Singer Without a Closet   97

Living Lesbian Nation   99
  Victoria Brownworth

Radical Spirit and Vision   108
  John Lauritsen

Radicalqueens Manifesto #1   113

Radicalqueens Manifesto #2   114

The Radicalqueens Trans-Formation   116
  Cei Bell

Pat Parker: A Woman of Vision   125

Sisters and Brothers: A Writer Hungering for Family
Finds GLF   127
  Perry Brass

DYKETACTICS!: Electrifying the Imaginations of
the Gay and Women's Communities   137
  Barbara Ruth

Simeon White: A Life of Seeing Connections   147

Fopping It Up: Former Cockette Rumi's Story   150
  Interview with Rumi Missabu

Gay Raiders   156
  Mark Segal

REVOLUTION AROUND EVERY CORNER

Between Bohemia and Revolution *163*
    Flavia Rando

Gay Liberation Front: Report from London *168*
    Richard Bolingbroke

Sylvia Rivera: A Woman Before Her Time *172*
    Liz Highleyman

Two Songs by Blackberri *177*

Honey, We Unshrunk the Shrinks! *182*
    Pam Mitchell

The Radicalesbian Story: An Evolution of Consciousness *190*
    Ellen Shumsky

The Woman Identified Woman Manifesto *197*

Berkeley & the Fight for an Effeminist, Socially Transformative
Gay Identity *203*
    Nick Benton

Two Poems by Dajenya *210*

The Effeminist Moment *213*
    Steven F. Dansky

DYKETACTICS!: Notes Toward an Un-Silencing *218*
    Paola Bacchetta

Two Poems by Barbara Ruth *232*

The Baltic Street Collective *234*
    N. A. Diaman

Gay Pagans and Atheists Manifesto *242*

40 YEARS AFTER STONEWALL

Looking Back from the Mexico-U.S. Border *249*
    Roberto Camp

A Letter from Huey Newton to the Revolutionary Brothers and Sisters about the Women's Liberation and Gay Liberation Movements *252*

Making History *255*
    Sidney Brinkley

Marsha P. Johnson: New York City Legend *261*

Lessons from the ENDA Mess *263*
    Doug Ireland

Happy to Be Childless *269*
    Allen Young

The Gay Community in Crisis *273*
    Don Kilhefner

Stonewall Was a Riot—Now We Need a Revolution *282*
    Merle Woo

Gay Liberation Media *295*

Glossary of Terms *299*

INTRODUCTION

Tommi Avicolli Mecca, Editor

"We are a revolutionary group of men and women formed
with the realization that complete sexual liberation for all
people can not come about unless existing social institutions
are abolished. We reject society's attempt to impose sexual
roles and definitions of our nature."
—New York Gay Liberation Front Statement of Purpose

It seemed like a sudden transformation, but it wasn't: Queers had
gone from a small movement of properly dressed "homophiles"
(men in suits, women in dresses) marching around Independence
Hall in Philadelphia every July 4 to a rowdy bunch of militant drag
queens, long-haired hippie men in jeans and T-shirts, and lesbian/
feminist women who refused to bake the bread and make the coffee, either in the gay liberation or in the women's movement.

It had been brewing for decades, at least since 1949, when
Communist Party labor organizer Harry Hay brought together a
rap group for gay men that became the Mattachine Society. A lesbian organization, Daughters of Bilitis, followed a few years later.
With McCarthyism and sexual repression the norm, the '50s were
not an easy time to gain support for anything unorthodox.

Relief was on the way. The '60s ushered in an era of sexual
freedom previously unimaginable in America. Young people rejected the conservative values of previous generations and asserted
their right to their bodies and their sexuality. Queer radicals took
a bit longer to demand their place in the revolution. In the mean-
time, they did what many other young people were doing: They
listened to rock music, grew their hair, hung out in jeans and T-
shirts, moved to farms, lived in communes, made lots of love and
turned on and dropped out.

They also risked their lives down South with the Freedom
Rides, marching alongside Dr. Martin Luther King Jr. and the thousands of others who demanded an end to segregation. Some, like

Simeon White of Kinston, North Carolina, mobilized against racism in their own hometowns. Many of them were in the crowd in Washington, D.C., when King made his historic "I have a dream" speech. In fact, a gay African American man, Bayard Rustin, helped organize that march.

They hitchhiked from all over big- and little-town America to play protest songs or read stream-of-consciousness poetry in Greenwich Village or North Beach cafés. They spoke out at Berkeley for free speech with Mario Savio and others who ushered in a new era for America's college students. They were teargassed while defending People's Park or marching on campuses against the unjust war in Vietnam.

They organized and fed poor people as part of the Black Panthers. They were members of the Young Lords (a Puerto Rican group) in Philadelphia or Chicago. They were part of the United Farm Workers movement in California. They joined the SDS (Students for a Democratic Society) to stop the war in Vietnam and prepare for the revolution that would change America. They came to San Francisco wearing flowers in their hair for the Summer of Love.

At least one of them, beat poet Allen Ginsberg, declared that he was "putting his queer shoulder to the wheel." While he was a hero to many, few were willing to follow his lead and break free of the closet.

The signs of a more militant queer spirit were always there among the most vulnerable queers, the street queens who couldn't pass as anything other than what they were. Tapping into the anger of the times, they rose up and fought back at Cooper's Donuts in Los Angeles in 1959, Dewey's Deli in Philadelphia in 1965, and Compton's Diner in San Francisco in 1966.

The fourth rebellion was the charmer: In June 1969, a routine police raid on a West Village gay bar called the Stonewall Inn sparked several days of unrest that gave birth to the modern queer movement. It was this incident that overnight would send thousands of counter cultural types, many from the civil rights, feminist and antiwar movements, racing out of their closets. It prompted Ginsberg to remark that queers had finally lost "that wounded look."

The first manifestation of post-Stonewall activism was the Gay Liberation Front (GLF). Unlike the homophile organizations of the '50s and '60s, the new group wasn't afraid to speak its name or its politics proudly. The name "Gay Liberation Front" was derived from the National Liberation Front, the Vietnamese group that fought the U.S. occupation of its country. The new movement saw itself in solidarity with all other struggles for social justice.

As Len Richmond and Gary Noguera, editors of *The Gay Liberation Book*, a pioneering anthology published by Ramparts Press in San Francisco in 1973, wrote: "Gay liberation is a radical movement that advocates a radical change in society—its social structures, power structures, its racism and sexual dogmas. We have a commitment not just to homosexual liberation but to total human liberation."

Activists with fabulous chosen names such as Blackberri, Hibiscus and Sweet Basil Razzle Dazzle marched, organized and generally made trouble. They wore outrageous outfits and paraded the street in what was then called "genderfuck," a form of dress that turned upside down society's notion of gender. A bearded man in long hair, an evening gown, makeup and army boots was a sight to be seen on the streets anywhere in America in 1969 or 1970. David Bowie and the New York Dolls, among others, stole their gimmicky looks (and made tons of money) from the "genderfuck" of those early gay liberationists.

At antiwar protests, gay men used campy new tactics to fend off cops and defuse tensions. As Kiyoshi Kuromiya relates in *City of Sisterly and Brotherly Love* (Marc Stein, Univ. of Chicago Press, 2000), "We'd go up to a line of cops with tear gas grenades and horses and clubs. And link arms and do a can-can. Really threw them off guard."

Beyond the outrageousness, gay liberation was about defining a new form of community and politics for queers, one based on tearing down all boundaries. Gay liberationists chanted as they marched in the streets: "Two, four, six, eight, smash the church, smash the state." Gay men chanted "Ho-ho-homosexual, the ruling class is ineffectual," while lesbians were yelling, "Hey, hey, ho, ho, male supremacy's got to go."

Those early trailblazers were not looking for marriage and corporate jobs or acceptance into the military or the church. They were into communal living and multipartnered sexual arrangements outside of the jurisdiction of the state and the family. They flaunted their difference. They made no apologies. Like their hippie, yippie and countercultural counterparts, they believed in sex, drugs and rock 'n roll. Not to mention truth, justice and a redistribution of wealth.

It wasn't just about meetings and demonstrations. Music, art, poetry and performance marked the new gay consciousness. For the first time ever, out queer artists packed coffeehouses and conference halls with appreciative fans.

It wasn't all a bed of roses. Sexism, transphobia and racism within the nascent movement led to split-offs by women, transgenders and people of color. Women, who suffered a dual oppression, preferred struggling with the homophobia of their straight sisters to dealing with the sexism of their gay brothers. Transgenders felt unwelcome at many gay organizations and were eventually left out of proposed gay rights legislation. Issues raised by people of color were ignored or deemed unimportant. The movement often acted as if it were a private party for white boys.

The result was a multitude of split-off groups that included Radicalesbians, Third World Gay Revolution, STAR (Street Transvestite Action Revolutionaries), Radicalqueens, and Lesbian Feminist Liberation. Eventually, the more reformist-oriented Gay Activists Alliance would take over the reins from the semi-anarchistic post-Stonewall, consensus-run organizations.

Despite its shortcomings, gay liberation succeeded in making coming out a queer rite of passage. It was a political strategy that affirmed the feminist adage that the personal is political. It was also a revolutionary act at a time when polite company didn't discuss sex, let along someone's sexual orientation.

My own coming out had all the drama of an Italian opera. How appropriate, considering I come from a working-class, immigrant, southern Italian family in South Philly. Despite a conservative Catholic upbringing, I became radicalized by the time I was 16 or 17, sneaking off to civil rights and antiwar marches.

In the fall of 1969, I started college at Temple University, mainly to avoid the draft. Within no time at all I joined the campus SDS (Students for a Democratic Society), an antiwar group. Then I discovered that the Gay Liberation Front held weekly coffee hours. It was a perfect fit. Filled with revolutionary fervor, I made the queer movement my life. Within weeks, I was secretary, then chair of the group. (Though nonhierarchal, we had to have officers to fulfill the requirements of being a student group.)

One of our key campaigns was pressuring the university to stop funding aversion therapy at a nearby psychiatric institute. A popular form of behavior modification, it involved attaching electrodes to the genitals of gay men, showing them slides of naked men and then shocking them with electricity, so that they would "lose" the impulse to be aroused by men. It didn't work, but that didn't stop the mad doctors. Our campaign eventually got the attention of a local late-night talk show. As chair, I was invited to debate an aversion therapist on the program. Of course, I agreed.

I told my mother the day before. I didn't tell anyone else. My father freaked when my uncle, a cop, called to say that I had been on TV, wearing blue eye shadow no less! It was not the way to come out to *la famiglia*. My godfather never spoke to me again. My father eventually threw me out of the house. I was lucky: My siblings and my mother became strong supporters. (My father and I made a teary-eyed peace 15 years later, just months before he died of a massive stroke.) Puccini would have had a field day.

The university eventually stopped funding aversion therapy.

At Temple GLF, we continued pushing the envelope as much as we could, running a drag queen for homecoming queen to protest the objectification of women inherent in such competitions. To mess with the minds of the campus ROTC (Reserve Officers Training Corps) recruiters, I approached their table at a student fair in genderfuck one day and asked to sign up. When they refused, several others who'd planted themselves in the room raced to my aid, yelling and causing a very public scene. Terrified, the recruiters packed up and left.

By far the most controversial thing we did was set up a "Kiss a Queer" booth on Valentine's Day 1973 outside the student bookstore. We were ahead of our time in using the word "queer." The booth drew few kisses, but such hostile reactions from students that the Temple News dubbed it the "Saint Valentine's Day Massacre." Not only were we taunted and called names, but we also had coins and rolled-up paper tossed at us. To add to the mayhem, mainstream media from near and far showed up after a group of straight jocks put up a "Kiss a Straight" table across from ours and called the press.

Conservative legislators in Harrisburg, the state capital, weren't too pleased and threatened to cut off funding to the university. I was called into the Office of Student Affairs and read the riot act. Fortunately, the school couldn't really do anything. We were a sanctioned student group. We had filled out the proper paperwork. At one point the administrator said to me, "You're not helping your cause any by doing things like this."

"What cause is that?" I asked.

"To be accepted as normal."

But we weren't trying to be "normal"!

Forty years later, I find that "being normal" is more popular than ever. The predominant cry within the LGBT community these days is no longer "smash the church, smash the state." It's inclusion (and ordination) in the churches, synagogues and other religious institutions that still oppress us. It's "marriage equality" for queer couples so that they can have the many benefits the state awards to heterosexual pairings. It's ending "Don't Ask Don't Tell," to allow LGBT soldiers to be out of the closet while killing for oil in the Middle East. It's home ownership, adoption and a lavender picket fence in gentrified neighborhoods where working-class folks used to live.

In many ways, the new millennium gay movement is the antithesis of the early '70s gay liberation. It cavorts with politicians who may be good on gay issues, but not on concerns affecting other disenfranchised communities. It is in bed with the Democratic Party establishment that gave carte blanche to George Bush to wage two illegal and immoral wars in the Middle East. It courts corporate support for its gala events, even its pride parades, which used to be protest marches and celebrations of the Stonewall Riots. Now those marches seem more of a market than a movement.

The queer movement still hasn't entirely gotten its act together about sexism, racism or the exclusion of transgenders. The recent controversy over the nixing of transgenders from coverage in the Congressional Employment Non-Discrimination Act by the Human Rights Campaign demonstrates once again that the struggle goes on as much within the community as outside of it. Racist carding policies still exist in some gay bars, as evidenced by a report from the San Francisco Human Rights Commission in 2005 alleging that a bar in the Castro discriminated against African American men.

As we mark the 40th anniversary (June 2009) of the Stonewall Riots that sparked gay liberation, let us remember the radical roots of our modern LGBT movement. Thanks to the efforts of radical queers, '70s activists passed gay rights bills, got positive images on TV and in the movies, forced the shrinks to drop homosexuality as a psychiatric disorder, halted police raids on gay bars and abolished some state sodomy laws, not to mention making "the love that dare not speak its name" a household word.

We still have a long way to go, but there's no denying the impact a generation of activists had when they took their lead from a crowd of rowdy patrons of a West Village bar and demanded an end to this country's homophobic business as usual.

Those brave souls, many of whom are contributors to this book, could never have realized what they were creating when they began meeting in church basements, on college campuses, and out in the streets. Though many have died of AIDS, this collection is a tribute to all of the early activists who blazed trails in those years just after Stonewall.

I still cling to many of the same ideals I had back then. Not only in terms of wanting an end to war and social injustice, but also in believing that the queer movement needs to concern itself with more than strictly gay rights or hate crimes legislation.

According to a study by the National Gay and Lesbian Task Force Policy Council and the National Coalition for the Homeless, 20 to 40 percent of homeless youth in this country identify as LGBT. In San Francisco, the "gay Mecca," it's 30 to 35 percent. In a city where queers are easily elected to office and the mayor defies state law to marry queer couples, 75 percent of transgenders don't have full-time employment. In that same city, touted in the late '80s as a model of caring for people with AIDS, 14 percent of people with the disease are homeless.

As long as queer people are homeless, hungry and without jobs or medical coverage, as long as LGBT workers don't receive a living wage, as long as the wealth of this country is in the hands of a few, as long as the means of production are owned by that very same monied class, we queers will

Tommi Avicolli Mecca, 1973

© Jo Hofmann

never truly have achieved what gay liberation set out to do four decades ago.

This book represents a snapshot of that moment in time when queers weren't obsessed with tying the knot or picking up a rifle to go off and fight "terrorists." Revolution was in the air. We truly believed that a united front with all oppressed peoples would help us create a better world, one built on inclusion and an equal distribution of wealth and resources.

Relive that dream within the pages of this book.

Tommi Avicolli Mecca
San Francisco, April 2009

Antiwar rally in Bryant Park, New York City, 1970.

© John Lauritsen

OUT OF THE BARS AND INTO THE STREETS

Militant Foreshadowings

Susan Stryker

Editor's Note: Even though this is a book about the gay liberation movement that grew out of the Stonewall Riots, generally considered the beginning of the militant phase of the gay movement, I thought it important to include an excerpt from Susan Stryker's Transgender History *(Seal Press, 2008) on three acts of queer rebellion that predate June 1969. They were important steps towards our mass coming out in the '70s.*

In a 2005 interview, John Rechy, author of *City of Night* and other classic mid-twentieth-century novels set in the gritty urban underworlds where sexual outlaws and gender nonconformists carved out spaces they could call their own, spoke of a previously undocumented incident in May of 1959, when transgender and gay resentment of police oppression erupted into collective resistance.

According to Rechy, it happened at Cooper's Donuts, a coffeehouse that stayed open all night on a rough stretch of Main Street in Los Angeles, which happened to be situated between two popular gay bars. An ethnically mixed crowd of drag queens and male hustlers, many of them Latino or African American, frequented Cooper's, along with the people who enjoyed their company or purchased their sexual services. Police cars regularly patrolled the vicinity and often stopped to question people in the area for no reason at all. They would demand identification—which, for transgender people whose appearance might not match the name or gender designation on their ID, often led to arrest on suspicion of prostitution, vagrancy, loitering or many other so-called "nuisance crimes."

On that night in May 1959, when the police came in and arbitrarily started rounding up the drag queen patrons of Cooper's Donuts, the rest of the customers decided to resist *en masse*. The incident started with customers throwing donuts at the cops, and ended with fighting in the streets, as squad cars and paddy wagons converged on the scene to make arrests. In the ensuing chaos, many people who had been arrested, including Rechy, escaped into the night.

The disturbance at Cooper's seems to have been a spontaneous outburst of frustration, with no lasting consequences, and it was no doubt typical of other unrecorded and previously unremembered acts of spur-of-the-moment resistance to anti-transgender and anti-gay oppression.

A similar, though nonviolent, incident took place in Philadelphia in 1965 at Dewey's, a lunch counter and late-night coffeehouse much like Cooper's, which had been popular since the 1940s with gays, lesbians, drag queens, and street prostitutes, as a place to go after the bars had closed. In April of 1965, Dewey's started refusing to serve young customers who wore what one gay newspaper of the day euphemistically described as "nonconformist clothing," claiming that "gay kids" were driving away other business.

Customers rallied together to protest, and on April 25, more than 150 patrons were turned away by the management. Three teenagers (two male and one female) refused to leave after being denied service, in what appears to be the first act of civil disobedience over anti-transgender discrimination. They, along with a gay activist who advised them of their legal rights, were arrested (and subsequently found guilty on misdemeanor charges of disorderly conduct).

Over the next week, Dewey's patrons and members of Philadelphia's homosexual community set up an informational picket line at the restaurant, where they passed out thousands of pieces of literature protesting the lunch counter's treatment of gender-variant young people. On May 2, activists staged another sit-in. The police were again called in, but this time made no arrests; the restaurant's management backed down and promised "an immediate cessation of all indiscriminate denials of service."

The Dewey's incident, like the one at Cooper's, demonstrates the overlap between gay and transgender activism in the working-class districts of major U.S. cities, in spite of tensions and prejudices within both groups. The Janus Society, Philadephia's main gay and lesbian organization at the time, issued the following statement in its newsletter following the events of May 2, 1965:

> All too often, there is a tendency to be concerned with the rights of homosexuals as long as they somehow appear to be heterosexual, whatever that is. The masculine woman

and the feminine man often are looked down upon . . .
but the Janus Society is concerned with the worth of an
individual and the manner in which she or he comports
himself. What is offensive today we have seen become
the style of tomorrow, and even if what is offensive today
remains offensive tomorrow to some persons, there is no
reason to penalize non-conformist behavior unless there
is direct anti-social behavior connected with it.

The Dewey's incident further illustrates the extent to which
the tactics of minority rights activism cross-fertilized different
movements. Lunch counter sit-ins had been developed as a form
of protest to oppose racial segregation in the South but proved
equally effective when used to promote the interests of sexual and
gender minorities.

It would be a mistake, however, to think that the African
American civil rights struggle simply "influenced" early gay and
transgender activism at Dewey's, for to do so would be to assume
that all the gay and transgender people involved were white. Many
of the queer people who patronized Dewey's were themselves people of color, and they were not "borrowing" a tactic developed by
another movement.

By the middle of the 1960s, life in the United States was being
transformed by several large-scale social movements. The post–
World War II baby boom generation was coming into young adult-
hood at the very moment the U.S. war in Vietnam was beginning
to escalate. A youth-oriented cultural rebellion began to unfold,
where countercultural styles in music and fashion—rock music,
psychedelic drugs, mod clothing, free love—offered significant
challenges to an older generation's notion of acceptable gender and
sexual expression. Long hair on men and button-fly blue jeans on
women actually made political statements about the war, the military draft and the general drift of mainstream society.

The African American civil rights movement was reaching a
crescendo, buoyed by passage in 1964 of the Voting Rights Act and
other milestone legislation, as well as by the birth of a radical new
Black Power movement. Similar ethnic pride and liberation movements were beginning to vitalize Chicano and Native American
people.

To a certain extent, the simultaneous white gay liberation and
radical feminist movements modeled themselves on these ethnic

movements, conceptualizing homosexual people and women as oppressed social minority groups. National political life, which had been thrown into turmoil following the 1963 assassination of President John F. Kennedy, reached a tragic low point with the 1968 assassinations of his brother, Robert F. Kennedy, and the Reverend Martin Luther King Jr.

The 1966 Compton's Cafeteria Riot in San Francisco's Tenderloin neighborhood was similar to earlier incidents at Cooper's and Dewey's. For the first time, however, direct action in the streets by transgender people resulted in lasting institutional change.

One weekend night in August—the precise date is unknown—Compton's, a 24-hour cafeteria, was buzzing with its usual late-night crowd of drag queens, hustlers, slummers, cruisers, runaway teens and down-and-out neighborhood regulars. The restaurant's management became annoyed by a noisy young crowd of queens at one table who seemed to be spending a lot of time without spending a lot of money, and they called in the police to roust them—as they had been doing with increasing frequency throughout the summer.

A surly police officer, accustomed to manhandling Compton's clientele with impunity, grabbed the arm of one of the queens and tried to drag her away. She unexpectedly threw her coffee in his face, however, and a melee erupted: Plates, trays, cups and silverware flew through the air at the startled police officers, who ran outside and called for backup. Compton's customers turned over the tables and smashed the plate glass windows, then poured out of the restaurant and into the streets.

The paddy wagons arrived, and street fighting broke out in Compton's vicinity. Drag queens beat the police with their heavy purses and kicked them with their high-heeled shoes. A police car was vandalized, a newspaper stand was burned to the ground and—in the words of the best available source on what happened that night, a retrospective account by gay liberation activist Reverend Raymond Broshears, published in the program of San Francisco's first Gay Pride march in 1972—"general havoc was raised in the Tenderloin."

The small restaurant had been packed when the fighting broke out, so the riot probably involved fifty or sixty patrons, plus police officers and any neighborhood residents or late-night passersby who jumped into the fray.

Several important developments for the transgender movement

took place in San Francisco in the months after the 1966 Compton's Cafeteria Riot. The Central City Anti-Poverty Program Office opened that fall as a result of the Tenderloin neighborhood organizing campaign. This multiservice agency included an office for the Police Community Relations liaison officer to the homophile community, a police sergeant by the name of Elliot Blackstone.

One afternoon shortly after the agency opened, a transgender neighborhood resident named Louise Ergestrasse came into Blackstone's office, threw a copy of Benjamin's *Transsexual Phenomenon* on his desk and demanded that Blackstone do something for "her people."

Blackstone was willing to be educated on the matter, and soon took a leading role in changing police treatment of transgender people. Another group of transgender Tenderloin activists, led by Wendy Kohler, started working with activist doctor Joel Fort at a unit of the San Francisco Public Health Department called the Center for Special Problems. A few months later, in early 1967, a group of transgender people began meeting at Glide Memorial United Methodist Church in the Tenderloin, where they formed a COG, "Conversion Our Goal," the first known transsexual peer support group in the United States.

The "Stonewall Riots" have been mythologized as the "origin of the gay liberation movement" and there is a great deal of truth in that characterization, but as we have seen, gay, transgender and gender-variant people had been engaging in violent protest and direct actions against social oppression for at least a decade by that time. Stonewall stands out as the biggest and most consequential example of a kind of event that was becoming increasingly common, rather than as a unique occurrence.

By 1969, as a result of many years of social upheaval and political agitation, large numbers of people who were socially marginalized because of their sexual orientation or gender identity, especially younger people who were part of the Baby Boom generation, were drawn to the idea of "gay revolution" and were primed for any event that would set such a movement off. The Stonewall Riots provided that very spark, and inspired the formation of Gay Liberation Front cells in big cities, progressive towns and college campuses all across the United States.

Ever since the summer of 1969, various groups of people who identify with those who participated in the rioting have argued about what actually happened, what the riot's underlying causes were, who was most affected and what the movements that point back to Stonewall as an important part of their own history have in common with one another.

Although Greenwich Village was not as economically down-and-out as San Francisco's Tenderloin, it was nevertheless a part of the city that appealed to the same sorts of people who resisted at Cooper's, Dewey's and Compton's: drag queens, hustlers, gender nonconformists of many varieties, gay men, a smattering of lesbians and countercultural types who simply "dug the scene."

The Stonewall Inn was a small, shabby, Mafia-run bar (as were many of the gay-oriented bars in New York back in the days when homosexuality and cross-dressing were crimes). It drew a racially mixed crowd and was popular mainly for its location on Christopher Street near Sheridan Square, where many gay men "cruised" for casual sex, and because it featured go-go boys, cheap beer, a good jukebox and a crowded dance floor.

Police raids were relatively frequent (usually when a bar was slow to make its payoffs to corrupt cops), and relatively routine and uneventful. Once the bribes were sorted out, the bar would reopen, often on the same night. But in the muggy, early morning hours of Saturday, June 28, 1968, events departed from the familiar script when the squad cars pulled up outside the Stonewall Inn.

A large crowd of people gathered on the street as police began arresting workers and patrons and escorting them out of the bar and into the waiting paddy wagons. Some people started throwing coins at the police officers, taunting them for taking "payola." Eyewitness accounts of what happened next differ in their particulars, but some witnesses claim a butch lesbian resisted police attempts to put her in the paddy wagon, while others noted that African American and Puerto Rican members of the crowd—many of them queens, feminine gay men, or transgender women—grew increasingly angry as they watched their "sisters" being arrested, and escalated the level of opposition to the police.

Sylvia Rivera, a transgender woman who came to play an important role in subsequent transgender political history, long maintained that she threw the beer bottle that tipped the crowd's mood from playful mockery to violent resistance, after she was jabbed by a police baton. In any case, the targeting of gender-variant people, people of color and poor people during a police action would fit the usual patterns of police hostility in such situations.

Bottles, rocks, and other heavy objects were soon being hurled at the police, who began grabbing people in the crowd and beating them in retaliation. Weekend partiers and residents in the heavily gay neighborhood quickly swelled the ranks of the crowd to more than 2,000 people, and the outnumbered police barricaded themselves inside the Stonewall Inn and called for reinforcements. Outside, rioters used an uprooted parking meter as a battering ram to try to break down the bar's door, while other members of the crowd attempted to throw a Molotov cocktail inside to drive the police back into the streets.

Tactical Patrol Force officers arrived on the scene in an attempt to contain the growing disturbance, which nevertheless continued for hours until dissipating before dawn. That night, thousands of people re-gathered at the Stonewall Inn to protest; when the police arrived to break up the assembled crowd, street-fighting even more violent that the night before ensued.

One particularly memorable sight amidst the melee was a line of drag queens, arms linked, dancing a can-can and singing campy, improvised songs that mocked the police and their inability to regain control of the situation. Minor skirmishes and protest rallies continued throughout the next several days before finally dying down.

By that time, however, untold thousands of people had been galvanized into political action.

Sources

Gay L.A.: A History of Sexual Outlaws, Power Politics and Lipstick Lesbians, Lillian Faderman and Stuart Timmons (Basic Books, 2002)
City of Sisterly and Brotherly Love: Lesbian and Gay Philadelphia, 1945–1972, Mark Stein (University of Chicago Press, 2000)
Stonewall: The Riots that Sparked the Gay Revolution, David Carter (St. Martin's Press, 2004)

"Militant Foreshadowings" from *Transgender History,* Susan Stryker (reprinted by permission of Seal Press, a member of Perseus Book Group)

Susan Stryker is Associate Professor of Gender Studies at Indiana University–Bloomington. An out queer transsexual and founding member of Transgender Nation activist group in 1992, Stryker earned a Ph.D. in United States History at UC Berkeley, held a postdoctoral research fellowship in sexuality studies at

Stanford University, and has been a visiting professor at Harvard University. She was nominated for Lambda Literary Awards for Gay by the Bay: A History of Queer Culture in the San Francisco Bay Area *and* Queer Pulp: Perverted Passions in the Golden Age of the Paperback, *and won for* Transgender Studies Reader. *Her Emmy-winning public television documentary* Screaming Queens *recounts the history of the 1966 transgender anti-police riot at San Francisco's Compton's Cafeteria. Her introductory text,* Transgender History, *was published by Seal Press in 2008.*

Eighth Grade Epiphany

Kenneth Laverne Bunch

My father was a survivor of a Nazi slave labor camp called Berga.

Dad was not Jewish, gay, Slavic or a revolutionary communist. He joined the U.S. Army in 1944 and was shipped off to Belgium in December 1944, just in time to be captured in the Battle of the Bulge (the largest land battle in the history of the U.S. Army).

Dad and 200 other U.S. soldiers were imprisoned in the worst German POW camp (Stalag 9) north of Frankfurt, Germany. The SS came to his lieutenant and demanded to know who the Jewish servicemen were. They had all thrown away their crosses and Stars of David. Having refused the inquiry, the SS chose those they thought "looked Jewish" and sent them to a slave labor camp at Berga, Germany.

In those days, prior to the naming of Post Traumatic Stress Disorder (PTSD) by the U.S. government, soldiers were simply tossed back into society without therapy. My father's PTSD manifested itself by his beating me every day of my life before I turned 18 years old and escaped to college.

My father was an "Archie Bunker," exhibiting the anti-Semitic, racist, homophobic and sexist upbringing that was common in pre-1960s Iowa. I remember sitting down in our living room to watch *All In The Family* one night. Dad entered the room and sat across from me. I thought, "This is going to be interesting, seeing how he reacts to Archie." Archie would say something bigoted and Dad would answer, "That's right!" Then the audience would laugh at Archie, implying the foolishness of the statement. After 10 minutes Dad realized the audience was not only laughing with Archie, but also at him. "Change that channel!" he shouted.

Everything was shouted in our house. One of my least favorite shouts was: "Is Queenie finished in the bathroom?"

"Queenie" was his nickname for me. I was an unconsciously effeminate boy. Junior High School in Des Moines, Iowa, was torture. "Girl" became my moniker among my classmates. It was said with all the venom of "nigger" and "queer." I hadn't a clue what

11

attracted such vitriol, until one day a fellow student, in a moment of compassion, told me, "Boys don't hold their books like that. Only girls hold them like that." I had been carrying my books across my chest instead of under my arm at my side. This inaugurated years of attempts to self-masculinize my behavior. Still, I had no friends until college.

It was in an eighth grade social studies class in that Mennonite school that I had a life-changing epiphany. Mennonites are a socially conservative branch of Anabaptists. In the 1960s though, radical, socially liberal teachers were emerging from Mennonite colleges to teach in Mennonite high schools across the U.S.

One day Mr. Brenneman asked our class a simple question: "Do you think the United States of America will last forever?" A wave of shock swept through our classroom. Intellectual light bulbs were popping. We hadn't ever considered this proposition. From that moment onward I began questioning assumptions that I, others and society held.

In 1970 I headed for a Mennonite college in Hesston, Kansas. The Free Speech Movement, anti–Vietnam War struggle, women's liberation, and assorted radical movements made their way into Mennonite universities and colleges in the late 1960s. Professors denounced the violence of war and emphasized Mennonite pacifism with antiwar vigils and demonstrations. Two friends and I realized the college needed an underground student-run newspaper, free to discuss issues that administrators might deem too "controversial." It was decided that I would write the cover article.

Our newspaper was called *The Fifth Column* and the cover article I wrote was titled, "Homosexuality: A State Of Being." The piece was so shocking that it left even the most radical professor speechless. College administrators promptly suggested that I should leave. And so I did.

In 1972 I moved to the liberal oasis of Iowa City, Iowa, home to the University of Iowa, to investigate its Gay Liberation Front. It took me calling and hanging up three times to summon enough courage to speak my name to the GLF contact on the other end of the phone.

At that time, gay life in Iowa centered around a handful of bars. In Iowa City there was a straight bar that turned "sort-of gay" after 10 p.m. on the weekends. Cruising the library or Greyhound depot was all that many gay men could tolerate.

GLF sponsored dances at the local Unitarian Universalist

Church once a month that were attended mostly by men. I remember standing at the first few dances, glued to the corner wall, frightened and intimidated by the level of freedom and abandon I saw. Disco was just coming into vogue, expressing a new sense of sexual freedom. Women had already separated into a lesbian feminist separatist community and wouldn't speak with gay men. In 1970 the local queer community was comprised of countercultural straight men and women, lesbians and gay men, all exploring their identities and experimenting with novel relationships.

Sondra Smith, a straight woman, had two twin girls. Lesbians came to Sondra and said, "OK, if you are serious about raising nonpatriarchial, nonsexist, nonhomophobic children, you will let your two daughters live with us." They promptly shaved the girls' heads and tried to indoctrinate them with "butch" behavior. Sondra agreed to an unofficial joint custody. After a short time, she realized the foolishness and the experiment ended.

On one occasion, I was in an elevator with one of those women, who was then a professor at the University of Iowa. She was extremely secretive about conversing with me. Ostracism by the rest of her community would be the penalty if she were discovered. This highly educated woman looked me straight in the face and said, "We are all planning to move to San Francisco, change our names, take up guns and start the socialist revolution." Then, in 1975, Patty Hearst happened and made a farce of the whole scenario.

While growing up, I had always looked forward to Halloween, the opportunity to don a wig and a dress without problems. In the early 1970s, there emerged a form of drag called "scag drag" or "genderfuck" in which an obvious man could wear a dress, usually to make a political statement. I knew instinctively that this would be my method of wreaking revenge for so many years of being harassed for being effeminate. From 1973 to 1976 I would race home from work and strut my stuff down the streets of Iowa City, purple polka dot housecoat and shoulder-length hair flowing in the wind. Psychological train wrecks greeted me at every turn. What a combination! Revenge and social change.

At the same time, I joined forces with a friend, Fred Brungard, and we planned and produced three Midwest Gay Pride conferences with the financial support of the university. The conferences attracted hundreds of people from the region and consisted of films, discussion panels, celebrity speakers, theater and workshops over one weekend. The Midwest premiere of John Waters's *Pink Flamingos* attracted a thousand attendees, mostly straight, to the university's "Film Night." The violent reaction of the straight males in the audience to the scenes of cross-dressing convinced me I was on the right track in using genderfuck to confront prejudices and assumptions.

For the 1975 conference I decided we needed an eloquent keynote speaker who could address the issue of gender identity. Searching through a catalogue of national gay organizations I found a listing for the Radical Queens in Philadelphia. Their fierce activist Tommi Avicolli Mecca spoke to a spellbound audience that year.

Subsequently, I traveled on a Greyhound bus to Philly to visit Tommi and met a plethora of stunning transgender activists. In those days, I felt I needed to live a life that confronted social prejudices 100 percent of the time, so I traveled in drag. I took risks to my physical person that today astound me. Boys would be waiting to attack me in shop doorways. How I escaped serious physical injury is beyond my comprehension.

Following the 1976 conference I decided we were continually speaking to the converted and needed to reach the 99.9 percent of Iowans who thought they had never met a gay person. I asked Tracy Bjorgum to join me in applying for a marriage license. We were assisted by the American Civil Liberties Union (ACLU) in Des Moines. Our slogan became "a fag in every living room." I was sure this action would be broadcast statewide by the media and promote the gay visibility we sought. Sure enough, it did. On Wednesday, March 9, 1976, we appeared on page 3A of the *Des Moines Register*. This is also how I "came out" to my parents.

In 1974 I moved into a three-story Victorian on Iowa Avenue in Iowa City with Pat Tranmer, Don Engstrom, Rick Graf and Dick Phillips. A wave of "back-to-the-land" movements was sweeping through parts of fledgling gay communities nationwide. The movement became known as the "Radical Faeries." The first issues of *RFD* (the radical faerie magazine) were conceived and produced in our attic, with articles on gardening, home construction and mysticism. Each issue contained hand-stuffed packets of pansy seeds and were sent out to addresses across America.

Eventually, four of us rented a farm outside of Iowa City and put an *RFD* lifestyle into practice, growing our own vegetables and sponsoring naked volleyball games with a diversity of friends. All the while we maintained our city jobs. We lived there for two years.

In 1975, the gay male community was split into activists and apolitical party boys. Sensing we needed more than once-a-month dances to socialize, I found a local African American bar that was suffering financially. Speaking to the owner, I convinced her to play more disco and started encouraging gay friends to patronize the Boulevard Room every weekend. Hundreds of patrons soon turned the business profitable.

Needing more of a theatrical outlet for my energies, I gathered four other theatrically minded friends together and formed The Sugar Plum Fairies, a traveling drag troupe. We performed in bars across the state. Tracy Bjorgum, Susan Short, Mike Salinas (who later would become editor of the *Bay Area Reporter*) and a man living as a transvestite hair stylist, Lisa, comprised the troupe.

Sitting down to plan one of our performances, Susan said, "I know these nuns in Cedar Rapids, and when a nun dies they save her habit. The Mother Superior is a friend of mine and if I tell her we're doing *The Sound of Music* she might loan us some habits." As soon as we hit the stage in habits and pom-poms, dancing to the music of the University of Iowa's fight song, the audience would jump to their feet screaming. These habits would soon make history.

Pat Tranmer planned a trip to San Francisco in January 1977. I asked to go along. Everyone said, "You're not coming back. You ARE San Francisco!" I thought they were insane. I hadn't been west of Colorado. But they were right: I returned to the farm six months later to collect my clothes. While discarding all my drag into the dumpster (I was getting out of drag and wearing more butch "Castro clone" attire) I came across those nun's habits. History can change in one moment and with one decision. I decided to keep the habits as insurance. Someday I might be bored with all this new butchness.

During my first week in San Francisco, Harvey Milk marched 5,000 (mostly white men) through the city protesting Anita Bryant's attempts to repeal a gay rights ordinance in Miami, Florida. Thousands of gay refugees were arriving in the city every week from all parts of the nation. I saw this mass exodus in Iowa City: Suddenly, as though a psychic clarion call had been broadcast, gays were leaving, three-quarters to go to San Francisco and one-quarter to New York City.

In San Francisco, an explosion of political, artistic and sexual freedom energy engulfed the Castro district. With the assassination of Milk in 1978 and the light sentence that his killer Dan White received, the community exploded with anger. Ten police cars were burned (one of which I set afire).

That same May, the day before Easter (Holy Saturday) I realized I was over the conformist attitudes and attire in the city. I told Fred Brungard, my roommate at 272 Dolores Street: "I'm bored, and the only thing different I have are these nun's habits. Let's put them on and go out and have some fun." The shock and awe in liberal unconventional San Francisco when we appeared on the streets surprised us. It was apparent that we had tapped into some powerful unresolved issues in this society revolving around gender, sexuality and religion, and the habits were our stick of dynamite. Gathering together 15 of our friends, The Sisters Of Perpetual Indulgence was born. The group was dedicated to "the promulgation of universal joy and the expiation of stigmatic guilt." The Sisters have since expanded to include numerous orders on all continents, in many countries and across the United States. Our commitment is to social service, social activism, artistic expression and spiritual renewal.

My epiphany in my eighth grade social studies class in 1967 has evolved in ways I never could have imagined. For that, I am eternally grateful.

Kenneth Laverne Bunch, a contemporary and comrade of Harvey Milk, was active in GLF prior to moving to San Francisco and was a founder of The Sisters of Perpetual Indulgence, a troupe of gay male nuns that now has chapters all over the world.

Kiyoshi Kuromiya: Integrating the Issues

Liz Highleyman

Kiyoshi Kuromiya was among the few pre-Stonewall homophile activists who made the transition to the gay liberation movement. One of the first openly gay Asian activists, he participated in the civil rights, antiwar, free speech and AIDS movements. An account of Kuromiya's life reads like a history of social justice struggles in the latter half of the 20th century.

A child of second-generation immigrants, Kuromiya was born May 9, 1943, at the Heart Mountain Relocation Center in Wyoming, a World War II internment camp for people of Japanese descent. After the war, his family returned to the Los Angeles area. Raised by conservative Christian parents, Kuromiya (who at the time went by the name Steve) later said he knew he was "different in about 20 ways from the other children." Nevertheless, he was regarded as a brilliant student and was chosen as class president.

In the early 1960s, Kuromiya went to study architecture at the University of Pennsylvania in Philadelphia, the city that would become his lifelong home. While a student, he wrote a popular restaurant guidebook that brought him considerable income and financial freedom.

Though Kuromiya had same-sex attractions from an early age—he later recalled that he spent time in a juvenile detention facility at age 11 after he was caught having sex with a 16-year-old boy in a public park—the gay movement did not provide his entry into activism.

As an undergraduate, Kuromiya joined Students for a Democratic Society and worked with the Congress of Racial Equality, leading sit-ins at a segregated restaurant in Maryland. After hearing Martin Luther King Jr.'s "I Have a Dream" speech at the 1963 March on Washington and meeting King soon thereafter, Kuromiya joined the wave of young activists who went to the South to do civil rights organizing. With so much of his time devoted to activism, he never completed a degree.

Even after he was beaten unconscious by deputy sheriffs at

Kiyoshi Kuromiya in 1991

a 1965 voter registration demonstration in Montgomery, Alabama, Kuromiya persevered and went on to march with King in Selma.

In the mid-1960s, Kuromiya also got involved with the nascent gay rights movement. He took part in one of the first-ever gay demonstrations on July 4, 1965, at Philadelphia's Independence Hall, politely marching with men in suits and women in dresses to protest discrimination against homosexuals in federal government employment and the military.

Kuromiya—then in his early 20s—was among the youngest homophile activists, and he grew increasingly radical, reflecting the changing tenor of the times. It wasn't long before he was criticizing subsequent "annual reminder" protests seeking gay and lesbian admittance into the establishment.

"The white middle-class outlook of the earlier [homophile] groups, which thought that everything in America would be fine if people only treated homosexuals better, wasn't what we were all about," he later recalled. "On the contrary, we thought, 'Screw that attitude.' We wanted to stand with the poor, with women, with people of color, with the antiwar people, to bring the whole corrupt thing down."

Consistent with that commitment, Kuromiya participated in many of the well-known movements of the era. On one occasion, he distributed an announcement that a dog would be napalmed on the Penn campus; when 2,000 people gathered to protest, he said he wished they were equally concerned about the people of

Vietnam. He took part in the protests outside the 1968 Democratic National Convention in Chicago and was charged with obscenity for distributing a poster he designed proclaiming "Fuck the Draft."

In 1970, a year after the Stonewall Riots, Kuromiya cofounded the Philadelphia chapter of the Gay Liberation Front, which met at a gay collective store on South Street called Gazoo. "Homosexuals have burst their chains and abandoned their closets," Kuromiya wrote in the local newspaper *Free Press*. "We came battle-scarred and angry to topple your sexist, racist, hateful society. We came to challenge the incredible hypocrisy of your serial monogamy, your oppressive sexual role-playing, your nuclear family, your Protestant ethic, apple pie and Mother."

The same year, as an openly gay delegate, he attended the Black Panthers' Revolutionary People's Constitutional Convention at Temple University, which endorsed the gay liberation struggle. Solidarity notwithstanding, he criticized homophobic slurs by some Panther members and associates including journalist Mumia Abu-Jamal. "We're no longer going to sit back when the Black Panthers call the pigs and rednecks 'faggots and cocksuckers,'" he stated in the *Free Press*.

In 1972, Kuromiya attended the first Rainbow Family Gathering in Granby, Colorado. A few years later, he was diagnosed with cancer and underwent surgery to remove part of one lung. When he recovered, he volunteered to work with renowned architect and philosopher Buckminster Fuller. For several years, Kuromiya traveled with Fuller (until the latter's death in 1983) and coauthored some of his books, including *Critical Path*, which proposed that mankind could control its destiny through technology. Kuromiya also found time to become a gourmet cook, a master of Kundalini yoga and a nationally ranked Scrabble player.

In the 1980s, Kuromiya turned his attention to AIDS activism, well before his own HIV diagnosis in 1989 (which he attributed to having made the circuit of bathhouses in Los Angeles, San Francisco, and New York years earlier). He cofounded some of Philadelphia's key AIDS organizations, including We the People Living with AIDS, the Critical Path AIDS Project, and ACT UP/Philadelphia—one of the few chapters still active 20 years later.

Viewing health care as "the new civil rights battleground," Kuromiya advocated tirelessly for grassroots education and empowerment, with an emphasis on disenfranchised communities in the United States and in developing countries. "His dedication

20

brought him to every major speech at every AIDS conference, hoping for another morsel of knowledge that might help someone in need," HIV treatment writer Lark Lands recalled.

Kuromiya ran a "community medicine chest" providing free drugs, started a medical marijuana buyers' club called Transcendental Medication (he was later lead plaintiff in a class-action lawsuit challenging the federal government's prohibition of medical cannabis) and sat on a National Institutes of Health panel on alternative therapy. But no matter how many panels he served on, said Julie Davids, one of the many young activists he mentored, "Kiyoshi still believed in the power of people in the streets." Indeed, he continued his civil disobedience up until the year before his death, protesting U.S. trade and patent policies that limit access to medications in low- and middle-income countries.

Kuromiya was among the first activists to grasp the power of the Internet as a tool for education and organizing. Under the auspices of Critical Path, he started one of the earliest HIV treatment Web sites and offered free Internet access to people with AIDS, as well as personally answering hundreds of emails and hotline phone calls from individuals seeking information and support.

In 1996, arguing that his Web site provided life-saving safer sex information, Kuromiya was among the co-plaintiffs in an American Civil Liberties Union lawsuit against the Communications Decency Act, a Congressional attempt to restrict sexually explicit content on the Internet that was ultimately struck down as unconstitutional by the Supreme Court.

Shortly before he died of complications from AIDS and cancer in May 2000, Kuromiya told a friend that he had principles he believed in all his life, and that he had never deviated from them. He called himself a "comprehensivist," Fuller's term for young people who had not yet become specialists in a particular field and retained their ability to look at the big picture. Over four decades, Kuromiya's life and work exemplified the interconnections between the GLBT movement and other liberation struggles.

References
The People of This Generation: The Rise and Fall of the New Left in Philadelphia,
Paul Lyons (University of Pennsylvania Press, 2003)
City of Sisterly and Brotherly Loves: Lesbian and Gay Philadelphia, 1945-1972.
Marc Stein (University of Chicago Press, 2000)

"Slicing Silence: Asian Progressives Come Out," in *Asian Americans: The Movement and the Moment*, Daniel Tsang (UCLA Asian American Studies Center Press, 2001)

Liz Highleyman is a freelance journalist who has written widely on LGBT issues, sexual politics, civil liberties, and progressive activism. From 2002 through 2008, she authored Q Syndicate's queer history column Past Out. As a medical writer, she focuses on HIV and hepatitis. A San Francisco resident since 1994, Liz lives with her partner and two beagles.

A Consciousness Raised

Hal Tarr

Upon being asked to write for this book, I took a look at some articles I wrote during the time I participated in the Gay Liberation Front (GLF). I must have been nuts to have written for my college newspaper that gay liberation meant that all men could love each other and that heterosexual relationships were sort of passé. But the atmosphere of the times, with the presence of Black Power, women's liberation, hippies, the peace movement, the drug culture and radical student actions, made anything seem possible.

I got involved with gay liberation because I attended a GLF course in consciousness-raising at the Free University, a collection of free courses offered by various individuals and groups at the University of Pennsylvania in Philadelphia. The classes were held in university buildings, even though the courses were not sponsored by the university. Such was the spirit of those times.

The course offered me my first connection with young gay men. Prior to this, I had gone to meetings and activities of the Homophile Action League (HAL), a somewhat older gay organization. All the others who attended were women and older than me. In fact, the other members decided they needed to discuss whether I, as a person under 21, could attend their meetings. I felt more akin in spirit to those GLF men, whose politics matched the leftist orientation of my campus, than I did to HAL, which was not born in the hippie atmosphere then so prevalent at American colleges.

Consciousness-raising groups were the heart of GLF. The impetus was to create a new gay identity that would stem from gay men's experiences and not from the negative attitudes towards homosexuality that were held by all the main institutions of society. This was a departure from the approach of HAL, which would react to the negative attitudes of those institutions but not attempt to foster a new identity. GLF's approach was similar to that of the other liberation movements of the times, which started with the premise that the personal was political and that individuals must be changed in order for the institutions to change.

22

"On Our Own," an article on consciousness-raising (CR) by a New York consciousness-raising group, defined its mission: "Everywhere we find hostility, prejudice, condescension, even amongst ourselves. Most gays accept the straight man's mythology that says we are sick, immature, perverse, deviant, and thus should hide our love away in tea-rooms, park bushes, on cruising streets, and in Mafia or otherwise pig-controlled bars. . . . These institutions keep us isolated and distrustful of each other. We are learning (through CR) what has been forbidden to us—to relate to one another with respect and love. We as gays must redefine ourselves . . . from our own heads and experience. Thus we use CR . . . to evolve a politics out of our experience."

As for the process: The "format of the session consists of each person's testimony on a given topic. . . . After everyone has given testimony, the group compares the evidence of their experiences." The list of suggested topics included "sex roles, cruising and bars, masturbation, monogamy, what kind of men we're attracted to, class background, religious training."

"We found that our problems are not individual illnesses, but are generated by our oppression as a class. This discovery negated one of the most effective weapons of our oppressors, the false division between the personal and political."

The basic ideas of CR were consistent with existentialism, the prevalent philosophy of the time, although we in Philadelphia GLF never referred to it by name. Existentialists argued that obtaining certain knowledge was an impossible ideal and that people must decide right and wrong for themselves without objective standards. Similarly, the philosophy of the consciousness-raising group emphasized the importance of one's own experience rather than the legal, psychological or religious standards of the time.

We eventually decided to hold our CR group meetings in the large apartment of one of our members who came from a well-to-do family. The most influential member of our group and of Philadelphia GLF was Basil O'Brien. Sometimes calling himself Basil Razzle-Dazzle or Basil Collamore, he had long blond hair and dressed at times in androgynous clothes. He had dropped out of Goddard College, a school known for its experimental approach. He related to us that pansexuality (experimentation with all kinds of sexuality) prevailed at the school. Basil had been greatly influenced by the writings of Edward Carpenter, a British philosopher and gay activist of the late 19th and early 20th centuries.

The other influential man in GLF was Kiyoshi Kuromiya, who was about 30, somewhat older than most of the rest of us. He had been involved in all sorts of left-wing organizations since attending the University of Pennsylvania. Later, Kiyoshi would become assistant to Buckminster Fuller, the engineer and visionary. He also became known for his AIDS activism and as a major player in a number of cases that were decided in the U.S. Supreme Court. His having being born during World War II in an American concentration camp for Japanese Americans may have accounted for his mischievous, fuck-the-establishment style.

Kiyoshi offered a Free University course on tripping (using psychedelic drugs such as LSD or mescaline). I enrolled in that course. During the first class, my trip went bad. I was afraid to go down a stairway, and I became separated from the others. When my behavior became erratic, I was arrested and spent the night in jail. After I was released the next day, I bumped into Kiyoshi on the street. I still hadn't come down from my trip. Kiyoshi invited me to come with him to a recently opened high-rise dormitory at the University of Pennsylvania to visit a gay magician. The man had hair down to his waist and wore a cloak and perhaps a pointy hat—not the sort of person I expected to find in that modern center of student life. Kiyoshi left me with him. I believe I allowed the magician to give me an injection. In any case, the magician was able to bring me down from my trip.

My first big adventure with Philadelphia GLF was my participation in the Revolutionary People's Constitutional Convention (RPCC) in Washington, D.C., over Thanksgiving weekend, 1970. The RPCC had been more or less organized by the Black Panther Party, a black power organization recognized by many as the leading revolutionary organization of the time. GLF people were very pleased to have obtained recognition from the Black Panthers and to have been invited to participate in planning the revolution.

There was a sense within GLF that the kind of culture we wanted required so much change that it could only be realized through revolution. Although it's impossible to know how most GLFers perceived the revolution, I'd guess that they saw it as a hippie, cultural affair rather than a violent, political uprising.

I started the weekend by visiting my parents for Thanksgiving. At dinner, I told them I was gay and that I'd be going to D.C. the next day for the RPCC. My parents were bewildered. My mother thought I was just saying I was gay to aggravate her. She asked me, if I was gay why wouldn't I be quiet about it? My father was more or less silent. When I got to the convention, I found GLF people at our home for the weekend, the modern chapel of American University. Sleeping bags were laid out on the floor.

Tall Victor of Chicago commanded the most attention as he paraded serenely around the chapel with his towering Afro, stately striped robes and shorter retinue. Brightly colored, hand-crocheted berets (like the kind the Panthers wore) were the popular fashion accessory that weekend among the GLF crowd. We must have had quite a few meetings, although I don't remember any specific one. There were some GLF newspapers and GLF pamphlets. One of the ones I read, and which impressed me the most, declared that it was demeaning to give blow jobs to straight men.

One night, we went over to zap the Zephyr, a bar where, earlier in the day, a GLF man wearing lipstick and some of his friends had been refused service. About 40 of us entered the bar. Some of us sat; others milled around. When the manager recognized the gay men he had thrown out earlier, he shouted that everyone should get out. At first, there was some confusion as to whom he was addressing. Then some of the bar employees and straight male patrons attacked two black gay men and a Puerto Rican gay man. Gays fought back. The fighting escalated and moved into the street. Police arrived, and also the media. The police seemed frightened of the media and released four gay men they had arrested. But when the media was gone, police caught up with a van of gay men who had left the scene. These men were arrested and charged with assault, illegal entry and destruction of property. They became the D.C. 12. Some of the men, particularly the black and Puerto Rican ones, were detained until the trial on December 23, when all were released. Some of the gay men involved were proud to have been part of perhaps the first action in which gay men from different parts of the country joined together in this way.

On the last day of the convention, we attended the big rally organized by the Black Panthers. We all looked forward to hearing Huey Newton's speech. Newton was considered to be the Black Panther leader most welcoming to GLF. There were even rumors that he was bisexual. I don't remember Newton's speech. I had little contact that weekend with the Black Panthers. Some GLFers complained about being largely ignored by the Panthers.

A few months later, Philly GLFers decided to attend a radical peace conference in Ann Arbor, Michigan. Kiyoshi felt that the peace movement should acknowledge the connection between gay identity and peace. In midwinter, about 10 of us piled into a Volkswagen minibus and headed off. Soon after we started out, the van tumbled over on the icy road. Thank goodness no one was hurt. We righted the van and proceeded. We took along some copies of the *Gay Dealer*, the Philadelphia GLF newspaper, of which Basil was very proud. He had worked with the *Plain Dealer*, a Philadelphia leftist newspaper, and convinced the others involved to put out an entirely gay issue called the *Gay Dealer*.

The paper covered rather well a variety of issues including the bars, the police, psychiatrists, transvestites, consciousness-raising, sex roles, how to crochet a beret, Radicalesbians and minority (then called Third World) gay men. Unfortunately, no more issues of the *Gay Dealer* or *Plain Dealer* were published.

GLF held dances that were well attended, especially by African Americans. GLFers were sometimes asked to speak at forums and classes as representatives of the new homosexuals. I participated on a panel in a graduate sociology class and one in the university's Christian Association. HAL representatives also participated. With Basil's encouragement, I went to two classes in drag one day. There wasn't much of a reaction on campus.

One night, we GLF men decided to go to a straight bar to dance. Kiyoshi, who was known in Philadelphia bars and restaurants for his *1968 Collegiate Guide to Greater Philadelphia* (under the name Steve Kuromiya), was able to get us a table, in spite of our somewhat scruffy appearance and the fact that most of us were under 21. When we started dancing together, no one bothered us. I sensed that the straight people thought it was hip to have gay men dancing among them. On another occasion, we decided to go to the Philadelphia Flower Show, a very big event in the city, although none of us had much money. We told the security guard at the entrance that we all were pansies and part of the show. He was so flustered that he allowed us to enter without paying. The things we did followed no particular plan. But we believed that all of our actions were helping to create a new culture and that we personified the new gay men.

I wrote two letters to the college newspaper about gay liberation. They were probably the paper's first positive pieces on homosexuality. Both were published as op-eds. Upon the publication of the first one, the leading leftist professor at the university eagerly offered to speak with me. Before this, I was unable to make an appointment with him.

So much seemed to be changing in men's and women's roles that it was not clear how far it might go. Sexuality was changing, too. More men were coming out. Who knew how many more might still come out? In GLF, we were suspicious about male athletes, especially football players. We had heard stories about physical closeness in locker rooms which involved patting each other's asses. There were also rumors regarding Joe Namath, the star playboy football player of the time. So I got the bright idea to explore the possible gay connection with athletics firsthand by visiting Penn's biggest football fraternity.

One morning, I walked up to the frat house door and rang the doorbell. I was greeted by a few of the brothers. I told them that I was representing the Gay Liberation Front. I said that I had heard some stories about football players and wanted to invite fraternity members to come out and join us. They were instantly amused and ushered me through the large first-floor rooms paneled with dark woods and decorated with sturdy, dull-burgundy-colored furniture. They asked me some questions about sex, but I told them I really wanted to speak to all of the brothers together. They discouraged me from doing that. They said they knew of certain brothers who might be interested. They invited me back to the house to play cards.

I returned for a friendly card game and was introduced to some of the others. The one I was most encouraged to speak to turned out to be the captain of one of the most prominent university athletic teams. He was entertained by my project. He was quite friendly, but noncommittal. He gave me his phone number. It was unfortunate that I never used it. I felt there was too wide a gulf between his world and mine. I never returned to the frat after that. But some of the brothers and I continued to greet each other when we passed on campus.

A while after my visits to the frat house, I learned about a cruisy men's room, which was located off the beaten track so that no one would go there except to cruise. I decided to see what it was like. Whom did I see in there? None other than the team captain from the frat.

Many years later, a prominent gay elected official and Penn alumnus from my graduating class came to speak to the gay group at Penn. He said that he had been a member of the same frat I visited. He told the audience how isolated he felt as a gay man. Sadly, when he attended Penn, he did not know some of the things some of his frat brothers and I knew about some of the other members of his frat.

I myself was a member of a fraternity, although not one known for jocks. I was very fond of one of the other members. We were good friends during our sophomore year, 1969–1970. Seven of us started out our junior year living together in an off-campus house. But after I went to class in drag, wrote op-eds about gay liberation and told this frat brother that I loved him, the pressure between us built up until one evening we had a physical fight. After that, it was decided that it would be best for all concerned if I moved out.

Socialism was supported by GLF and appeared in the platform of the Third World Gay Revolution, a racial minority caucus. Philadelphia's GLF was very mixed racially. GLF groups in other places may have been less so. Some GLFers eventually became disenchanted with socialism when it was discovered that Communist Cuba had been placing gay men in concentration camps.

GLF's closest relative in the social change movement was not the Black Panthers but rather women's liberation, from which GLF borrowed consciousness-raising and the questioning of gender roles. GLF challenged the idea that behavior traditionally associated with males was superior. It favored androgyny. To seem more androgynous, I began to use my full name, Halley, rather than my nickname, Hal.

The women's liberation movement and GLF extolled egalitarian relationships rather than those in which one party was dominant. GLF favored respectful relationships between gay men and opposed what it saw as the meat-market environments of the gay bars, park bushes and tearooms (men's bathrooms). The traditional family was seen as preserving a dominant/submissive relationship, with the husband/father being dominant and the wife/mother submissive. We saw this as a microcosm of the dominant/submissive relationship structure of the capitalist system. Furthermore, the traditional family made no place for the gay person. Thus it was derided. The commune, a part of hippie culture, was seen as the alternative to the family. In a commune, it was thought, people would treat each other as equals and there would be no room for dominant/submissive relationship patterns to develop.

For a while, my roommate Frank and I had a sort of commune

in our studio apartment in Center City Philadelphia. When I first met him, Kiyoshi was living with another man, who was sort of his lover. But things didn't work out well, and in late 1971, Kiyoshi had nowhere to live. My roommate suggested that Kiyoshi stay in our apartment and sleep on a mat on the carpeted floor in the little changing room between our main room and our bathroom. So Kiyoshi lived with us for the next five months.

While Kiyoshi was living in our apartment, we decided to start a gay coffee hour at the University of Pennsylvania. The coffee hour was a big hit, attracting large crowds every week, although most of those who attended were not Penn students. For a while, I tried to remedy this by putting up flyers in the men's dormitories. But the flyers never stayed up for very long. I remember one time seeing a flyer defaced with remarks referring to GLF men as non-fucking faggots. I always wondered what the sex life of this author was like and how it compared with my own.

The relationship between Philadelphia GLF and HAL was strained. GLF people saw HAL members as having an outdated outlook and not being part of the revolution. One HAL member apparently criticized GLF people for merely sitting around and contemplating our navels. Perhaps she was referring to CR groups.

There was also a huge gap between GLF men and the much larger number of guys who socialized in gay bars. GLF did little to attract new men into the organization. It had no clearly identified program of action. Then, too, political ideology did not necessarily match real feelings. For instance, although GLF touted androgyny, it was not unusual for GLFers to be attracted to masculine men.

GLF was created with the idea that the country would experience a revolution of some sort. As that did not seem to be taking place, the framework of GLF seemed more and more separated from reality.

Thus were born new, less radical organizations that could better relate to the larger number of gay men who spent time in bars and were not ashamed of it. Those organizations expended less of their political energy on ideological arguments and had more defined programs. However, the attitude of the new Gay Activists Alliance was different from that of HAL. GLF had challenged the foundations of the old institutions, as had the other liberation movements, so that GAA could take on the institutions from a greater position of strength.

Now on July 4, as I sit comfortably among fellow members

of Frontrunners Philadelphia, a gay running group, at the home of two of our members, I reflect on the conversations between us tonight and on our many Saturday runs and the brunches that follow them. I think that although our relatively thin but otherwise average appearance may make us look different from my GLF comrades and myself years ago, the egalitarian, respectful qualities of our give-and-take and the self-assurance of our personalities represent what we GLFers had in mind for gay men in 1970 when the opportunity for this type of contact and this sort of personality among gay men was less common.

Hal Tarr works and lives in Center City Philadelphia and travels around almost exclusively by bicycle. After being raised in the New York City area, he's lived most of his life in Philadelphia except for the two years he lived in Australia, another year and a half in Manhattan, and a half year in Israel. He enjoys working on the outdoors events committee of Philadelphia's LGBT community center. In 1998, as part of his job working at the central branch of Philadelphia's public library, he was asked to create the first permanent gay/lesbian collection in the system. The honored guest at a benefit for the collection was the most notable former member of the then-defunct Homophile Action League, Barbara Gittings, who had also been very active in the American Library Association. A second but larger gay/lesbian collection was later created in her name at one of the branch libraries.

Coming Out and into the GLF: Banned No More in Boston

John Kyper

I came out at the very end of 1969. I had learned about the Stonewall revolt several months after the patrons of that famous Greenwich Village gay bar resisted a police raid and fought back against New York's Finest from a *Newsweek* article with the sneering title "Police and the Third Sex."

A year of freshman ROTC at the University of Vermont had turned me against the unending war in Vietnam and impelled me into political activism. Two years later, in mid-1969, I dropped out of college and moved to Boston because I was sick to death of the isolation of Vermont, especially after spending my childhood in the small towns and cities of northern New England with a Calvinistic family dominated by a cruel minister father notably unsympathetic to my inchoate sexual yearnings.

I became a conscientious objector, deciding to fight it out with my friendly local draft board because (in part) I didn't yet have the nerve to "check the box" and tell the powers that be that I was homosexual. That was soon to change: Conscientious objection was leading me, inexorably, to gay liberation, and I would come out a mere two weeks after starting a two-year alternative service at a local hospital. By my refusal to "measure up" as a man and become a trained killer for the state, I had come to the realization that my manhood was dispensable. To assume an unnatural machismo would be self-destructive of all that I most valued.

I can never forget the December night that I first walked into Sporter's Café at the foot of Beacon Hill. I was high with this first exposure to gay energy, and I kept going back to Sporter's nearly every night for a month. But I quickly tired of the bar games: standing around for hours in a cramped, smoky room, staring at other men, trying in my shyness to start a conversation with a stranger without feeling like an utter fool. I sensed there had to be a better way. Several early gay liberation articles, syndicated by the underground press and reprinted in Cambridge's monthly *Broadside/Free Press*, had helped me find the courage to completely come out. Now I looked around anxiously to see what gay political activism might exist in Boston, but there was nothing immediately in sight.

In January 1970 I answered an ad in the weekly *Boston After Dark* seeking people interested in starting a Student Homophile League. I was frightened the first time I walked into an SHL organizational meeting with 10 other people, in a remote conference room at Boston University's George Sherman Student Union. I quickly discovered I had nothing to fear; an exciting chapter of my life was opening before me, and there was no turning back. SHL was soon holding socials at BU every week, providing (or trying to provide) a relaxed and open alternative to the dark, secretive places where gays had been accustomed to meeting.

Perhaps appropriately for this Puritan/Catholic city long notorious for banning books (and just as we were getting under way, for trying to shut down the rock musical *Hair* when it came to the Wilbur Theater), Boston had had little history of gay militancy, unlike New York or San Francisco. Attempts to form a local Mattachine Society in the 1950s had floundered because of the abrasive personality of Prescott Townsend, its eccentric Yankee Brahmin founder. At the time there were only two other gay organizations, the Homophile Union of Boston (HUB) and the Daughters of Bilitis (DOB), each predating SHL by less than a year. In the beginning these three groups were dedicated principally to providing services and social functions in a city where little but the bars and cruising areas had existed before.

Political activism was an afterthought to most of the people involved in these early efforts, consisting solely of an appearance before the legislature's Judiciary Committee to argue for reform of the state's draconian sex laws. Codified in Chapter 272 as "Crimes Against Chastity, Morality, Decency and Good Order," they are still on the books today, even though Massachusetts courts would make them a dead letter many years before the U.S. Supreme Court's 2003 *Lawrence* decision would eventually do the same to the laws against gay sex in every state that still had them. No one bothered to oppose us, and we were scarcely noticed, save for a passing mention in the back pages of the Boston *Globe* that identified us only as a collection of anonymous "homophile organizations."

For many in SHL, these modest actions were not enough. In March, half a dozen of us started the Boston Gay Liberation Front, not as a splinter of the slightly older organization but instead as a political extension of it. We desired to emulate all of the enviable things that New York's GLF was doing, and the negative reactions of more conservative gays only fueled our enthusiasm. One HUB member I spoke with seemed convinced that we had been sent to infiltrate the gay community, apparently by the Communists. Taking our name after the National Liberation Front of Vietnam—the Viet Cong—only heightened the notion. GLF-NY had evolved out of the Yippies, and the counterculture energy was contagious when I visited New York in early April. Nine months later, Stonewall was still a fresh memory, a common reference point that the people I met spoke of with excitement. The group was doing all sorts of things that we in Boston could only dream about: demonstrating in the streets, publishing a tabloid newspaper (*ComeOut!*), and planning a community center, among them. While I was there I attended a GLF dance held at Alternate U, a countercultural school near Union Square. It was exhilarating!

Our first action was to have a contingent in the April 15, 1970, moratorium on Boston Common protesting the ever widening war in Indochina. Our signs—"Bring the Boys Home/Gay Liberation Front"—scandalized traditional pacifists and leftists, and even some gays. I continued to hear about it for several years afterwards. Even though a splinter of the larger rally ended up marching off to Harvard Square where people rioted and smashed shop windows, it could not dampen my enthusiasm for what we had just pulled off.

Next we decided to hold a dance. I had never witnessed same-sex dancing in Boston outside of the murky confines of The Other Side, a bar on the edge of Park Square in Bay Village. At the end of April, GLF pulled off our first openly gay dance, in an abandoned Harvard lecture hall that had been taken over by a group of street people calling themselves "Free U," shortly before it was demolished to make way for the University's new Science Center. We held another dance Memorial Day weekend at the Charles Street Meetinghouse, much to the outrage of some prominent Beacon Hill residents, allegedly including a closeted couple living next door.

Although dancing between members of the same sex was said to be illegal in Boston, the police did not bother us. During both dances, however, the band insisted upon playing "Under My Thumb," a Rolling Stones male supremacy diatribe, infuriating the women and presaging the later fracturing of GLF over the summer.

A second Meetinghouse dance three weeks later was cancelled after an emissary from Mayor Kevin White visited the minister to convey his displeasure.

Our plans for a Gay Pride dance were similarly frustrated. The local Homophile Coordinating Committee proclaimed June 28th, the first anniversary of Stonewall, "Gay Liberation Weekend." Desiring a dance as the highlight of our activities, we contacted all of the area colleges and churches that we thought might be sympathetic. Nothing. Some of the excuses were truly grotesque: The University of Massachusetts, then located in Park Square, the center of local gay nightlife, deemed us "inappropriate" for its neighborhood. The administration at the Massachusetts Institute of Technology (MIT) referred our request to a staff psychiatrist, who opined that its innocent students would be too threatened by our dance to continue functioning! The student association was so insulted by this illogic that it donated $600 to GLF.

Several alternatives for the dance were discussed at GLF. People talked with varying degrees of seriousness of seizing a building at UMass, or liberating a park. We had to discourage a couple of militants who simply wanted a confrontation with the police. Los Angeles's GLF had recently held a successful "gay-in" when hundreds of people defied police harassment in Griffith Park by showing up on a sunny weekend day to kiss and hold hands in public. Bereft of other options, we finally decided to put on a similar performance at the weekly Sunday afternoon rock concert on Cambridge Common next to Harvard Square.

Boston Gay Pride 1970 was very disappointing. After it was over, I wondered if we all should have gone instead to New York's first gay march, held the same weekend. That seemed to be where the action was, as precious little was happening in Boston! We held a series of seminars, "Dialogue with a Straight World," Saturday afternoons in the basement of St. John the Evangelist Episcopal Church on Beacon Hill, attracting maybe 30 people, all but two openly gay. It didn't feel like much of a dialogue. The next day a dozen of us held our "gay-in" in Cambridge, gathering around a banner and passing out balloons emblazoned "Gay Is Love." We held hands, danced and waved to the tourists in the passing Gray Line buses, who stared at us as if they thought the whole scene on the Common was a zoo. "Nothing like this in Sioux City!" we joked.

A week later HUB sponsored an attempted July 4th march through Provincetown that was stymied by the town's refusal to grant a permit. It ended in a peaceful standoff between demonstrators and police. The town subsequently reconsidered (perhaps after a court challenge) and granted a permit for a Labor Day march down Commercial Street to the Town Field. A couple hundred of us attended, including a sizable contingent from New York's Gay Activists Alliance.

The rest of the summer was anticlimactic, save for finding space at last for a dance in August, at BU. SHL was floundering, moving around to different area campuses as it struggled to attract new people and keep from losing those it already had, while GLF was slowly drifting apart. As we all worked out of SHL, GLF was never able to achieve a separate identity and remained in the shadow of the other groups. We held desultory meetings at MIT throughout the summer, hampered by heavy turnover. In September I returned from a week's vacation to discover the group no longer existed; the women had walked out, charging that the meetings were male dominated. What was left reconstituted itself as Gay Male Liberation (GML).

Relating to the community and to the larger society proved a difficult task. Here the women may have been more successful than the men. Through the fall and winter GML was preoccupied with its own problems and was scarcely able to relate to anyone outside itself. Its attempts at self-definition and consciousness-raising became an obsession, and disagreement was discouraged by the more-radical-than-thou guilt games that had come to characterize much of the contemporary New Left. Many of us who had been connected with GLF drifted away because we could no longer identify with the group. What power there was had shifted from the "college people" to the "street people," now headed by a domineering male going under the nom de guerre "Rebel"—who soon decided that he was a "radical femme" and renamed himself Rebelle.

Disillusionment began to set in for others in the group when several members returning from the Revolutionary People's Constitutional Convention, held in Philadelphia at the end of 1970, reported homophobic treatment from some of the Black Panther Party vanguard. But the establishment and collapse of a community center at the turn of the year was the "great leap forward" that nearly destroyed GML. With the gift from MIT, the group rented a large house on Prospect Street in Cambridge, near Central Square. The center was meant as a social and political focus for gay males, a place where individuals could interact freely.

The community center collective seemed cursed from the beginning. One of its members, a mysterious individual who called himself "Wade," absconded after being trusted with several hundred dollars—a stunt he then allegedly repeated with several other GLFs around the country. It was a disheartening echo of the commonplace oppression by blackmailers and other rip-off artists. Laxity with its finances was typical of the collective (only two of its members were employed), and it quickly amassed a deficit of $800.

But money only symbolized the deeper problems of living together. The prevalence of animosity among its members prevented the community center from contributing to its community (which had given it some support, but not enough) and proved that gays, no matter how liberated they thought they were, had yet to learn how to trust one another.

The center's motives were noble, to be sure, but the members of GML could not overcome the ghetto mentality that encourages homosexuals to despise themselves and each other. That the community center broke up in February, only a couple of months after it had been formed, should have been no surprise. Certainly GML was not alone. The problem of trust was manifest throughout Boston's early gay movement. Relations between the organizations were usually tenuous, and misunderstandings were commonplace. At times the militants and their more conventional counterparts in HUB and DOB were barely speaking. Women were often angered by male dominance of common projects and refused to cooperate when they felt their wishes ignored. Thus planning for a Gay Solidarity Day in April 1971 disintegrated when it became obvious there was precious little solidarity to celebrate—punctuated by a few men muttering about "those goddamn bitches" at a planning meeting the women had boycotted.

At first, prospects for a second annual Gay Pride hardly seemed any more promising. But our early efforts had begun to pay off. Not only were the different groups finally able to cooperate, but many more people were now willing to participate in a public program. Our visibility had grown immeasurably following an impromptu GML picket in February outside Ken's Restaurant, a popular after-hours gathering spot in Copley Square, after the management had ejected two men for kissing. Then the *Globe* discovered the movement, publishing a photo of the picket to illustrate its story.

Gay Pride Week 1971 was a celebration of what we had accomplished, and an attempt to reach more people. We sponsored a successful week of seminars, culminating in a sidewalk march of more than 200 people through downtown to four institutions deemed symbolic of our oppression: Jacques bar in Bay Village, the Boston Police Department headquarters on Berkeley Street, the State House, and St. Paul's Cathedral.

While we were rallying on Boston Common across from the State House, those ubiquitous Gray Line buses again appeared. Elaine Noble, who would make national news several years later when she was elected to the legislature, was addressing us at the moment and had us turn our signs around to face the passing tourists. We then headed to the Parkman Bandstand for a poetry reading, a symbolic "book dumping" of antigay works and a "closet-smashing" ceremony. That night we held our first Meetinghouse dance since we had been stopped the year before. This time we were not bothered by the mayor or by the police.

Not all the omens of this first Gay Pride Week were pleasant, however. With our modest success we discovered we could be ripe territory for exploitation by all sorts of newfound "friends." The Trotskyist Socialist Workers Party (SWP), which until recently had expelled gays from its membership—"homosexuality is a bourgeois disease that does not exist under socialism" was the official line—suddenly discovered us as a promising new source of recruits. The party hierarchy seemed consistently incapable of viewing new movements in any other way, as many feminists had already discovered.

Our misgivings were quickly confirmed when SWP presented its own "Forum on Gay Liberation" without the planning committee's prior knowledge. It was scheduled to conflict with a regular SHL meeting. The first any of us learned of the event was from handbills that suddenly appeared on light poles around Beacon Hill and implied it was a part of the week's activities. Its promised representatives of the local gay movement, however, turned out to be a party member who had attended one SHL meeting and a political candidate imported from New York. Evidently we couldn't be trusted to present ideas on gay liberation to the party's satisfaction. By the time SWP members represented themselves to the media as spokespeople for our organizations, we had had enough. A Gay Pride Week symposium at Old West Church turned into an ugly confrontation after SWP tried to place its pamphlets on the table with our literature. The same scene, we soon learned, was playing out in other cities, including New York and San Francisco.

Even heavier was the realization that a somewhat eccentric associate might be a police agent. He wasn't, it turned out, but that brief burst of paranoia was unnerving. Recently purloined FBI documents had spoken of creating the sense "that there is an FBI agent in every mailbox." One GML member had spent a short term in jail after refusing to testify before a grand jury "fishing expedition" against the Mayday Collective, which had just tried to shut down Washington with a massive antiwar protest. Repression was becoming an omnipresent reality.

After a year and a half, I was rapidly burning out. Gay liberation in Boston felt like it was coming to a standstill. More seemed to be happening in smaller places like Rochester, N.Y., or Minneapolis. Closer to home, the Kalos Society of Hartford was publishing a monthly newsletter, *The Gryphon*. I despaired that we would ever get together a monthly gay paper in Boston.

Aside from literary endeavors like the *HUB Quarterly*, DOB's journal *Focus* and GML's newly formed *Fag Rag* (which would publish sporadically for nearly two decades), Boston had seen only a short-lived SHL weekly that lasted 10 issues and never outgrew the mimeograph machine. I had wearied, too, of the factionalism I was witnessing in SHL and HUB, and I quietly dropped out of both organizations. When a GLF-founded study group finally disbanded that fall, I realized that I no longer belonged to any gay groups. A stage of my life had ended.

Unlike some others, however, I was not embittered. Instead, I was grateful for the valuable lessons I had learned through gay liberation. Political revolt was the therapy that had changed my life for the better. If the gay movement was ever to amount to anything in Boston, I realized, other people would pick up the ball.

I was right. Within two years I would be more deeply involved in gay activism than I had ever been before, with the first efforts to pass antidiscrimination legislation in Massachusetts, bird-dogging of the local and national media for antigay bias, and the founding of the weekly *Gay Community News*.

It turned out I had never left gay liberation at all.

John Kyper moved to Boston in June 1969 after dropping out of the University of Vermont to become a conscientious objector during the Vietnam draft—and soon jumped feet-first into the city's early gay movement. For many years he wrote for Boston's pioneering weekly Gay Community News, *also from San Francisco and Mexico City. His 1974 deportation from Canada as "a member of the prohibited class of persons described in Paragraph 5(e) of the Immigration Act in that you admit that you are a homosexual and your admission to Canada has not been authorized by the Governor-in-Council" helped lead to the reform of that country's antigay immigration laws. In the mid-1970s he was a member of the Fort Hill Faggots for Freedom collective in the Roxbury, Massachusetts, neighborhood where he still lives. Now he works variously as a municipal bureaucrat, naturist, public transit advocate and Sierra Club activist.*

My Adventures as a Gay Teacher

Tom Ammiano

The Gay Liberation movement was transformational for me. The gift of self-affirmation around my sexual orientation was significant and life-changing.

In 1963, I left the confines of a decidedly not gay-friendly North Jersey for San Francisco. New York was too close, too familiar, Los Angeles too spread-out, Berkeley too intellectual. I had read about some kind of bathhouse for men in San Francisco. For a 40-dollar Greyhound ticket, why the hell not? Grad school at SF State was oppressive, but provided eye candy. SF was damp and more parochial than I expected. Where was that damn bathhouse? Why was I still closeted? How come men I thought were gay were so threatened and not friendly?

Even with those disappointments, it was still San Francisco. People were talking about a little neighborhood called the Castro. I was one of those who was not out, but everybody knew, or suspected, or pitied, or wanted to maim and kill me. Thank God for hormones and the need for physicality. They gave me the courage to step into my first gay bar, the Missouri Mule. I was so nervous I didn't trust myself to order a drink, but I felt a camaraderie there and an edginess I was craving. I knew I would be back.

Politically, San Francisco was a city of civil rights marches, the women's movement, antiwar die-ins, and a percolating, self-empowering gay movement. My involvement started with a mimeographed flyer on a telephone pole. "Tired of being discriminated against? Tired of not being able to speak out about who you really are?" and most riveting of all, "Tired of the bars overcharging, and being racist and sexist in their admission policies? Come to this meeting!" All of it resonated with me.

I had been teaching for seven or eight years. I heard the same stale, homophobic notions and remarks from teachers and parents, not to mention administrators. I applied for a vice principalship in the '70s wearing an earring. You can guess the outcome. I went to the meeting. It resulted in an organization called BAGL (Bay Area

Gay Liberation), a name suggested by Jim Gordon, a nudist. It only
lasted for one year—too many sectarians ruin the stew—but what
a year it was! We took to the streets. We picketed. It was exhilarating and effective.

I decided to come out as a gay teacher, which at the time
would have meant losing my job immediately. Teachers were being fired all over the state for being gay or being suspected of being
gay. Credentials were being revoked at the state level. There were
many witch hunts, and the unions were not being helpful.

I called my African American lefty friend, the late Yvonne
Scarlet Golden, and asked, "How do you call a press conference?"
She told me the basics, and we were off to the races. The press turnout was tremendous, considering the release was mimeographed
and a bit smeared. While most of the questions were snide, there
was an unmistakable current of legitimacy. Our beef was that the
school district refused to print announcements of a gay teachers'
meeting, and that there was no protection of the rights of gay
teachers. The School District's antidiscrimination policy did not include sexual orientation.

While the coverage generated the usual hate mail, there
was also an outpouring of support. Jim Wood of the *San Francisco
Examiner*, God bless him, wrote a sympathetic front-page banner
headline story complete with photo! Through the efforts of many
teacher friends, both straight and gay, we organized a protest outside the school district before the meeting of the Board of Education. It was quite daring and captured the imagination of more
than a hundred people, straight and gay. Queer Blue Litter, an
early video group, captured it. The reel is still around.

The Board postponed the vote on including sexual orientation
in the nondiscrimination policy and allowing notices of gay teachers' meetings to be included in the district's newsletter.

We went into high gear a week later. A couple hundred people
packed the boardroom on June 17, 1975. With tensions rising, the
board dicked around, then took the vote for gay rights, and voted
7-0, unanimous in our favor. They were rather stiff and flummoxed
bureaucrats, and Lord have mercy, we were so damn happy. The
place naturally exploded. It wasn't only the women's mascara that
ran. Queens of every type were hugging.

Of course, the hard part, the implementing of programs, was
yet to come. We would be sabotaged along the way by closeted
gay teachers, who were afraid and mean. One of them tipped off

a reporter from a tabloid that I would be speaking to a high school class. The reporter snuck in the class. Later, there was a large headline claiming that Tom Ammiano, perverted teacher, shows students gay positions. Now we have the Fox network for that.

Soon after that, Harvey Milk began his historic run. The times were ripe for the gay movement to have a leader, a real spokesman for the people. After a few fumbles, this tall, charismatic, former New Yorker attracted attention and respect. The story of his brutal murder was depicted in the Academy Award–winning documentary *The Times of Harvey Milk* and in Gus Van Sant's movie *Milk*. They are important vehicles for preserving our history.

Inspired by Harvey Milk, I went on to run successfully for School Board, Board of Supervisors and now the State Assembly. My early activism shaped my political career and I have always been grateful.

Tom Ammiano was involved with Bay Area Gay Liberation and the fight for recognition for gay teachers in the SF Unified School District in the '70s. He is a former president of the San Francisco School Board, and served for 14 years on the San Francisco Board of Supervisors. He is now a California State Assemblymember representing the state's 13th district.

Pre-Now

James C. Roberts

Looking back over the years—more than 40 of them—I do not see a world that is so remote that it feels like Jurassic Park. Instead, I see an era that was a culmination of what came before and that presaged what was to come. That includes both the triumphs and the tragedies, the comings of age and the transitions to alternate universes, and the coming of what the ancient Mayans and present-day seers tell us will be either an apocalypse or a new, perhaps Atlantean, golden age.

The late 1960s was a time of enormous upheaval and change. JFK, Malcolm X, Martin Luther King Jr. and Robert Kennedy had been removed from the scene through the decade. The Civil Rights Movement was morphing into the Black Power movement. Even the Supremes were abandoning their Audrey Hepburn-esque wigs for Afros. Women were beginning to find a sociopolitical voice that would lead to a continuing ascendance in the corporate and legislative arenas. The Vietnam War—which led directly or indirectly to the murders of the four aforementioned icons—was at its height.

Who knew that a similar folly would be inaugurated in the Middle East in the early 21st century just as Vietnam is becoming an Asian tourist attraction? Will we see five-star tour packages to Baghdad 30 years from now?

Amidst the ashes of the Eisenhower faux Pax Romana, and the backlash against what the so-called "Silent Majority" saw as an increasingly hedonistic America, gay liberation began to emerge. It does not need detailing in this limited space. That same sexuality has existed in all eras and on all continents with varying degrees of tolerance and/or celebration. But back in the days before Will met Grace, the very topic was still anathema.

For example, you could not be gay and work for the FBI. That is quite ironic when you consider that a director reputed to be a drag queen with a live-in male lover ran it. Same-sexuality was still considered to be a psychological disorder in the United States. Of course this was also a time when mixed-race marriages were still illegal in a large number of states. In the late 1960s even my home state of Pennsylvania was a little more than a decade away from allowing its sodomy law to expire. That was a law that could have consigned *homosexualists* (a term that Gore Vidal coined) to prisons where they could have more access to gay sex than they could outside of prison.

As a young college student I viewed this Richard Nixonian world from the perspective of someone who grew up in a predominantly African American working-class neighborhood called North Philadelphia. In fact, at that time it was at least 95 percent African American. As of this writing, however, the area is undergoing extensive gentrification. The children of the people who once would not think of even driving through our area are now buying and rehabbing the late-19th- and early-20th-century row homes. These are homes that were originally built for middle-class and upper-middle-class White people who abandoned them en masse for the near, then far, suburbs.

Growing up in North Philadelphia in the 1950s and 1960s, I had a very limited impression of what it meant to be gay or lesbian. One archetype was the "Sissy," a man who seemingly embraced or exaggerated the feminine side of his persona; and the other was the "Bulldagger," a woman with a fondness for flannel shirts, corduroy slacks and (possibly) cigars.

In a male-dominated society many saw it as less threatening to acknowledge a woman who openly embraced traits thought to be masculine than a man thought to be converting himself into a woman. Today, many who conform to these archetypes might be placed under the umbrella term transgender. But that term was not in common use 40 years ago—if at all.

Of course, there was a great deal of same sex lovemaking, just as there is today. It was common knowledge in the neighborhood which boys "messed around," even if they did not consider themselves to be gay or bisexual. Due to the overwhelmingly fundamentalist religious beliefs of our parents and grandparents—most of whom were just a generation, or less, from their roots in the South— it was viewed as a phase to be outgrown. Many repressed their urges to be same-gender-loving by becoming hyper-heterosexual. Some married or engaged in serial heterosexual relationships while still having gay or lesbian relationships on the sly. The Down Low may be a fairly new term, but it is an old activity.

As I came of age, so to speak, I began to realize that there was a black gay community—or rather black gay communities. There were numerous black gay bars like the Ritz (one of Johnny Mathis's hangouts when he came to Philly), Sk's and Mommies that existed literally in the shadow of City Hall. There were black gay cruising places.

There were black gay rent parties. If you knew enough people it seems that there was a different one every weekend. For a few dollars you could get a fried chicken or fish platter complete with greens, macaroni and cheese, corn bread and beer. It was soul food on the cheap that also served to pay somebody's apartment rent. There was sometimes reefer smoking. Dancing was not discouraged. The one thing you were not likely to find was White people.

About this same time I began attending Temple University. Temple is also located in North Philadelphia, only a few blocks from where I grew up. I was even born in Temple University Hospital. Our family had moved to the Germantown section of Philadelphia from North Philadelphia during the summer between my high school graduation and the start of my Temple freshman year.

After a couple of relatively uneventful years at Temple I made two important decisions. The first was to change my major from Political Science to Communications. My original intent was to become a lawyer. The dramatic courtroom oratory I saw in such television shows as *The Defenders* and *Perry Mason* had swayed me. That changed, however, after I saw a Temple Theatre Department production of Rodgers and Hart's *The Boys from Syracuse*. I was immediately hooked. I soon realized that if it was drama I craved, where better to find it than in the theater? Thus began a performing arts career on stage, on radio and in front of television and movie cameras that is currently in its fourth decade.

That same year I saw a sign in the Temple Student Activities Center. SAC is what we used to call it. The sign announced the weekly meetings of the recently formed Gay Liberation Front's Temple chapter. I knew then that I would attend the very next meeting. I did. That is where I met Tommi Avicolli Mecca. I was far less nervous about going to that meeting than I was about going into a gay bar for the first time. The first such establishment that I ever went into was a modest little place on Atlantic City's New York Avenue called Val's. I do not remember how many times I walked up and down that block before I got up the nerve to take my underage self in there. But walk in I did, and bought my first bottle of beer, which I clasped tightly in my hands until it was time to drive home in my used, $400 1963 Plymouth Fury.

I was not the least surprised when I went to my first Gay Liberation Front meeting and discovered that there was no one there I knew. Practically all of the other attendees were male and White. Of the 20 or so people there, a few were female or African American. None were both.

It was mostly a social affair that featured light refreshments, casual conversation and some harmless flirting. As the weeks and months passed, the tone of the consciousness-raising sessions—as they were called then—grew more serious and more personal. These young people talked about the coming-out process and the repercussions that it had on their families, their friends and themselves. Since there was no local African American gay community organized around political issues at the time, this was all new to me. Also, coming from a political science curriculum—and growing up in the Civil Rights era—this was fascinating.

Then I came upon a group called the Gay Activist Alliance.

That was a group that met in Center City, downtown Philadelphia. The group's members were older than those in the Temple group. The vibe was not nearly as lighthearted or as optimistic. The one meeting I remember most vividly was one in which there was a discussion led by a White lesbian. After the agenda had been attended to, there was an open discussion period.

I kept my hand raised for quite some time before I was called upon to speak. I spoke about some of the negative experiences I had in some of Philadelphia's gay establishments. Specifically, I spoke about not being able to gain entrance into bars even after producing proper identification proving I was legally of age. Some establishments, I told them, would not even accept a valid driver's license as proof of age. I then mentioned that while I was being denied entrance, White men who appeared to be younger than me were allowed in without having to show *any* identification.

The woman in charge abruptly told me that was not an issue about which the group was concerned. She then turned the floor over to a middle-aged man who complained that no one to whom he was attracted should have the right to turn him down once he made the offer of sex. This prompted a discussion that seemed to go on forever.

That night ended my participation in gay rights activism for the next seven years.

James C. Roberts is a lifelong resident of Philadelphia. His history with gay liberation dates to the beginning of the 1970s. He has been an HIV/AIDS activist since the mid-1980s. He currently resides in the West Mount Airy section of Philadelphia with J. Edward Murray, his partner of two decades, and Smokey, their chocolate Labrador retriever.

My Memories as a Gay Militant in NYC

Néstor Latrónico

A Brief Introduction

I arrived in New York City in 1968 from Argentina as an English student, full of enthusiasm for everything that was happening there at that time. I was a gay man in my early 20s, carrying in my brain and body a huge amount of ignorance about the city. New York fascinated and horrified me. After a few years, the horror was gone, but the fascination stayed. The horror had to do with the poor neighborhoods, the ghettoes, the violence. I didn't have enough money to rent an apartment in a nice part of town, so my first apartment was in the East Village, in the Lower East Side, 11th Street and Avenue C.

For those who knew that area in the late '60s, you may know what I mean: That street used to be called Saigon. Great experience! I was happy there for a few months, in spite of the squalor and danger. I realized it was dangerous but, for some reason, nothing and nobody ever hurt me. I think I looked at things and people with pure eyes, with some sort of innocence. I remember I even had a glimpse once of Allen Ginsberg, whom I admired immensely (I had read his *Kaddish* and *Howl*) and who lived in the area.

Recognizing the Territory: A World of Images

It was there that I had my first gay experience. Imagine: summer, rain and heat . . . Out of nowhere came, crossing the street to where I was, a beautiful Puerto Rican boy. Our eyes met, and almost without any words we climbed the stairs to the apartment I was staying in. We made love in a way new to me, a way that I could now call wild, even savage, but also delicious and wonderful. It was purely sexual, no affection, no kisses, no caresses were exchanged. But the pleasure was immense . . .

I soon realized that everything I was interested in was happening on Chistopher Sreet in the West Village. I rented a room in the Alton House Hotel at 7th Avenue and 14th Street. It was easy to meet boys and take them there for sex. I was amazed at the fact that nobody paid any notice to whatever I did or wherever I went, so I could take there anybody I liked. I also ventured to 42nd Street. A world of masculine images! I was transfixed. Magazines, posters, books showing men in all their beauty piled up in every shop between 7th and 8th Avenues.

Tremor in Manhattan

The June 1969 events took me by surprise. I had been to the Stonewall a few times as a regular guy looking for a beer and for someone to have sex with. I *could* have been there when the police arrived that night. Fate decided otherwise, so I wasn't even a witness to the events that were to become the basis of the worldwide Gay Revolution that ensued.

Soon I was in the midst of it, mixing with everyone, enjoying the new life that could be felt by any sensitive mind on Christopher Street. Joy is the word that best describes for me the feeling that permeated those summer days. Sometime later, pride summarized the feeling most of us had, very rightly so, I think. I already had a kind of social consciousness that was struggling to develop inside me, and this breath of fresh air after the storm, this moment of unity and love, this clamor, this acceptance of oneself and one another as who we were, this coming out in the open for the first time as brothers and sisters was a turning point in my life. Nothing would be the same after that.

A dance organized by the GLF became my first real contact with the new life and the new people, aside from the joyful life in the streets. The atmosphere there was totally different from that of the bars. People were really friendly, loving. There I met a young man who became my lover, my teacher, my loving, unconditional friend, my guide in the midst of all those frenzied GLF meetings. He was one of the founders of the GLF. His mind seemed to encompass the universe. He was (still is) a beautiful man whose knowledge and warmth sustained me through the different pathways the movement was taking.

Constant updating was crucial to being part of the movement. Every day brought something new, something challenging. Never before had I met so many gay men. Meetings, demonstrations, consciousness-raising groups. . . . The atmosphere was exhilarating. The world felt new, as if it had just been created.

June, 1970: The First Lesbian Gay Transvestite March

It didn't take me by surprise, because I knew it was being organized to celebrate the Stonewall Rebellion. It attracted me like a powerful magnet. I knew I had to be there, and I joined it on 22nd Street, delayed because two of my gay friends were afraid to come with me. That day became my day of initiation, the day I became a full person, out in the open, under a glorious sky and a marvelous sun. As I said, that day the joy was immense, and just like what happens with natural phenomena, I don't think words could ever describe it.

I must say, however, that this first Gay March was the one and only for me. I compare it with the first meeting of two lovers. It was ecstasy. And one will always remember that first time you made love as something unique. I enjoyed the March, or the Parade, as it was later called, in the following years too, but I felt that, although gaining in glamour and glitter, it had lost part of its splendor because the bars had moved in and were now part of it too: Without losing its purpose, the March had become something more commercial. Soon, the freedom we had dreamed of became just freedom from harassment and persecution by the police (yes, a great, wonderful achievement, of course, considering where we were coming from!), but we still were not considered equals, and the gay ghetto continued to exist.

Branching Out: The Third World Gay Revolution

This was the name of a Black and Latino gay group I was a part of during its brief existence. In the spring-summer of 1970 a small group of a few Black gay men and Lesbians, together with Latinos, started this group out of a feeling that our oppression was not represented in the GLF. Being gay to us was just one of the things that oppressed us, and not the one we could focus the most on, considering that racism, poverty, hunger, the marks of slavery, dictatorships (supported by the United States) in many of our countries (including mine), political persecution, were most important in our minds. We felt it was necessary to do something about these oppressions, which also included national identity for those coming from Third World countries (today, "developing" countries), and national independence (Puerto Rico). Although never put in writing, our purpose was to deal with all of this, mainly within ourselves, so we mostly talked to each other about what we suffered *directly*, something we felt was not the case in the GLF. What we mostly did was some sort of consciousness-raising, although we didn't call it that.

It was not that the GLF didn't deal with racism, but as its members were practically all White, they were not the "receivers" of racism except in a reflected form. This does not mean they were insincere, on the contrary. But in the real world, in every aspect of daily life, racism was something that was happening to others, including your friends and lovers. The GLF made an immense effort to deal with racism and oppression in all of its forms, and I think it did so successfully. But again, African American and Latino American people saw things differently. As I said, we saw and experienced a different world where being gay was just one of our oppressions. Even if we could not solve them, they were there, and we didn't see that represented in the gay movement as it was. The GLF, though, was the only group to address these issues and to make them part of its fight against oppression.

We added the word Revolution to the name of the group because it made us feel like brothers and sisters of the national revolutionary movements that were happening all over the world at the time. With gay banners we went to a few demonstrations, mainly in support of the Black Panther Party and the Young Lords, but our small numbers made it difficult to have an impact on our communities, including the gay community, and a lot of the time we just talked about politics and had lots of fun. I think we were trying very hard to find our gay identity within the Black and Latin community, and to fight discrimination not only there but even within the gay, mostly White, movement. Action remained a blurry issue for us; that is, it was something we talked about a lot but we didn't know how to confront directly. We felt something had to be done, but we knew we didn't have the strength to do it. The Third World Gay Revolution did not last more than a few months, and it folded in the fall. It was not the result of a decision we made, but rather something that happened naturally. Being part of this group deepened my political awareness, and it made me feel I understood better what racism was really about.

A Gay Territory: The 23rd Street Collective

Later, around the end of November 1970, something very new and exciting was awaiting me and five other men. I remember walking with them under the first season's snowfall to the loft on 23rd Street between 6th and 7th Avenues, which was to become our new home, taking with me a few belongings and feeling the happiest man in the world. The 23rd Street Collective (or "Milkcrates, Crafts and Graphics," as Paul Aginsky called it, because Juan Carlos Vidal was the graphic artist and craftsman, and with milk crates he had built a wall) had been created. We were venturing into the unknown.

The Collective seemed to have a great impact on many people—on the movement and on me and on the other five men who were part of it. It was an experiment, an experience where the six of us shared everything we had. The world had become gay, a real communion. There seemed to be nothing outside something that had become our creation. We related only to ourselves and to others who were also gay. Was this a mistake? I don't think so. At the time, being gay-identified was a most important issue. The collective felt wonderful, loving and a politically risky thing to do. For the first time (or so it seems), six gay men were living together, as brothers, as lovers (not necessarily sexual), in the context of a movement whose main aspiration was love, freedom and equality. Personal objects and money were all shared, even if one of us didn't have any.

This was the closest one could come to an ideal life, absolutely superior to family life, with its roles and programs and calculations. The names of those men: Dan Smith, Paul Aginsky, Juan Carlos Vidal, Earl and Pat (I'm sorry that I can't remember now their last names), and myself. Pat was a beautiful guy who didn't stay very long in the Collective. Paul Aginsky was the center and one of its founders, and his generosity I had never seen the likes of.

The intensity of the experience in the Collective was so great that my life in it seemed much longer than it really was. This was a real school for all of us. We struggled to do things together politically, but adapting to each other took some time. The loft we lived in was big, so we all had plenty of room to be alone if we wanted to. The main thing is that we were happy and got along very well. We even had a cat (a tuxedo cat), whose name was Gato.

Like many of us, I was lucky to be at the right place at the right time. I think much of what I learned from this whole experience is part of who I am today.

At some point in 1972, I think, Dan, Paul and Earl moved to

San Francisco along with half of my other friends. That city had become a new, powerful magnet, and the Gay Movement seemed to split up into these two cities. Juan Carlos and I stayed on, and other gay men joined us, but the spirit was practically gone, and I was the last person to leave the loft where so many parties, so much fun and joy were now just memories. I found a new apartment and moved out. This was about October 1972.

Remnants of That Great Tremor . . .

. . . that great movement, remained for some time. I met new people who wanted to do something around gay issues. They had a really high political consciousness. Among them were Mark Berenson, Stuart Finkelstein, Bruce Gottfried, Robert Simpson, who are my friends to this day, and Juan Carlos Vidal, who died in the summer of 1985. A new group got together, around the idea of making a movie or writing a book. But nothing materialized, and soon we just stopped meeting as a group beyond our individual friendships.

The move to San Francisco by so many gay people who had been real bastions in the NYC GLF, I think now may have had an effect in its becoming weaker, to the point of disappearance. I feel tempted to compare the Stonewall Rebellion to the scientific theory of creation, the Big Bang. At the beginning everybody was very close, but with time we started leaving the center as separate beings. This is just a thought that occurs to me after so many years. But who could have stopped such an exodus? And would things have been different if they had stayed? The word spread like fire, and in no time many people were leaving. It's still a mystery to me how this happened. Some of them came back to New York, only to leave again soon, while others remained. Others never came back, except for a brief vacation. They felt the lure of a new city that promised so much, and this meant a new life, a new happiness. I never felt this attraction; otherwise I would have moved too. But it made me feel pretty lonely.

A Last Word

I wish I could have, with these words, embraced all that was happening simultaneously from 1969 onwards in the Gay Movement. This seems too ambitious for a small article. But I'm leaving out so

many people, so many events! What I'm offering is just a glimpse
of those days, although a huge movie (life itself) is rolling on before my eyes. Basically, I only wanted to talk about my feelings,
more than about politics, as I feel them after so many years.

Today I live in Buenos Aires, Argentina. I'm a teacher, photographer, poet. I've published four books of poetry in Spanish,
among them, in 2008, an anthology of gay poetry together with
three other gay poets, called *Poesía Gay de Buenos Aires* (*Gay Poetry
from Buenos Aires*). Such a book is the first of its kind in this city,
probably the first in Latin America, a small revolution in itself. By
publishing it, I felt I like a militant again.

*Néstor Latrónico was a member of the New York City GLF and the 23rd Street
Collective (1970–1972). Today he is a bicultural resident of Buenos Aires,
Argentina, where he works as a teacher and translator. He is also a poet and
fine art photographer.*

From the Closets of New Haven to the Collectives of New York GLF

Jason Victor Serinus

I remember reading about the Stonewall Uprising of late June 1969. I was working in New Haven at the time, doing part-time community organizing. Just as I was exiting The Pub, the gay bar across from Yale affectionately known as The Pube, I caught the headlines about Stonewall in the *Village Voice*.

In 1969, I was still in the closet. My internalized homophobia ran deep, fed by years of conditioning. I had spent four years at Amherst College, then an elite all-male school of 3,000, agonizing over whether I was homosexual, heterosexual, or bisexual. I was so consumed with angst that I found studying difficult and spent many vacations virtually alone on campus, where I could catch up on schoolwork without the distracting sight of other men.

By age 23, when I arrived in New Haven, I felt so ashamed of my attraction to men that I couldn't look anyone directly in the eye. In fact, the only reason I had entered The Pub was out of desperation. I felt that if I didn't do something, anything, I would die a dirty old man, slinking through the streets, unable to hold my head up high.

My shame became the impetus for my activism. During the summer of 1965, I spent seven weeks in North Carolina doing civil rights work with the Southern Christian Leadership Conference (SCLC). I felt the need to act after reading a book on racism by Nat Hentoff that described the alienation black people felt when they walked past white people who either looked through them as though they didn't exist or treated them as though they were less than a whole person. I deeply identified with their plight: How black people were treated was exactly how I sensed I would be treated if people knew I was homosexual. But because I knew of no gay liberation movement or political ideology that justified my right to exist, I projected my internal struggle onto black people and went off to help them instead of fighting for my own civil rights as a gay man.

When I returned to Amherst College that fall, I searched for information that could help explain my hidden attraction to men. Certainly I couldn't turn to organized religion for support. The three major religions all treated homosexuality as an abominable crime against nature.

Soon I found a book by psychiatrist Irving Beiber titled *Homosexuality*. A lot of good it did. It was filled with classic stereotypical explanations of how "the homosexual's sickness" was the product of a dominating mother and emotionally absent father. Even after GLF began, the best-selling book *All You Ever Wanted To Know About Sex But Were Afraid To Ask* by Dr. David Reuben surfaced as a "hip" source of misinformation about homosexuality, mocking and belittling us. It took a dozen more years of activism to get the American Psychological Association to reverse its stand on homosexuality, and to get positive, gay-affirming books on the market.

Forward to 1969. At virtually the same time I learned about Stonewall, I met my first lover, Bruce. After five months of living together in the closet, during which time I worked in Yale's Sterling Library while ironically exhorting my female coworkers to join the ranks of women's liberation, I spent two months cutting sugar cane in Cuba on the first Venceremos Brigade. Because I was one of the best cane cutters in our camp, I was given the honor of cutting cane in the same field as Fidel.

In Cuba, I engaged in several uncomfortable discussions about homosexuality with representatives of the Cuban Communist Party. They assumed that anyone who said anything positive about homosexuality or bisexuality must be gay. I've often wondered if the Communist Party official who approached me to propose an aborted private meeting had something other than talk on his mind.

My last interaction with a Party member transpired in January of 1970 as I was leaving the ship on which we returned from Cuba. As I was walking off the gangplank, I planted what I intended as a fond good-bye kiss on the cheek of translator Anna Gonzales. Anna immediately covered her cheek with her hand, uttered *"O, mi madre,"* and ran off. I think she felt tainted because she had just been kissed by a homosexual.

When I returned to New Haven, I briefly entertained the notion that homosexuals like me were a product of capitalist decadence and would never exist in a revolutionary society. Bruce moved out shortly thereafter, replaced by four other members of a political collective that provided support to Bobby Seale and the Black Panthers during Seale's famous New Haven trial.

Still closeted, still thinking that there must be something better than the passion for men that seized my being, I snuck off one spring night to attend the first gay dance ever held at Yale. There I saw a gorgeous man whom I had lusted after each time I participated in ostensibly "straight" folk dancing sessions at Yale. The realization that I was not alone made me wonder once again if perhaps there was something good about my sexual orientation.

Later that night, as I was eating with other gays at Olivia's, the 24-hour dive where Yale professors and street people met for more than Coca-Cola, I was approached by Carl, the Methodist minister who was an ally of our community organizing group.

"Just come from the dance?" asked Carl, matter of factly.

"Dance? What dance?" I responded, with choked voice and blank expression.

"The gay dance at Yale."

"Oh, a gay dance at Yale?" I replied, as though I had never heard of such a thing.

"Guy [as I was named then], we need a Gay Liberation Front in New Haven, and you're the right person to start it."

"Me, start a GLF? Why me? And how did you know I was gay?"

Boy, did I have a lot to learn.

A few weeks later, I found myself in a room in Dwight Chapel, waiting for people to respond to posters I'd placed around town announcing the first meeting of the New Haven GLF. The Panthers were meeting down the hall. Seeing me, several walked in, only to be told that they were at the wrong meeting. I ignored their snickers as they exited quickly to saunter down the hall.

It didn't take too many meetings for me to realize that I didn't know enough about gay life to be the head of a gay organization. So I decided to take a crash course in gaydom. After an exploratory meeting or two, I moved to New York City in the summer of 1970 to live in Manhattan's pioneer 17th Street Gay Men's Collective. There were 10 of us, all in one large, open 12th-floor loft that offered little private space. We were all anticapitalist, antiracist and antisexist, but that didn't mean that we all liked each other.

Our numbers included loft owner Carl Miller, a famous textile designer; Allen Young, formerly of Liberation News Service and the future author of several major books on the gay movement; Jim Fouratt, now a fellow music/movie reviewer who had worked alongside Abbie Hoffman and the Yippies before fighting at Stonewall; Punit Auerbacher, a San Diego–based bodyworker and actor; and Bob Bland, who recently ran for political office in Vermont. Three of our members had survived incarceration in mental institutions because of their homosexuality, and were carrying deep wounds.

Along with the Baltic Street, 95th Street and 23rd Street Collectives, we attended meetings of New York's Gay Liberation Front. Thanks to Allen Young, our collective published several issues of *Gay Flames*, a free paper that attempted to organize street people and hustlers into a radical movement. We also helped organize GLF's short-lived Gay Community Center.

GLF catalyzed a huge wave of political, social, personal and attitudinal transformation. We fought to get the *Village Voice* to use the word "gay" in advertisements for our meetings. We worked relentlessly to get the *New York Times* to use our preferred word "gay" instead of the medical term "homosexual." We even had to stage a sit-in and picket to get New York University to allow gay people to have a dance! Allying ourselves with the women's movement, the civil rights movement, and the antiwar movement, we saw gay liberation as a key element in transforming society and making the world a better place for all.

Early GLF meetings were often pretty chaotic. New Yorkers are an argumentative bunch to begin with. Many of the men had never been confronted on their sexism, and had lots to learn about women. Our meetings were open to anyone, and each meeting brought fresh men who cut women off in mid-sentence, spoke in louder voices and deferred to those with the deepest voices and biggest muscles.

At the first meeting I attended, on a Sunday night in June of 1970, one of my lesbian sisters was using a softball bat she had brought from regular Sunday women's softball games as a gavel to call meetings to order. While I vividly recall one of the women grabbing that bat, walking around the circle, and nonviolently swinging it in the direction of some offending men in an attempt to drive home the point that women deserved respect, others' memories differ. Perhaps I was simply overwhelmed by the extreme polarization that was taken for granted in factional New York politics.

No matter how hard the women and their male allies tried, instantly educating men steeped in the sexism of American life was an uphill battle. Soon after that meeting, a number of women split off to found separatist organizations and collectives. I totally supported their move. They needed to find their own power and identity as lesbians, and we men needed to drop the patriarchal attitudes we had inherited and find a new way of being in the world. In short, we each had to discover anew and learn to live the vision of equality that Harry Hay, as well as Del Martin and Phyllis Lyon (founders of the Daughters of Bilitis, a pioneering lesbian organization), had espoused in the years before GLF.

The early days of GLF were a time of great awakening. We were learning to accept ourselves as we were, and to proudly proclaim our newly embraced identities. Central to that process was learning to love ourselves and treat each other with respect.

In order to discover more about our true natures, GLF members formed consciousness-raising groups. A small number of us would convene in a circle and pick a topic. One week it would be our mothers, the next playing sports, the next relationships with our siblings. Each of us would take a turn telling his story. Thus we discovered just how many of us had played right field, had been beaten to a pulp because of high voices or "sensitive" natures, loved Judy Garland and ballet and Leontyne Price, and didn't have the stereotypical dominating mother and emotionally absent father that Irving Bieber and other hideous homophobes had proclaimed as the "cause" of our homosexuality.

One special consciousness-raising group called itself the Radical Femmes. The name derived from the butch/femme dichotomy that sometimes manifests in lesbian and gay relationships. The term was new to me. When I lived with Bruce, I didn't know anything about butch or femme, top or bottom. We just did what felt right, without any restraints other than the big bad closet inhibiting our love.

In some ways, my newfound knowledge was a curse. Categories such as butch and femme lead to divisions of roles and power. To the extent one believes in any category that separates human beings from each other, one perpetuates the antagonism and division that currently threaten our very existence on Planet Earth.

I certainly didn't feel like a Radical Femme, even though in a conscious effort to undermine patriarchal models of gender correctness, I walked through the streets of NYC wearing long women's earrings, nail polish and unisexual clothing, and modeled for art school classes where male students drew me with huge breasts. In fact, I had inherited the unfortunate nickname of Venceremos Butch, and was forever barred from attending Radical Femmes circles by men who simultaneously resented me and found me attractive.

Eventually, the Radical Femmes changed their name to Femmes Against Sexism. Then they concluded that calling oneself "femme" was in itself sexist, and self-destructed. Soon thereafter, Venceremos Butch was no more. One who is not busy being born is busy dying.

One of my fondest memories of life in the 17th Street Collective was the time that Punit sat naked near the window, listening to music on headphones. A woman across the street from our loft, horrified at the sight, called the police to complain of a naked man wearing earmuffs. Thankfully, by the time the police entered our loft unannounced, we were all clothed, hanging out in a huge, pterodactyl-shaped, tie-dyed tent that Carl had designed. Spying no earmuffs, and stunned by the sight, they shuffled their feet and left. The old paradigm had stared the new paradigm right in the face, and didn't know what to do.

Eventually the 17th Street Collective disintegrated. Punit and I, along with Henry Ferrari and Jimmy Clifford (now both dead of AIDS), founded the 12th Street Collective, where we continued our work. Allen and Carl (dead of AIDS) moved to Butterworth Farm in Massachusetts, where Allen still lives. I left NYC on my birthday in 1972, moved to San Francisco, became active in Bay Area Gay Liberation (BAGL), and helped start Pacifica radio's Fruit Punch, the first gay men's radio show in the United States. On our first "gay music" program, I insisted on playing Maria Callas singing the aria "Suicidio" because so many gay men, buying into their internalized homophobia, continued to kill themselves. Given that the aria was in Italian, not everyone got the connection.

Then the process of reification began. The essence of gay liberation, which is love, became a thing, a marketable commodity you could wear around your neck or paste on your bumper or hang out your window. Even your dog could sport a rainbow collar. The gay love that was sacred and inviolable became love for sale. Eventually we ended up with gay organizations filled with so-called leaders who, in an attempt to gain power, pandered to straight people and dumped on the very "perverts" who fought at Stonewall and made them look less than respectable. Hence, almost four decades later, we witnessed a movement for gay marriage in California that paid millions for ads that featured straight people rather than gays talking about marriage equality.

Eventually I came upon the Radical Faeries, a group of counterculture gay men convened by gay liberation father Harry Hay, his lover John Burnside and a few other renegades. I spent many years sitting in faerie circles, working to build faerie sanctuary, before becoming involved with other heart-centered gay men's communities such as the Billies.

On June 16, 2008, I was married to David James Bellecci in a public ceremony in Oakland City Hall officiated by two of my civil rights heroes, Oakland Mayor and former U.S. Rep. Ronald V. Dellums and Rep. Barbara Lee. I remain actively involved in community building, still extol the praises of Maria Callas, and still hold the vision of a world where all can unite as sisters and brothers. If all goes well, David and I will be in Cuba in the summer of 2009 as participants in the 40th Anniversary Venceremos Brigade. As the faeries are wont to say, the circle is open, but unbroken.

Written with the assistance of Allen Young and Stuart Timmons.

Jason Victor Serinus is a music and audio critic who writes for Carnegie Hall, Stereophile, Opera News, American Record Guide *and many other publications. He edited* Psychoimmunity & the Healing Process: A Holistic Approach to Immunity & AIDS *(Celestial Arts, o.p.) and whistled Puccini as the voice of Woodstock in an Emmy-nominated Peanuts cartoon. Allen Young collaborated with lesbian writer Karla Jay to edit three gay liberation anthologies, including* Out of the Closet: Voices of Gay Liberation *(NYU Press, in a new edition); and a national gay survey called* The Gay Report. *He also authored* Gays Under the Cuban Revolution. *Stuart Timmons authored* The Trouble with Harry Hay: Founder of the Modern Gay Movement *(Alyson Press).*

Even Iowa Homos got the Blues

Dennis Brumm

Ames, Iowa, was not a hotbed of homosexuality when I left my small Midwestern hometown in 1970 to attend Iowa State University.

I was not even in the closet at age 17. I was in a vault. At about age 12, I'd recognized I was attracted to other guys, but I had none of the teenage experiences so many do, and was convinced that nobody else, anywhere, was feeling the same thing I was. I never would have imagined that within two years my life would change dramatically.

In the spring quarter of my first year at school, a human sexuality group on campus had invited two men come to campus to talk about sexuality. One was Frank Kameny, an early gay civil rights activist in the 1960s "homophile" movement. He was brought to talk about homosexuality. This had to be "balanced" by another man, whose name I've long since forgotten, who spoke on the "heterosexual" viewpoint. I'm sure heterosexuality didn't needed to be promoted, as it was already quite endemic. They "balanced" it because very few people would have felt comfortable going to the presentation had it been only about homosexuality.

For some reason, a number of guys I was hanging out with in the dorm decided this homo/hetero discussion would be an "interesting" thing to go to. I was still in the vault, and found even attending it a bit threatening. I pretended I'd be interested too, purely from a sociocultural perspective of course, and went along.

That afternoon was the first time I ever saw anyone in the flesh who was open about his or her homosexuality, and the first time I ever heard anyone talking openly about it without all the trappings of adolescent discomfort I was used to. Kameny's part of the talk was entirely from a civil rights perspective. He said nothing about cultural overlays that caused his oppression. Mostly, it centered on the discrimination and firing gay men and lesbians faced when discovered in government jobs, which had happened to him.

I think the hetero man made some offhand comment about

"heterosexuality must be working out—there are so many of us."
He was not very interesting to listen to after Kameny's speech.

It was intriguing that those of us who went said very little at
all about the lecture after we left. It was as if we'd seen a man from
Mars. I suppose on many levels we didn't know what to make
of the Martian, or how to process what we'd heard. I moved the
whole experience over into my safe vault.

That summer, during the horror of the Vietnam War, I got my
draft number. I was not one of the lucky ones. My number was
32, meaning that if I didn't keep a student deferment I would most
certainly be drafted, as almost everyone up to number 150 or so
would be.

Between July and September of that summer, a patchwork of
events (my distrust and fear of the war, and an illness that had kept
me home over the summer) coalesced in me, probably egged on
a bit by raging hormones that were making me increasingly frustrated, and I (thankfully, finally) managed to face and deal with
my attraction to men. By September 1972, I managed to tell a lifelong friend from my hometown whom I grew up with that I was
a "homosexual." Soon, I did the same with a friend in the dorm
whom I'd known for three or four years. Fortunately, both were
supportive, but they were as clueless as I was about the subject or
what I should do next, as none of us had ever before dealt with gay
people or homosexuality in any paradigm other than uncomfortable joking.

One day at a laundromat I found the 1971 Year in Review
issue of *Life Magazine*. The lead story (the only part I remember)
was titled, I believe, "Homosexuals in Revolt." I read the issue over
and over. One of the pictures was of Jack Baker, an out-of-the-
closet gay man who had been elected president of the student government of the University of Minnesota. The magazine featured a
story as well as his campaign poster, which showed a very "typical"
college student of the time, wearing jeans, sitting on the floor, but
also in high heels. The poster had a caption on it that said, "Put
yourself in Jack Baker's shoes." I decided to write him a letter.

I wish I had a copy of the letter I sent, but didn't think to
save it at the time. It was, I'm sure, a missive mixed with hope
and despair. I do still have the letter that he sent back to me. Jack
suggested I come to Minneapolis for a weekend (about a 200-mile
trip), and hang out in their local community center, talk to people,
and "get my head together."

One of the two friends whom I'd told I was gay insisted I do this. On a Friday after a genetics class, I drove to Minneapolis, found the address of the gay center from my letter, parked the car and stood across the street and watched.

People were going in and out of the building, but I was paralyzed. I couldn't go in. I guess it was too much to cross that final hurdle from the life I pretended to have and the person I pretended to be.

I phoned my friend back at the dorm in Iowa. He said I couldn't "just leave," since "people were expecting me." (No doubt my arrival wasn't the focus of their plans, but at age 19 I didn't realize the whole weekend wasn't supposed to revolve around me.)

Afraid of offending or disappointing people, I followed my friend's advice. I called the center, and some words spewed out about how I'd come there, was expected, was sorry, but couldn't go any further. I couldn't enter the building, and was thinking about just leaving. A very nice, calm man asked me where I was, and if he could come out and talk to me. Scared shitless, I said yes. I told him where I was, near a park bench. I sat on it and waited.

We sat on the bench, and probably talked for over an hour. At first I felt as if I were meeting a Martian. I had no idea what to expect, but he was very kind, reassuring, patient and understanding. Finally, he asked if I wouldn't like to go in and talk to some other people, and since I felt calmer by that point, I had the resolve to face myself and my fears. Somehow, the Martians weren't what I'd been led to believe they were. The closet door creaked open a lot more.

For two or three hours, I listened and talked to people. Whole groups of them were apparently interested in my story. I doubt if it was every day some young, clueless Iowan arrived. I went back the next day and talked more, feeling increasingly more comfortable with my new tribe of very kind Martians.

Then the whirlwind began.

While in Minneapolis, I got the address of the gay liberation group at the University of Iowa in Iowa City, and I called or wrote to them after I got back home. One of the people there told me that he'd been in touch with a man in Ames who was thinking of starting a gay liberation group on our campus. I met this man and through him met other people. In December 1971 I went to the very first public gay liberation meeting on the Iowa State campus. Since the location and time of the meeting had been published in the paper, there were rumors that people with guns were going to come and kill us.

I was still living in the dorm, quite un-gay to all the people I lived around except for one, my friend. Yet I managed to get enough courage up to go to the meeting. I honestly don't know how I did it, but I think again it was probably because I felt that my new friends were expecting me. I was probably the only virgin (and still a virgin for a while longer) who even considered going. The meeting was fairly short, with a campus newspaper reporter and maybe a dozen folks in attendance. The tension, or at least the tension I felt, was almost unbearable. I didn't say more than two or three words, if that, during the entire meeting.

We had no more public meetings during the course of that year. Instead, there were gatherings where we discussed all of what was still new and important for me and the rest of us: how we had been oppressed as gay people, what this stemmed from, and how to cope in a hostile world. By the end of the spring, I'd really made a lot of personal progress. My worldview and political view had changed immensely. I had told my father I was gay (and been kicked out of the house for it, which I pretty much expected). With a newfound support group, I was pretty happy my life was going to be quite different—and a lot better—than I'd imagined it only several years earlier.

Unlike larger cities with big gay populations, smaller towns, at least 30 years ago, had gay and lesbian subcultures that pretty much chose to remain unseen. Not many of us were willing to stick ourselves out and stand up for who we were. But it doesn't require a large number to make a statement. Our groups in Ames (the lesbian and gay men's groups early on were separate) at first tended to pass out leaflets at plays or other events that depicted gay and lesbian people in an unfavorable light. Even that was very radical in an environment in which people had always been able to pretend we didn't exist. I should note that I'm using the term "gay and lesbian" as a historical reference, as it was used at the time, not to be exclusionary.

The most theatrical event we managed during those early years was a protest against Campus Crusade for Christ. They were tabling in the student union on campus, passing out J. T. Chick "tracts" promising hell and damnation for just about anything that regular humans do. They had one tract called "The Gay Blade" that condemned homosexuals along with the rest of those they disliked.

Some of us decided to organize a march through the student union to express our displeasure. We got some help from other radical groups, called the university press, carried signs, sang and clapped. We had a very stoned Jesus carrying a cross leading us along our path to the Campus Crusade table. The good Christians went straight for our Jesus, terrified that he was the anti-Christ they so dreaded. I couldn't have hoped for any more drama than that. But he was so out of it he just smiled at them and led us on. We passed out our propaganda to students and faculty who were leaving or entering. It was indeed a joyous day. The press coverage was pretty good, probably because most people at the university, while they may not have totally empathized with our cause or theatrics, certainly didn't enjoy the other side either.

Not everything we did was so theatrical. Our groups at Iowa State worked together with gay and lesbian groups at the University of Iowa to put on three Midwest Gay Pride conferences in 1974, '75 and '76. These were indeed ahead of their time, considering the place and the obstacles. They had very good turnouts, with people attending from as far west as Nebraska and Kansas, as far east as Ohio and Michigan, as far south as Arkansas and as far north as Minnesota and Wisconsin.

The first conference in 1974 featured Mark Segal, leader of the Gay Raiders (later publisher of the *Philadelphia Gay News*); Tom Maurer of the University of Minnesota, a gay lecturer and counselor; and Mawalimu Imara, a Unitarian activist from Boston. In 1975, Tommi Avicolli Mecca, of Radicalqueens, and author Rita Mae Brown were the keynote speakers.

The conferences featured panels and workshops covering widely diverse subjects that directly affected people's lives, including the depiction of gays in the media, queers in prisons, gays and the Left, aging, religion and gender. There were also cultural activities including movies and plays, and a dance—a fine mixture of "work" and "play."

During my final years in Ames, I became less active in the campus gay group but still attended most of the meetings and helped whenever issues arose for which I could be of assistance. I was one of several people who spoke at a City Council meeting about getting a nondiscrimination clause added to the city's charter, and, though that didn't succeed then, a number of years later such a resolution was adopted.

By the late 1970s, I was eager to move on. I hated Iowa weather, both winter and summer, and there never was much in between the two to enjoy. I was a lot more confident than when I arrived green in Ames, a naïve 17-year-old. I'd traveled a fair amount to cities, where the numbers of gay people were so much greater, and felt the need to find one where I'd feel safer. In 1977, a friend and I drove to San Francisco for a few weeks of vacation. I went to see the city I'd heard was the epitome of what gay culture might be. I felt so comfortable with the general attitude and loved the hills, water and climate. What a big contrast from the Midwest! A year later I had moved permanently to San Francisco.

Dennis Brumm was one of the original members of Gay Liberation at Iowa State University in Ames, Iowa (1971). He grew up in a small Iowa town. While in college he came out during an era that was politically charged. Among his accomplishments: He is the editor/producer of several totally obscure movies and the composer of some completely unknown music. He moved to San Francisco in 1978, where he still lives in anachronistic splendor, while watching his city's headlong march into being a haven for the rich, mostly white and hip. In the past few years he has been actively involved with groups concerned about the effects of peak oil (resource depletion, environmental degradation, overpopulation, species loss and overall human quality of life).

There's a Certain Kind of Woman

Mara Math

At age 5, I spent my Sunday mornings cutting out women characters from the color funnies and rating them by "prettiest." (The Brenda Starr mermaid character always won. Then, as now, I was more drawn to faces than figures.)

At 11, I waited breathlessly for each *New Yorker*, eager to add to my collection of Peck & Peck's "there's a certain kind of woman" clippings: "There is a certain kind of woman who'd rather eat soutzoukakia in the Greek Isles than fondue in Stowe. For this woman, there is a certain kind of store: Peck & Peck." Those ads suggested what then passed for quirkiness and independence, spiced with a dash of sophistication, that had nothing to do with the clothing and everything to do with character—the closest exposure I had to any hint as to what elusive noncorporeal quality made women attractive.

At 14, half my daydreams were of some boy or other, and the other half were of saving other girls from male attackers. In junior high, I always wondered why some boy didn't notice how beautiful my best friend Anne was and scoop her up—but I never noticed that *I* was noticing. Whether I would have graduated to lesbianism without the spark of lesbian-feminist literature, however, is unfathomable—and so I remain eternally grateful.

What you have to understand is that I never had a sexual thought about another female until I read lesbian-feminist literature. As an incest survivor, I was so estranged from my body that I didn't have a clue: When I felt that way about a boy, that was a crush; when I felt that way about a girl, that just meant I wanted her to be my special friend. I still have my sixth grade diary, which records my first obsession with a girl: "Cynthia spoke to me today. "Cynthia was absent today." "Cynthia said hi today." "Cynthia smiled at me today."

I was 16 in 1972 when I first encountered feminism, and close on its work-boot-shod heels, lesbian-feminism. Feminism saved my life, and lesbian-feminism gave it shape. Lesbian-feminism is no longer the only or even the central prism through which I view the world, but it trained my ways of seeing so thoroughly that it will never be completely absent. It was a way of looking at the world that included a rejection of racism, classism, ageism, and just about any other stratification of inequity, a way of looking that embraced, rather than rejected, the natural world.

After I initially rejected feminism as unimportant compared to antiwar activism—"People are *dying* over there!"—what finally opened my eyes at 16 was a copy of *The Female Eunuch.* The classism and puffery of Germaine Greer's book embarrass me now, but reading it, I had my first Big Click, to use a *Ms Magazine* cliché of the day. Suddenly, it all made sense—the condescension of males, the unfair favoritism shown my little brother, the dearth of women authors in every high school anthology . . .

In grade school, I'd devoured every one of the blue-cover biographies that had a female subject, always vaguely dissatisfied when she was merely The Wife Of. And oh, how I longed to be Clara Barton, the pioneering war-front nurse to whose Baltimore home our classes were occasionally carted, never considering how I would reconcile that desire with my distaste for needles and blood. I didn't realize that what I most admired about Clara Barton was the tale of how, while she and another nurse were sleeping in a hayloft, CB fended off a drunken soldier who attacked her companion. (It would be another decade-plus before I learned that CB herself had proclivities that may have explained just what she was doing in that hayloft with another woman.)

Cultural role models were scarce indeed. I was shocked, in a blood-warming way, the first time I heard Linda Ronstadt sing, "I ain't sayin'/You ain't pretty/But . . ." Having been born too late for "Don't Make Me Over," probably the first feminist anthem, "Different Drum" was a revelation to me. She was singing to a boy! At that time I'd yet to hear the phrase "the male gaze," but this song taught me I'd been suffering under it. She was telling a boy he was pretty! And that *she* was a-movin' on! "Oh don't get me wrong/It's not that I knock it/It's just that I am not in the market/ For a boy who wants to love only me."

With the same inchoate hunger I'd had for biographies of women, as a kid I'd also loved Gale Garnett's "We'll Sing in the Sunshine" ("I'll sing to you each mornin'/I'll kiss you every night/ But darlin', don't cling to me/I'll soon be out of sight"). A woman being a free spirit! Far out!

Would I have been ready to have my eyes opened if my mother had not already scattered a few seeds in her scattershot way? It was less her role as a single mother, post-divorce, or her membership in Federally Employed Women (FEW, get it?) than her occasional acerbic comments. Maybe I'm imagining that she turned up the radio for "We'll Sing in the Sunshine," but I still remember my surprise at her hostility to my beloved oldie "Memphis, Tennessee," in which Johnny Rivers sang, "But we were pulled apart/ because her mom would not agree/And tore apart our happy home/ in Memphis, Tennessee." I loved the sentimental melancholy of a father missing his young daughter, but Mom glared at the radio and snapped, "Why is it always the woman's fault?" In that instant I was handed a new framework. (My parents would stay married for another two years.)

Although I can remember the first piece of feminist literature to get through to me, I don't remember which lesbian-feminist piece did the same—perhaps because I proceeded to read absolutely every bit of lesbiana I could get my hands on, from old copies of *The Furies* newspaper to trashy '50s paperbacks and Naiad Press novels (generally speaking, the equivalent of Harlequin Romances for lesbians).

I was part of the first generation to have more positive images of lesbians than negative ones. This made my experience, for all its difficulties, infinitely easier than that of any previous lesbian generation. As opposed to a genealogical generation, a lesbian generation, in that time of ferment, was about three years. That is, the dykes I knew who were three to five years older than I was had come out only after they had first gotten suicidal or electroshocked or married, while I worried about whether I was lesbian "enough." And when I was 22 and locked in a death-struggle with my first woman lover over what we variously termed "commitment" (her) or "aping heterosexual relationships" (me), my 18-year-old friend Sara shrugged and announced breezily, "Oh, monogamy, that's silly!" and bounced on out of the room.

I was thoroughly and viciously thrashed the first time I ever uttered a word of coming-out to a roomful of more-or-less strangers, an experience that delayed my coming into my lesbianism for five years. That roomful of near-strangers was a feminist studies group led by, and composed of, separatists, with whom my feminist politics had always passed muster. Until the evening we had to tell our coming-out stories, and I didn't have one.

I didn't know enough to admit to what I didn't know. I didn't understand that had I acknowledged my own inexperience, some of those women might have been all too happy to, er, take me in hand. Instead, I stuttered in a small voice that I was, "um, bisexual." I figured I must be bisexual, because at that time in Washington, D.C., the only choices were to be a lesbian-separatist or a straight woman, and I knew I was neither of those things. I said I was bisexual, but what that really meant was that I wasn't sleeping with anyone: I was too feminist for the boys, and too tied to the Left, too non-separatist, for the lesbians.

The separatists who made up the group promptly expressed their contempt ("Would the Bolsheviks sleep with the Czar?!" Juanita Weaver demanded) and cut me off from then on. This was painful, to have the only lesbians I knew reject me, and it made me wary for years to come of approaching other lesbian groups. I didn't want them to feel, as these dykes made clear that they did, that I was ripping them off somehow. Of course, this was a short-sighted strategy on the part of the separatists, as that was one of two times in my life I could most easily have become a rabid, frothing-at-the-mouth separatist. How do you get to be a lesbian if the lesbians won't talk to you?

In the radical political milieu in which I moved, the youngest antiwar activist in our avowedly—in retrospect perhaps "allegedly" would be a better term—revolutionary community, I never once viewed lesbianism as deviant, sinful, twisted, unnatural, suspect or bad. Having been raised in Reform Judaism, with its emphasis on the obligation to improve the world, primed me to be receptive to radicalism and thus feminism and lesbian-feminism.

Because it was lesbian-feminism and not plain old lesbianism, it was that much easier for many of us who took up the banner. We weren't lesbians because we were deviants who could not deny our sex-crazed urges, we were lesbians because we loved women and were making a revolution, we were transforming the world. We were anxious to love and honor women's minds as much as their bodies. We might have to whisper furtively about that song by Melissa Manchester called "Ruby and the Dancer," but our secret understanding of the song was exciting, privileged, not a sign that we were oppressed because "women's music" wouldn't be played on mainstream radio for another 20 years, and even then the pronouns had to disappear. Even having to be partially closeted at times seemed more of an enticing masquerade than a benchmark of danger, proof of membership in this secret society: It was as close as I would come to being Emma Peel, spy extraordinaire and my first filmic role model.

This group identity was an enormous boon to me and the women who came out at that time. We were united in struggle (or so we thought), we were generous and supportive to each other in "the" lesbian community. As I traveled around the country—"then I'll be on my waa-aa-ay"—I'd stay at the houses of strangers, but not really strangers, women who were listed as "Contact Dykes" in *Lesbian Connection*. "How do you always find a place to stay?" my mother asked, unaware of the fine, strong filaments of connection crisscrossing the country. I had the luxury, unsought but welcome, of joining the lesbian community when it was cool, not cool as in faddish, not as in LUG, Lesbian Until Graduation, but as in righteous, desirable, iconic.

When I did come out to my mother, I had for a safety net my touted belief that if she rejected me, "the lesbian community will be my family." I'm also eternally grateful that thanks to my mom's open-mindedness, I never had to put that dangerously naïve faith to the test.

I didn't feel any shame or guilt at being involved in this new world, only fear and shame over whether I was a "real" lesbian (thanks, Juanita and Charlotte!). Then again, in retrospect, it seems clear that if you're worrying about whether you're a real lesbian or not, that's pretty good evidence that you're a real lesbian.

As to that, my female cousins had only one question when I asked them if our step-grandfather had ever done to them what he had to me. At that time I'd yet to see the brilliant Gay Pride placard: "If being molested made you queer, this parade would be a lot bigger!" When my cousins each posed that predictable question, "Is that why you're a lesbian?," I heard myself telling the truth before I even understood it: "No, that's why I wasn't a lesbian *sooner*."

There were drawbacks, downsides, flaws, of course, in lesbian-feminism as I experienced it. There was the sacred text, Anne Koedt's *The Myth of the Vaginal Orgasm*, which criticized Freud for telling women that we feel something we don't, and went on to insist that we could not be feeling something that some of us were. There was the gay-straight split, which I was fortunately just young enough to miss, or I'd probably still be straight: A heterosexual roommate gave birth a year after participating in the world-changing women's takeover of the underground paper *The Rat*, and her dyke comrades in arms visited her in the hospital only to say, "You're lucky it was a girl, or you would have had to give it away." There was the pervasive sense that pure sexual attraction was invalid and invalidating, objectifying, *wrong,* which tainted my social life for longer than I care to admit.

But for all of that, I was just young enough for lesbian-feminism to inform and transform my life so utterly that I can barely imagine who I would be without it: A closeted lesbian drinking or drugging herself to self-medicate the shame away? A resentful wife, thinking to cure her marriage by falling in love with the first man who knows where her clitoris is?

I'm glad I'll never know.

Mara Math's editorials, arts reviews and investigative pieces have appeared in more than 70 publications, and she wrote the Readers Guide to Gay and Lesbian Studies *entry on San Francisco's queer history. She conducted her first interview, with activist Yvonne Wanrow, as a member of the* Second Wave *magazine editorial collective, 1976–78; currently an arts writer for the* San Francisco Examiner, *she has interviewed film principals including Felicity Huffman, Alan Ball, Ellen Kuras, Arthur Dong and Bill Maher. Mara's CineMedusa.com article on lost genius Marion Wong is used by the Academy of Motion Pictures and Sciences as their official handout on Wong's restored film. A tenant activist and former union organizer, Mara lives in San Francisco with Dina the Tree-Climbing Dog. She remains grateful to have missed the gay-straight split in the feminist movement.*

A POEM

Fran Winant

Fran Winant was a founding member of the Gay Liberation Front and Radicalesbians and appeared, with others, on GLF's Come Out poster made for the first gay march, described in her poem "Christopher St. Liberation Day, June 28, 1970." Fran edited and published the first U.S. lesbian anthology, *We Are All Lesbians*, published by Violet Press in 1973. Books of her poetry are *Looking At Women, Dyke Jacket* and *Goddess of Lesbian Dreams*, all published by Violet Press. Her poetry is in anthologies including *Poems From the Women's Movement* (Library of America, 2009). Her paintings were in the first gay artists' show at New York's New Museum in 1982 and are included in Harmony Hammond's *Lesbian Art In America* (Rizzoli, 2000).

Christopher St. Liberation Day, June 28, 1970

with our banners and our smiles
we're being photographed
by tourists police and leering men
we fill their cameras
with 10,000 faces
bearing witness
to our own existence
in sunlight
from Washington Maryland
Massachusetts Pennsylvania
Connecticut Ohio
Iowa Minnesota
from Harlem and the suburbs
the universities
and the world
we are women who love women
we are men who love men
we are lesbians and homosexuals
we cannot apologize

for knowing
what others refuse to know
for affirming
what they deny
we might have been
the women and men
who watched us and waved
and made fists
and gave us victory signs
and stood there after we had passed
thinking of all they had to lose
and of how society punishes its victims
who are all of us
in the end
but we are sisters and sisters
brothers and brothers
workers and lovers
we are together
we are marching
past the crumbling old world
that leans toward us
in anguish from the pavement
our banners are sails
pulling us through the streets
where we have always been
as ghosts
now we are shouting our own words
we are a community
we are society
we are everyone
we are inside you
remember
all you were taught to forget
we are part of the new world

photographers
grim behind precise machines
wait to record
our blood and sorrow
and revolutionaries beside them
remark

love is not political
when we stand against our pain
they say
we are not standing against anything
when we demand our total lives
they wonder
what we are demanding
cant you lie
cant you lie
they whisper they hiss
like fire in grass
cant you lie
and get on with the real work

our line winds
into Central Park
and doubles itself
in a snakedance
to the top of a hill
we cover the Sheep Meadow
shouting
lifting our arms
we are marching into ourselves
like a body
gathering its cells
creating itself
in sunlight
we turn to look back
on the thousands behind us
it seems we will converge
until we explode
sisters and sisters
brothers and brothers
together

This poem appears courtesy of the author. It appeared in Looking At Women, *by Fran Winant (1971, Violet Press, New York, NY).*

Chicago Gay Pride, 1975

© Harold J. Osler

TUNING IN

No Girl in My Soup

Thom Nickels

In the fall of 1968 I moved to Boston from Philadelphia to begin my alternate military service as a conscientious objector (CO). After securing CO work at Tufts–New England Medical Center and settling into a small room in Harvard Square, Cambridge, I was ready to check out the gay scene.

During my first few months in Boston-Cambridge I made up (in spades) for my sex-starved high school years. Although I was out at this point, the only men I seemed to be meeting were closeted Harvard men (some of whom dressed in opera capes) in downtown bars like the Punch Bowl. On the weekends I'd hitchhike from Boston into Cambridge after the bars closed hoping to get a lift from a willing prospect (sans opera cape, of course). In my Harvard Square rooming house I was meeting socialists, hippies—I especially remember a defrocked San Francisco Episcopal gay priest—and assorted "ivory tower" Harvard academics. The possibilities for friendship seemed endless.

Nineteen sixty-nine was a momentous year. On the morning of April 9, around 4 a.m., I was walking through Harvard Yard on my way to work when I ran into the SDS (Students for a Democratic Society, a radical antiwar group) occupation of Harvard's University Hall. Police vans were leaving in droves in an attempt to evict the SDS students who had occupied the building after evicting several of the deans. The scene was pure chaos, with screaming police and students hanging banners out of windows.

The police mistreatment of the protesters led to the radicalization of most Harvard students and a 10-day strike ensued. For 10 days Harvard Yard was filled with student protesters, musicians and famous people giving speeches about freedom of speech and student activism. One afternoon I listened as Nobel laureate George Wald defended the strike and demanded amnesty for the SDS occupiers.

In 1969 I was harboring (and bedding) AWOL soldiers I'd met in Harvard Yard. These ex-soldiers were refusing service in Vietnam or having second thoughts about being drafted. I'd feed and house these guys in my small room and then refer them to people I met at Tufts New England who knew "underground" safety routes to Canada. Usually I'd bring the AWOL soldier to a designated bar or café and he'd be taken to the next safe place on the new Underground Railroad. In this way I felt that I was doing my part for the "revolution."

After the events of June 1969 at New York's Stonewall bar, two new underground papers, *Lavender Vision* and *The Broadside Free Press*, appeared on the streets of Boston. Here at last were alternatives to the fag-bashing lefty publications like Boston's (SDS-controlled) *Old Mole*, the signature newspaper of radicals protesting the Vietnam War. These radicals championed prejudicial *Good Housekeeping*–magazine-style values when it came to homosexuality. The word "fag" was used widely in *Old Mole* articles.

There was considerable homophobia in leftist and antiwar communities at that time, but less homophobia in the street hippie/musician and drug scene. This was quite a shock to me, having just left Republican suburban Philadelphia for an environment I thought would be prejudice free and on the cutting edge of social change.

These radicals may have had beards and long hair and wanted the U.S. out of Vietnam, but when it came to the sexual revolution they were no more liberated than the Pennsylvania Amish.

Gay Liberation might have been new on the scene, but I felt that over time it would force many of the old guard radicals to change their tune. The birth of the women's liberation movement was certainly a sign that change was coming. Straight women would be instrumental in helping to change the consciousness of straight men when it came to issues of sexuality. This assured me that the fag-baiting days of the *Old Mole* were numbered.

As a young writer/journalist I was eager to write for *Lavender Vision*, Boston's first gay liberation newspaper. I had just joined the Boston Gay Liberation Front and knew that GLF had its work cut out for it: Not only did it have to change the way straight male radicals perceived gays—a revolution that supported the transformation of oppressive governments and illegal wars but did not oppose the oppression of homosexuals was only half a revolution—it also had to construct the building blocks for changing the larger society.

My first published piece in *LV* was "Straight Amerika, the Moon

Is on Your Crotch." Here I recounted an experience I had with three hippie-leftist "revolutionaries" whom I'd met in the Boston Common. These long-haired guys and I began a friendly chat until they noticed my Gay Liberation Now button. "Oh no—we can't go for that!" they said. I explained to them that if this was really what they thought, then they were no better then the people who owned and operated Boston's State Street Bank—in other words, the corporate enemy or the system imperialists behind the operation known as the Vietnam War.

Oppression is the same, I told them, whether it's found in the political or personal realm. I warned them that gay liberation was the beginning of a tidal wave that would eventually change the face of society.

Boston GLF held weekly meetings at MIT. When we weren't meeting together in conference rooms we'd occasionally go to the movies together. One night we went as a group to see a movie, *There's a Girl in My Soup*. As we were buying tickets I remember that I didn't want the woman cashier to think that we were straight. "There's no girl in my soup!" I exclaimed proudly. The inane comment caused a comic uproar of sorts, especially when a fellow GLFer jumped on my back and repeated the refrain for the benefit of the cashier.

"There's no girl in my soup!" he said, "and while we're at it, there's no girl in my bed, either."

With this Marx Brothers routine we had performed our first, albeit frivolous, zap. Many more would follow.

Gay liberation had become such an all-consuming passion for me that I stapled a sign—Join the Brothers and Sisters of the Gay Liberation Front—on the back of my leather jacket. It wasn't enough to wait until the group organized zaps.

They could as easily be done as solitary endeavors, anywhere or anytime. Whether it was showing up at the Brattle Theater in my leather jacket sign and making sure I placed myself in front of heterosexual couples in the ticket line, or dashing ahead of sailors on leave while they walked downtown with their parents, I relished the emotional impact the sign might be having on people walking or standing behind me.

A casual zap with "thunderous" consequences occurred when Boston poet Rudy Kikel and I decided to walk hand in hand down Charles Street one late afternoon. As we strolled along somewhat self-consciously we watched in horror as a car coming up alongside us crashed into a telephone pole. Obviously the driver was so discombobulated at our hand-holding that he lost control of the steering wheel.

When I wasn't working in the hospital I spent many hours hawking *Lavender Vision* in Harvard Square. I was especially eager to get the attention of the mustached male lefties walking by carrying rolled-up copies of the *Old Mole*. The male lefties never took a newspaper, but a number of women did. Those were real hippie/radical women in long commune-style dresses and Janis Joplin hair. Overall the reactions to my hawking the paper and shouting, "Get your gay liberation newspaper!" were pretty blasé. At the time I was trying to decide whether outright hostility would have been preferable to the sheer indifference that I encountered. I was at least hoping to get a phone number from a passing stranger, some perk for all my hard work, but nothing on that level ever materialized. At the time I blamed this on Boston's puritan heritage or my battle with chronic acne. But that's another story.

Since Boston GLF agreed to participate in the Black Panther Revolutionary Peoples' Constitutional Convention (RPCC) in Washington, D.C., in September 1970, we boarded a Ken Kesey–style Volkswagen bus for the nation's capital. We were scheduled to stay at the Gay Liberation commune for the weekend and then, along with scores of other GLFers throughout the nation—some 60 gay men and two dozen lesbians—present our case for equality and inclusion when the convention convened.

In the Gay Liberation commune we held roundtable discussions, slept on the floor in sleeping bags and danced in circles while holding hands. What was novel in the dance circle were the numbers of men in genderfuck dresses whipping it up faster than a team of whirling dervishes.

In Washington we worried about the Panthers' acceptance of gay liberation. While we knew that Huey Newton was a staunch ally of gay liberation (in an August 1970 edition of the Black Panther Party newsletter Newton made an appeal to oppressed groups, including homosexuals, to "unite with the BPP in revolutionary fashion"), there was trouble with the Eldridge Cleaver contingent. The Cleaver people believed that being gay was as sick as wanting to be president of General Motors. While in Washington we'd even gotten word that a sizable contingent of Panthers snickered at the GLFers (in dresses) at one of the pre-convention meetings. This caused considerable angst in the Gay Liberation commune. Some of us were very worried how we would be received by the general convention.

This proved to be a needless worry, because the convention adjourned early. There had been reports of in-fighting and disagreements, perhaps the result of FBI attempts to sabotage the convention. The disappointment we felt at the cancellation was tremendous, although the free time enabled us to perform a number of small zaps around Washington before heading back to Boston via New York City.

One such zap was a 7 a.m. impromptu dance-a-thon (thanks to a jukebox) we held in a local fast-food restaurant packed to the gills with contractors and blue-collar workers getting their morning coffee.

The workers' reaction was particularly blasé, as if they'd seen such displays a million times before.

In New York City we toured the Village and stayed in the warehouse apartment of a New York member. The New York and Washington sleepovers, at least for me, were always chaste events. Politics and ideas seemed to snuff out the libido's cravings, although I do remember attempting to live vicariously through the nocturnal lovemaking sounds of a monogamous interracial couple who had become our Boston GLF poster boys.

GLF didn't seem to mind the fact that the couple was monogamous, even if most GLFers weren't all that approving of monogamy. This was my first lesson in life's contradictions: Monogamy may have been condemned as an idea many equated (in consciousness-raising sessions anyway) with capitalist ownership, but when it came to two guys GLF genuinely liked and respected, GLF looked the other way. Our honorably monogamous GLF poster couple even had a special king-size bed sheltered behind a massive full Victorian-style canopy during our New York stay. Talk about *Good Housekeeping* moments! (Sadly, not even the peeping Toms among us got a chance to view the desired couple in action. In many ways Boston GLF was a highly moral group.)

After the botched Washington convention, I continued to write for *Lavender Vision* and joined my fellow GLFers in the 1970 Moratorium against the Vietnam War. With our striking Boston Gay Liberation Front placards we marched through hundreds of thousands of people gathered on the Boston Common, the crowds parting like the Red Sea as we became our own little army. I can easily recall the fascinated stares and dumbfounded looks we received then. There were no words of hostility directed at us, despite the fact that for most of the participants this was probably their first look at openly gay men marching en masse.

For me it was an especially proud public moment, in essence my first gay pride event, even if I kept wishing that our GLF contingent was much larger than it actually was.

Thom Nickels is a journalist/playwright and the author of eight published books including Philadelphia Architecture *and* Out in History. *He is the architectural writer/critic for the* Philadelphia Bulletin, *a weekly columnist for Philadelphia's* Star *newspaper chain and a contributing writer to the* Gay and Lesbian Review. *Nickels is the religion book editor for the* Lambda Book Report. *In 2005 he was the recipient of the Philadelphia AIA Lewis Mumford Architectural Journalism Award. His novel* SPORE *will be published in 2010.*

Coming Out as a Reluctant Activist in a Gay Maoist Cell who Mostly Just Wanted to Get Laid

Mark Freeman

As a not-yet-20-year-old, I was in the right places at the most interesting of times. Just up from Los Angeles Valley, the original Valley that is, home of our fair nation's first mall, made famous by Frank Zappa's kid, Moon Unit, who was ridiculing her straight peers in the song "Valley Girl." No gagging-with-a-spoon was required to encourage a still dorky proto-hippie tired of being harassed by jocks to finally escape those suburbs by hitchhiking to San Francisco for good in 1967.

The San Francisco Bay Area had been drawing my friends and me northward all through our high school hell years, via news of the Free Speech Movement at UC Berkeley, the Freedom Riders recruited to the South and then rumors of a new haven forming in a neighborhood called the Haight. We were the two or three "peace creep" weirdos in each high school in the L.A. area, finding ourselves and each other through a Unitarian Church group with the acronym LRY: Liberal Religious Youth. We met monthly for antinuclear rallies, light substance use and the usual adolescent bisexual intrigues at weekend-long parties at the home of whoever's parents would let us, or were out of town. But the Bay Area was our Mecca.

I was not gay, you understand, just definitely not straight, in the unhip square sense of the term. Of my first handful of sexual experiences, three merely happened to be guys—and each more or less connected to political happenings.

The first was on the floor of his parents' penthouse apartment, where we organized a boycott of Pacific Palisades High School after it passed a dress code outlawing our long hair. Another was an ex–junior high teacher of mine met while circle-dancing at midnight on the grass at the Valley Unitarian Church, while inside weird lights flashed and weirder individuals cavorted to experimental electronic music and one guy atop a stepladder speed-rapped nonstop. That, it turned out, was Neal Cassady, and they were the Merry Pranksters. Who knew? You can read about that big night in

Tom Wolfe's *Electric Kool-Aid Acid Test*. Yet another experience was with a Negro activist in his 20s, back when "Black Power" was a new term. After I attended a few meetings of the increasingly radical Student Nonviolent Coordinating Committee, SNCC decided that white folks could no longer be members. But I could still go to their wild mixed parties, which is where we did it.

It should be clarified that sex and sexual orientation back then were still something you had or did, and not something you were. I don't think there was any fewer instances of homosexual activity pre–gay liberation, and maybe there were more, as the only out queers were the few obvious bull-dykes or drag queens, but the hidden homos had far more sex, and quite often with straight folk. Of course, it was all very hush-hush.

My role models and roommates at my first dingy apartment in San Francisco were two politically engaged girls who'd graduated from my high school a few years before. One I met while she was working in a used bookstore, singing and strumming Joan Baez songs at the cash register, her hair aptly falling over her face and onto her guitar. The other was employed in the box office of the Victoria Theater, the last burlesque follies in the Mission. Only years later did I find out that Barbara and Val had been secret lesbian lovers all that time. No longer a mere folkie intellectual, by now I was officially a hippie, a diminutive of the beatnik hipster, the term coined by *SF Chronicle* columnist Herb Caen.

My first year in San Francisco began with the Gathering of the Tribes: A Human Be-In that filled a meadow in Golden Gate Park. It was joyous, stoned and spiritual, but was it gay? Here's the thing. To us, hippie meant pro-sex (also pro-living, pro-psychedelics, pro-freedom). Before Gay Lib erupted in 1969, there was no call to proclaim yourself in public. Nevertheless, along with Lenore Kandel, who'd just had an obscenity bust for her poem "To Fuck With Love," Allen Ginsberg was there and his poetry was overtly homoerotic. Timothy Leary was there, chanting his "Tune In, Turn On, Drop Out" mantra, but so was his partner in LSD research, Dr. Richard Alpert, soon to become known as Ram Dass and only much later to come out (he says talking about being homosexual might have distracted from his spiritual message).

The Dead were there, and maybe a quarter of their fans were homo- and bisexual. Or at least, like most every other hippies, embraced the idea of Do Your Own Thing, as in, "that's cool for you" or "whatever's right." Berkeley politicos chanted, "Out Now!," but the chief hippie slogan against our involvement in, Vietnam was "Make Love, Not War!," There were no rules and few judgments as to what kind of love that was. That year the national media announced the Summer of Love in San Francisco, but we'd already held a mock funeral procession through the Haight to mourn the "death of hippie" at the hands of media hype.

Now living at Dolores and Market Streets with two hip but hetero guy friends from LRY, I got together with my first long-term girlfriend. She came up from L.A. (where I had known and admired her in high school), arriving to discover why her boyfriend wasn't communicating anymore. Turns out he had taken up with a wild LRY girl who had been staying with me. So of course his now ex and I consoled each other. Don't ask, it's complicated at that age. Just let me admit that in all this mixed foursome, it was the boy I was most attracted to. Something similar had occurred with my very first female mate, Debbie Winston, when a partner-in-bed switch landed me with her gal pal, instead of with that girl's Mick Jagger–lipped boyfriend. I was so glad to be—and to be seen as— "normal" for a change, though she did later wonder out loud why "all the boys I have slept with have wanted each other more."

My new partner was beautiful, a bit like the Tenniel drawings of Alice in Wonderland, with long hair well below her behind. I was the curly-headed, skinny Jew-boy to her little hippie Earth Mama. We were both 18. Living in Bernal Heights, then a racially mixed working-class neighborhood, she taught pottery to local kids. I helped start a free film festival in the basement of the library (we'd double-bill *The Blob* with an anti–Vietnam War doc). Together we worked with the local branch of the Food Conspiracy, a buy-in-bulk no mark-up venture that sprang from the Haight hippie commune Kaliflower. It grew into San Francisco's premier collective, Rainbow Foods, which remains the only supermarket hip enough to close for a holiday on Gay Pride. (The first gay march here was in 1970 and was called a Gay-In, then it became Gay Freedom Day, and later devolved into mere Pride.) Is a picture emerging from out of the druggy mists? Being queer was a quiet part of a larger counterculture.

As a low-paying job I was hired by Arlene Goldbard at Draft Help, a draft counseling agency (as in, how to stay out of Vietnam) started by Steve Gibson at San Francisco State University (née College). During the Strike of 1968 we moved it to the corner of 18th and Dolores in the Mission. Carl Wittman was our military counselor for guys already in the service who were thinking of going AWOL. Best known for writing *A Gay Manifesto*, he was an early advocate of a gay activism closer to Black Power and Women's Liberation ("We're Here, We're Queer, Get Used to It!"), as opposed to the more mainstream homophile movement ("First-Class Citizenship for Homosexuals").

He'd report on small but stirring protest demos and told me (somehow or other he figured I'd be interested) about the "Purple Hand" protest, on Halloween of 1969, against the editorial policies of the *San Francisco Examiner*. They printed the names and addresses of men arrested in gay bars, for instance. When a bag of purple ink was dumped on the protesters by printers, the angry queers used the ink to scrawl "Gay Power" on the newspaper building and continued decorating with their hand prints.

To support Carl, my girlfriend and I wound up in a Civic Center convention hall at the 1970 American Psychiatric Association meeting with the small group of Gay Lib activists to disrupt it. The APA removed its "diseased" definition of homosexuality in 1973.

Among our Food Conspiracy cronies around town were several houses of gay men and lesbians in Noe Valley, a working-class white neighborhood next to Eureka Valley (which was not yet called The Castro). They considered me an enlightened straight guy, and we swapped recipes for granola. At another house in the lower Haight, a cute gay guy took me aside and gave me a copy of a novel from the Parisian Press, a bisexual pillow book that took place at actual places like the Ritch Street Baths and a bar called the Stud. How did he know I'd be into it? I did not share the book with my girlfriend, but kept my eye open for that bar.

After we broke up (or she broke off with me, to be precise) I thought I could relax into a quiet bisexuality. Little did I know that as soon as I acted on my gay feelings, the proverbial closet door would swing open for good. I made my way to a house of gay liberation guys in Noe Valley and got pounded that very day. Soon we were all in a gay Marxist study group, which morphed into the June 28th Union, named for the date of the Stonewall Riots in New York. Like all young firebrands, each of us wanted to be more radical than anyone else, and so like Chinese Red Guards we did Criticism/Self Criticism and considered ourselves Maoist. But among our crew (li'l Joey, Camomile, Ferd Egan, the Michaels Novick and Silverman) I was the one most considered an "immature leftist with bourgeois tendencies."

As gay activists, we leafleted the bars, and as gay libbers typically chanted "Out of the bars and into the streets!" as we marched by. I was more than a little interested in getting myself into the bars and between the sheets. In the Haight Ashbury there was the I-Beam and Gus' Pub, run by Malcolm, who would go on to open El Rio: Your Dive in the Outer Mission. While the Mission was always funky hip, the Haight style was ornate, teeming with thrift store treasures in Victorian excess. North Beach was the gay neighborhood during the beatnik era and well into the '60s with bars like the Savoy Tivoli and the delightfully named Anxious Asp. Downtown closeted businessmen applauded drag superstar Charles Pierce at the Gold Coast and gawked at sailor go-go boys in gilded cages at the Rendezvous. Even gayer (and more full of color) was Polk Gulch, with its piano and hustler bars on Polkstrasse, Black dance bar Oil Can Harry's and my fave, the Alley Cat, where you could almost be sure of a nightly fight, usually involving at least one lesbian. The downscale boys my age and young queens were like catnip to me.

We'd go to South of Market for, shall we say, easily accessible opportunities. There were baths downtown (Bull Dog) and in the Mission (Liberty Street), but none like the endless hallways of kinky fantasy found at the Folsom Barracks. Of the South of Market bars, our favorite was the Stud, founded by hippie George Matson in 1966—the first bar of any kind in San Francisco to play punk music. It was the hangout of Sylvester and the Cockettes and Etta James, and became the regular home to long-haired hippie bucks, New Wave hetero girls and drag queens who didn't even try to pass as women.

It was in one of the bathhouses, the unique bisexual Sutro Baths in the space Club 1808 now occupies on Folsom, that I first met Harvey Milk—dressed. Replete with ponytail from his days as hippie co-producer of the play *Hair* in New York and now running a haphazard camera shop on Castro Street, Harvey was making his first run for supervisor in 1973. He was at the bath's shop area, collecting funds for his campaign in a cardboard dairy container cut out to simply read "homo Milk." He was a doer, and despite my Maoist pals' disdain for mere electoral politics, Harvey and I hit it off. We later worked together against Proposition 6, the anti–gay teacher initiative, and on an anti–real estate speculation bill—even though many of the real estate wheeler-dealers were gay.

The Democratic Party did everything it could to keep Harvey

out of office. They already had their gay power-broker flunky and had him run against Milk to split the vote. But Harvey's power base were the new residents of Eureka Valley, welfare queens from the Haight, sweater queens from the Financial District and show-tune queens from Polk, who made the transition to being 501 Levi lovers and leather queens and became the newly "masculine" Castro clones. Harvey had to cut off his long hair to finally get elected, but the hippie roots of San Francisco Gay Lib never completely died out.

A new revolutionary trend was growing, nurtured by these undying roots. Carl Wittman contributed to the birth of this Radical Faeries movement, as it is called, but again somewhat indirectly. Carl was in a straight couple back then. He and his partner were to become political whores. Not party hacks, but literally prostitutes. They came out as a lesbian and a gay man, and each put an ad in the *Berkeley Barb* (like Craigslist now). With the money they made, they bought land in Wolf Creek, a small town in southern Oregon that was attracting fed-up-with-the-City emigrés. Carl and his lover Allan Troxler bought out the wife, and theirs became the first gay male farm in Wolf Creek. Up the road from Carl and Allan's place was a separatist feminist commune, only women welcome except for close friends like their two gay neighbors.

In 1976 Carl and Allan took over publication of *RFD: A Country Journal for Gay Men* from its Iowa founders. That same year, George Jalbert, also known as Crow and by his comfier nickname Chenille, bought land on the other side of Highway 101 in Wolf Creek. On July 4, 1976, as an alternative bicentennial event, the new gay farm hosted the Faggots and Class Struggle conference, where the Gay Men's Theater Collective first presented a version of their seminal (and often semenal) work, *Crimes Against Nature*. This was the land that became Nomenus, the first "fairy sanctuary."

Michael Starkman was an original cast member (and therefore co-writer) of that passionate group-theater piece. I met him during a new surge of San Francisco gay lib, the mass political organization known as BAGL (pronounced like the boiled Jewish bakery good but actually an acronym for Bay Area Gay Liberation)—a group aimed at labor coalitions and founded by three Trotskyist organizers in early 1975. Coming five or six years after other Gay Liberation Fronts, it soon took on a slew of isms, the focus getting re-argued week to week. As Michael puts it, "culling from so many progressive forces bubbling around us, feminism, Maoist class analysis (the most boring), anti-imperialist movements."

Starkman also recalls another outgrowth of Gay Liberation. "The Radical Faerie movement happened in a lot of cities at about the same time, despite the Harry Hay hagiography. I'm not sure that we were using that term before Hay issued his famous Call to the Desert in '79. But Arthur Evans, who would publish *Witchcraft & the Gay Counterculture*, was talking about pagans in his Faerie Circle. And there was a Radical Sissy study group I was in since about 1977, with Tede Matthews, a stubborn, generous drag and welfare queen doing genderfuck—and really classfuck, working-class drag when drag meant upper-class lady imagery, because really who wouldn't want to be Lana Turner? Tede later worked at Modern Times Bookstore, and you can see and hear him in the classic gay documentary *Word Is Out*. Also Silvana Nova, who actually made a mock run for supervisor, and quite a few others. Our analysis focused on masculinist imperialism, the patriarchal energy operating even in Gay Lib. I can still hear your crit/self crit, Michael dear, and can only reply "Guilty as charged."

Since we're already a bit afield of the date parameters of the original Gay Liberation movement, perhaps I can make one last untimely comment on our past and future. There's a word for those we lost in those times, and that word is heroic. Harvey Milk, a martyr who was anything but a saint. Allen Ginsberg, a joyfully lecherous Jewish grandfather for gay boys everywhere. Ram Dass, who worked with Tim Leary but grew up, came out and taught compassionate hospice care. Mike Silverstein, a suicide when rejected as too faggy by the privileged Maoist revolutionaries of Prairie Fire Organizing Committee. The first girl I ever slept with, Debbie Winston, shot and killed while pregnant by her boyfriend in Oakland. Ferd Egan, drug advocate and ACT UP firebrand. Gary "Shocky" Comfort, the most beautiful man I've ever met, who died before benefiting from Gay Asian Pride. Proto–Radical Faery Carl Wittman, Cockettes Sylvester and Martin Worman, HIV nurse George "Chenille" Jalbert. All died early of AIDS.

And the scores we lost later. Comrades and lovers and heroes all, I pass them on to you.

Mark Freeman is still living in San Francisco. He has spent the last two decades working as a Nurse Practitioner at Tom Waddell Health Center's Transgender Clinic and doing harm reduction work with folks on drugs. Before that he produced/narrated the radio show Healing Tales, *stories for people living with HIV and those who love them. His latest project is* Pop101: Now Then & Back When, *a cross-generational blogcast on pop music. He has been with Ken, the other most beautiful boy he ever met, for 20 years.*

Our Passion Shook the World

Martha Shelley

We were hot and rude, joyous and angry, utopian and opinionated. "Nuanced" wasn't part of our vocabulary. Question authority? We didn't even recognize it!

July 4, 1968, Philadelphia: A group of gays carrying neatly printed signs with slogans like "Equality for Homosexuals" picketed Independence Hall under the hot sun. The men wore suits and ties, the women wore skirts and nylon stockings. I hated the dress code, hated the passersby who treated us like a sideshow. I particularly remember a chubby boy in shorts who licked the drips off a vanilla ice cream cone as he gazed blankly at the freaks. I lusted after an ice cream, but we had to maintain an orderly, dignified picket line. At the end of the day, I swore I'd never do it again.

December, 1969, Greenwich Village: A freezing day, but I was reasonably cozy in a secondhand suede jacket with only one rip at the elbow. I held up my bundle of papers and cried, "Get your copy of *ComeOut!*, newspaper of the Gay Liberation Front." A straight couple went by, pushing a stroller. They gave me the freak-show stare, so I shouted, "*ComeOut!* on sale here—find out what your kid will be like when he grows up." To my delight, they jumped and ran off.

What happened between those two dates was the Stonewall Riot, followed by the founding of the Gay Liberation Front. The history of those events has been told elsewhere. Here I want to talk about our visions for the future and what became of them.

We were anarchic from the outset. Anyone who had a project in mind got together with others of similar inclination and made it happen: a dance, a demonstration, a newspaper. If we had anything resembling a platform, it was best expressed by the resolutions we proposed at ERCHO (the Eastern Regional Conference of Homophile Organizations) in November 1969.

We demanded freedom and self-determination for all minority groups. We condemned the persecution of elements of these minorities, specifically political prisoners and those accused of crimes without victims.

A member of the Mattachine Society described this resolution as "not even remotely pertinent to the homophile movement." In a way, he was right. The old homophile movement tried to present gays as just like straights but with a teensy difference—like being left-handed instead of right-handed. The gay liberation movement saw our oppression as one leg of the behemoth that stomped on us and divided our communities—the other legs being male domination, white supremacy and economic exploitation.

October 1970: Demonstrators, including GLF members, gathered in the streets outside the Women's House of Detention in Greenwich Village, shouting our support for Angela Davis. The inmates called down to us. Most of them had been accused of victimless crimes such as prostitution and possession of drugs. They set fire to bits of paper and waved them about, brief orange flickerings against thick black bars, thin brown arms. I wondered if any of those arms belonged to Angela, or if she was being held in a segregated cell.

A few blocks away, white middle-class lesbians gathered at the Duchess, a popular watering hole. An acquaintance told me how comfortable she felt there, where she didn't have to consort with the black and Hispanic lesbians who patronized the Big D farther downtown.

Our next resolution at ERCHO was to call for lesbians and gay men to protest the Vietnam War openly as homosexuals.

Before the Stonewall Riot, members of Columbia University's Student Homophile League (including me) joined an antiwar protest on campus. The other students kept their distance, as though we had measles. When New York GLF participated in a much larger antiwar march, a liberal newspaper columnist dismissed us as the "slim-waisted creeps of the Gay Liberation Front."

Today the issue the gay community is fighting for isn't being openly gay in the peace movement; it's being openly gay in the military. How much more antithetical to the original spirit of GLF can you get? Join an organization where you're expected to kill and die on command? Nobody could give us orders!

We had other resolutions. We demanded freedom from society's attempts to define and limit human sexuality. We called for dominion over one's own body, through sexual freedom without regard to orientation, through freedom to use birth control and abortion, and through freedom to ingest the drugs of one's choice.

November 1969, the ERCHO conference in Philadelphia: The venue was a lesbian bar with blacked-out windows, warm and a bit stuffy despite the season. Representatives arrived from organizations of vastly different sizes and influence. Mattachine, the largest, had hundreds of members; other organizations consisted of one gay couple and a mimeo machine. I was a member of the Daughters of Bilitis delegation and also caucused with GLF. Debate on the above resolutions was heated. The turning point came when Craig Schoonmaker of Homosexuals Intransigent denounced abortion on the grounds that lesbians don't get pregnant. People thought he was Catholic but he was just misogynist. (In 1977, he formed a political party. Its principles included banning abortion, amputating hands of third-time offenders, trimming the military by firing all women except nurses and secretaries, and reducing the price of phone sex.)

The older DOB women jumped to their feet and raised hell. I knew from private conversations that one of them had been raped and impregnated and had procured an abortion, at a time when that was illegal and dangerous. Craig's speech, and the fury of the women's response, tipped the vote in our favor.

We understood from the get-go that the right to control our bodies was central, and it was exactly what the powers that be wanted to take from us. Our youth gave us the courage of certainty, but left us blind to complexities that would unfold in the course of time.

In those days we demanded the right to be free of unwanted pregnancies. We couldn't have imagined today's demands: the right to inseminate, to adopt and to foster, or for parental rights to be based on raising children together, rather than on mere biology.

Back then, though we wouldn't have argued for heroin, some of us thought that ingesting psychedelic drugs was a positive good. Now I will admit that I could've done with a little less ingestion. But I think most GLFers would still agree that drug use should be decriminalized and the prisons emptied of addicts.

I am still perplexed about the transsexual issue. On the one hand, it is clearly subsumed under the right to control your own body. On the other, the essence of GLF thought (and where it intersected with feminist thought) was that we had the right to be anything we wanted with the bodies we had. That we could reclaim our bodies from a society that denigrated them, and learn to love them. That the whole gamut of human expression—clothing, gesture, emotion, sexuality—was permitted to anyone. Now it seems that there is considerable social pressure for young lesbians who would have been butch in the old days to alter their bodies, chemically and surgically, and become men. (I don't know whether effeminate men feel the same pressure.) Nobody knows what the long-term consequences of these medical interventions will be.

Despite the unforeseen complexities, the resolutions we drafted 40 years ago are amazingly relevant today. There's still plenty of work to do on all these issues. Yet I'm blown away by what our movement has done so far. In 1969 we couldn't hold hands in public, and now gay marriage is legal in four nations, civil unions in fifteen more. There are gay film festivals everywhere (even Siberia) and a lesbian prime minister in Iceland.

GLFers were young, hot-headed, sure of our own opinions. We quarreled with each other and dissolved into splinter groups: Radicalesbians, Red Butterfly, Third World Gay Revolution, the Effeminists, Street Transvestite Action Revolutionaries, the Gay Activist Alliance. Utopian quests are always short-lived. But if we hadn't exploded into existence, gays would still be pleading politely for acceptance, and the world would still be deaf to their pleas.

Martha Shelley was one of the founders of New York Gay Liberation Front and Radicalesbians, and a member of the collective that produced ComeOut! *newspaper. Her articles helped shape the ideology of the gay liberation movement. She currently lives with her wife Sylvia in Portland, Oregon, where they are active in the local Code Pink chapter.*

Sylvester: A Singer Without a Closet

Tommi Avicolli Mecca

David Bowie and other outrageous "glitter rock" performers in the early 70s may have seemed out because of their flamboyant performances, but none of them were actually out of the closet, or they briefly came out only to renounce their sexuality on their rise to the top.

Blues and disco singer Sylvester was out, proud and never had a closet. *Tales of the City* author Armistead Maupin once described him as "one of the few truly gay celebrities never to have renounced his gayness on the ladder to success."

Born in Los Angeles in 1947 into a middle-class black family, Sylvester followed his grandmother Julia Morgan's advice and learned to sing well. Morgan was a blues singer of the '20s and '30s. Sylvester became known early on as the "child wonder of gospel" because of his powerful and stirring church singing. After many conflicts with his mother and stepfather as a teenager, Sylvester took off for San Francisco in 1967. He would later say, "My life started when I moved to San Francisco."

"Here I felt free," he told *Rolling Stone* in an interview. "I could do anything I wanted because I had no past."

In San Francisco, Sylvester, like many of his generation, reinvented himself. He soon started performing in drag under the name Ruby Blue, utilizing the blues and gospel repertoire he developed in L.A. He sang around the city wherever he could, including with a then unknown girl group called the Pointer Sisters.

When he was invited to join the Cockettes, the outrageous hippie gay male theater troupe, Sylvester quickly made a name for himself with his collection of old Bessie Smith songs and dresses from his grandmother. His first performance with the troupe was in a show called "Hollywood Babylon." He appeared in one of the Cockettes' most famous and controversial movies, *Tricia's Wedding*, a takeoff of the nuptials of then-president Richard Nixon's daughter.

After gaining a huge San Francisco following, the Cockettes eventually took their act to New York, and though they failed to

Sylvester in the late 1980s, performing in Philadelphia

capture the hearts of the jaded big city, Sylvester's immense talents didn't go unnoticed. He ended up with a record contract with Blue Thumb, which put out two of his albums. His first featured a kick-ass version of Bessie Smith's classic "Gimme a Pigfoot." His backup group, the Hot Band, at one point included Martha Wash and Izora Rhodes, who would go on to become the Weather Girls.

Though he always said he wanted to be a Harlem jazz singer with a full orchestra backing him, Sylvester's career in the late '70s took him in different direction, as he explored dance music and eventually became a disco star. His huge hits, "You Make Me Feel (Mighty Real)" and "Dance (Disco Heat)," earned him the nickname Queen of Disco, a title that was equally shared by fellow disco singers Gloria Gayner and Donna Summers.

His fame spread. He made an appearance in Bette Midler's *The Rose*. He recorded backup for Patti Labelle and Sarah Dash, and in 1985 for Aretha Franklin's "Who's Zoomin Who?" LP. He sold out shows wherever he went. David Bowie once quipped that the reason his San Francisco debut wasn't sold out was because the city had Sylvester and didn't need him.

In December 1988, at the age of 40, Sylvester succumbed to AIDS, ending a short but accomplished career as an out gay black performer.

Living Lesbian Nation

Victoria A. Brownworth

In 1972, the year I finished high school, *Village Voice* columnist jill johnston published *Lesbian Nation*, a collection of her ruminative short essays on being a dyke. The columns were written between 1969 and 1971—the formative, foundation years of the gay liberation movement.

If you Google "Lesbian Nation" now, you do not get information on johnston or her book, but rather a host of meet-and-greet Web sites for lesbians, replete with information on the top 10 hotties from the popular TV show *The L Word.*

Four decades since the Stonewall Rebellion have brought us not the revolution of our then dreams, but the complacent assimilationism of looking for dates online and checking out the heterosexual actresses who play gay on TV. Whither Lesbian Nation, the amazon country of my youth?

Memoir is a complex entity. There is a critical juncture between memory and history, and that is where the convergence of events and activism begins to emerge not just as a burgeoning political movement but as actual history. Forty years after Stonewall, we are just beginning to truly write that history, and much of that history is built from memories still fresh, vivid and visceral.

My own memories of the movement that created lesbian liberation begin with a cold autumn night in 1970 above an adult bookstore on Market Street in what was then the Tenderloin porno/hustler/prostitution strip in Philadelphia. It was a school night, although I no longer remember if it was a Monday or a Thursday or one of the nights in between. I was 14 years old and in my coat pocket lay a carefully folded clipping torn from *The Drummer,* an alternative newspaper, which had been stuck in my locker by a classmate. The small announcement on the piece of newspaper gave the place and time for the founding meeting of Radicalesbians.

In their 1970 manifesto/mission statement, Radicalesbians, a political action group founded by and for lesbians after Stonewall, posed the following question: "What is a lesbian?" and answered it

99

with: "A lesbian is the rage of all women condensed to the point of explosion. She is the woman who, often beginning at an extremely early age, acts in accordance with her inner compulsion to be a more complete and freer human being than her society—perhaps then, but certainly later—cares to allow her."

At 14, I had no personal mission statement, nor did I completely understand how I had so easily become the youngest member of a radical political group that was as afraid of me (jailbait that I was) as it was welcoming of me (eager new recruit to the lesbian-feminist revolution). What I *did* know was that who I understood myself to be was described succinctly in those opening lines of the Radicalesbians statement of purpose. At 14 I had already been chafing at the restraints being female had placed upon me. I was the embodiment of that rage ready to explode, and as a consequence, even though I didn't understand the importance of it all clearly at that time, RL seemed very much the group for me.

In the months before attending that founding meeting of RL, I had come to realize, despite being only 14, that I was at the very least bisexual and far more likely, lesbian. But my personal experiences of lesbianism, which were born out of my Catholic school girlhood and expanded by the Summer of Love, did not make sense in any clear context that I could visualize for myself as a mere high school sophomore. The so-called "free love" of the era had made bisexual dalliance—at least among "girls"—a commonplace. Most of my classmates had engaged in some form of sexual flirtation with other girls. Yet none of those girls identified as lesbian.

At 14 I had a female lover, and she was not my first. I also had a boyfriend, actually several boyfriends, none of whom I was lovers with. In addition, I had serious crushes on several older women, including my French teacher, who had reciprocated my interest with some flirtatious specifics. I had a vague and discomfiting sense that my sexual life, in which women were dominant and men peripheral, was abnormal, but I was attending an all-girl's high school where lesbianism was an undercurrent that ran through both faculty and student body, charging the atmosphere with a latent sexuality that touched almost everything in covert ways.

Yet, because there was no actual mention of lesbianism, the overt expression of love or desire for other girls/women was still very much the thing that dare not speak its name. Many of us—students and faculty—were having lesbian affairs, but we didn't talk about it. Lesbianism remained a secret not to be revealed, even though we all knew it was there, barely hidden. My school had a feminist predicate, dedicated as it was to the education of smart, college-bound girls, but lesbianism was a wild card not to be factored into the final equation of that education. Perceived then as it often still is now, lesbianism was the dangerous and dark underside to feminism—the natural or unnatural, depending on the perspective—end point, if one is to truly embrace feminist concepts in their entirety, and thus alarming to both women and girls alike who could not or would not envision a life outside the world of heterosexual privilege.

The defining difference between radical lesbian feminism post-Stonewall and gay liberation was that radical lesbian feminism demanded that one eschew heterosexual privilege. That singular difference explained why gay liberation went in one direction while lesbian feminism went in another. Gay men retained their male privilege, while the only link women ever could have to male privilege was by association through heterosexual relationships. Once they jettisoned that position of attenuated privilege, they became marginal creatures.

What groups like Radicalesbians did then was provide an alternative to that heterosexual privilege paradigm that we as women had all been raised to believe was our incontrovertible legacy and future. RL took the women who belonged to the group to a place where lesbianism was all-encompassing, where it was not an offshoot of something else, not a side trip, but where it was everything, the journey itself. RL broke the silence on lesbianism that surrounded every other part of my life.

At RL, being queer was real life, not a dark corner onto which no light was supposed to shine. While life in the bar scene was strictly an after-dark affair, the politics of radical lesbian feminism could be practiced day or night. Therein lay the most simplistic aspect of our liberation—we needn't hide in the shadows any longer. We were building a civil rights movement, for women and for lesbians, in which we would no longer be second-class citizens wedded literally, figuratively, and as permanent chattel to the concept of male/heterosexual privilege.

The early 1970s in Philadelphia and New York, the two cities where I spent most of my time in those years and where I was involved with lesbian and gay groups, were fraught with the conflict between gay liberation and radical lesbian feminism. As a teenager,

I was inevitably drawn to both realms of the movement. In my initial search for gay life, I had developed a coterie of older gay male friends I met in the bars, and I was perceived early on, because of my age and my looks, as a potential fag hag. But it was in radical lesbian feminism that my politics and the beginnings of my theories on gender and sexuality began to coalesce. For me, gay liberation was like nonstop recess—dancing, drinking, being wild at the bars and clubs, repeating lines from old movies and plays, being dramatic—this is what hanging out with gay men was like. Radical lesbian feminism was like a challenging school that only a few could enter, providing an education I desperately needed and could not get elsewhere—an education about myself as a lesbian woman.

In the first few years post-Stonewall, I moved back and forth between those two worlds—the gay male world where the only women were drag queens and fag hags, of which I was neither—and the radical lesbian feminist world where I was a student of serious politics that were being developed into a movement I believed would ultimately lead to a cultural and social revolution of sorts.

One of the many ways 1970 differed from now is that queer youth—lesbian, gay, transgendered, even bisexual—were not honored, embraced or even accepted except as sexual playthings. We were told, repeatedly and often not very nicely, that we were unsure, game-playing, too young to have made up our minds (this was in the days when being queer was perceived as choice rather than orientation) about our sexuality, yet we were desired, which only added to the confusion of our status. These conflicting messages made becoming part of the burgeoning post-Stonewall movement all the more difficult to navigate for someone as young as I was when I moved into that circle of older queer men and women.

In addition, the movement was, and remained for many years, male dominated and male focused. Those used to the LGBTQI political buffet can't imagine what it was like when it was merely G. That G-is-for-gay was expected to include anyone and everyone, regardless of gender or orientation, and include them—men, women, transgender people and bisexuals—under what often felt like a repressive and exclusionary male rubric.

The world Radicalesbians opened for me was one at an almost breathtaking variance with the rest of my life. The women in RL were predominantly women in their 30s and 40s, some of whom had been married to men but who had left their husbands and sometimes even their children for other women. Others were women who were stone butches who had never been with a man in any context and never would be, because women were their life. All, however, were hard-core feminists with a perspective that was defined by the surety that women were not second-class citizens but were, in many if not all respects, superior to men.

There was a self-confidence and self-acceptance in the women I met when I was a teenager in RL that was not reflected anywhere else in my life: Not at my all-girl high school, not in the gay bars I frequented with my fake ID and ready lies, not from my Seven-Sisters-college-educated mother, nor from my female teachers. The time I spent in RL helped mold me into the radical lesbian feminist I still am today, but I would not know that until much later.

In my college years, reflecting back on my days in RL, I drifted toward lesbian separatism and began to clarify for myself as well as for other women through my writing and activism, what it meant to be a lesbian in a gay male liberation movement. I needed to immerse myself in women, in lesbian feminist theory, in a world that was as removed from the patriarchy as we could create within a larger patriarchal society. It was a heady and difficult time, and many other women I knew were struggling to achieve this balance between the male-dominated heterosexual world and the gay liberation movement of which we were a presumptive part.

In the period when RL was functioning in Philadelphia, we held weekly meetings focused on political action and consciousness-raising. I met lesbians who would lead the movement in Philadelphia with me. Clarifying our position as lesbians who were feminists, as opposed to lesbians who were male identified, was central to who we were as a group and as a model for the movement we were building—our lesbian nation. We read, we discussed, we planned, we got angry with men and with male chauvinism and with the subjugation within our own movement. We began what I would later come to view as a stultifying, smothering rhetoric about the politics of sexuality that left little room for interpretation and which defined lesbian sexuality from the Andrea Dworkin vantage point: Penetration = subjugation = heterosexual mimicry. In our quest to denounce all things heterosexual and male, we had also inevitably denied ourselves the kind of expansive sexuality that gay men were concomitantly reveling in as we built our theory and our politics and they fucked their way through the decade post-Stonewall, forging a politics through sexual experience, rather than the de-sexualizing of theory.

The context of sexual liberation was limited in this lesbian-feminist, consciousness-raising, politically correct world to simply the right to be coupled with another woman, while over in the gay liberation movement it was defined as a continual debauch—sex with anyone and everyone, with a big fuck you! to the hetero-sexual paradigm under which gay men had, pre-Stonewall, been forced to live. For radical lesbian feminists, the goal was different: It was to eradicate the taint of men and heterosexuality and patri-archy from our lives in every way possible, from lipstick and bras to high heels and penetration. We were all engaged in the same lib-eration movement, but the things that we saw as essential to that liberation were so different that one radical lesbian feminist de-clared that we would always have more in common with straight women than with gay men, because those women could share the common bond of our oppression, which gay men never could.

This was the conflict that kept Radicalesbians and Daughters of Bilitis separate from groups like Gay Activists Alliance and Ho-mophile Action League. Sexuality was the bridge that connected us, but gender was what separated us. How could radical lesbian feminism and gay liberation meet, meld and ultimately coalesce into a larger, workable model for a civil rights movement?

My formative years in RL were destined to define me as the quintessential man-hater: The patriarchy was my enemy and the enemy of all women. How could I then embrace the gay male lib-eration movement? How could both sides of the queer spectrum meet, when gay men had no interest in women or feminism and lesbian feminists had been so damaged by the patriarchy that deal-ing with men had caused and continued to cause many of us actual physical pain?

This conundrum haunted me as a teenager and well into my college years. I hung out at the gay coffeehouses and political ac-tion meetings of queer groups on the University of Pennsylvania campus at Hillel House and Houston Hall. I was also part of the gay and lesbian group at the college where I spent my undergraduate years, Temple University. There I met gay men with whom I would forge lasting political bonds.

RL didn't last very long in Philadelphia and soon I was left seeking other political venues for my expanding queer conscious-ness. I had attended the first-ever gay pride march in New York in the summer of 1970, and I periodically took the train to New York and went to meetings of political groups like Daughters of Bilitis and Gay Activists Alliance, neither of which had branches in Philadelphia at that time. I read jill johnston avidly and sought out other lesbian writers and lesbian venues.

While New York seemed to be a nexus of gay and lesbian liberation movements, Philadelphia seemed fractious and unsure of its political direction. As soon as Gay Activists Alliance formed a branch in Philadelphia, I joined. There I was one of only three women—one of whom identified as a fag hag—and about 40 men. Again, I was the youngest member of the group, and again I wondered what the connection between lesbians and gay men really was.

I have mulled over the question of what lesbians and gay men have in common for nearly four decades and have yet to form a cogent answer. As a consequence, I realize now how defining my time in Radicalesbians was, even though I spent far more time in the ensuing years in mixed LGBT groups from Gay Activists Alliance to ACT UP and Queer Nation.

The theoretical basis of my radical lesbian feminist politics began to form on that chilly night in 1970 when I first realized that there was a lesbian world women were creating outside the closet established by the pre-Stonewall era and that in that world lesbians were free and equal and powerful and in no way subservient to men—straight or gay.

There was no place for men in that lesbian nation because it was men we were trying to escape. Not gay men, per se, but men as a gender class, men as the provocateurs of the patriarchy that had turned so many of us into survivors of, at the very least, sexual harassment and second-class status and at the worst, rape and incest and other violence.

In 1970, I was not the only "girl" in the Radicalesbian room—every woman there, no matter what her age, was still referred to as "girl," was still infantilized by the society at large while also being reduced to the sum of her genitalia and breasts. One of the reasons our sexual manifesto—spoken and unspoken—decried all hints of heterosexualized sex was because so many of us had been the forced victims of it. While gay men presented no real sexual threat to us, they still were representative of what threatened us.

Most of my queer life I have spent working with and for a combined movement of lesbians and gay men. Just as I wasn't in those first few years post-Stonewall, to this day I have never been truly convinced that we all want the same things. There is still no place at the table for lesbians, while gay men have ascended to power despite their sexual orientation. The oxymoron of the gay Republican, for example, is a definitively male experience; it presupposes a privilege lesbians can never have—still.

Do I yearn for the Lesbian Nation in capital letters that I envisioned for my future? Not really. I find I have, as have most of the women I know who have retained their radical lesbian feminist roots, created my own lesbian nation as a microcosm of the larger queer community.

When I think back to those halcyon days post-Stonewall when we were so intent on building not just a movement but a revolution, I see how vital that time was to my understanding of who I would become as an adult lesbian, all because of what those RL women taught me. Ultimately I would reject and replace some of the rhetoric, particularly that which defined lesbian sexuality so narrowly, with my own perspective. But I have never denied or rebuked what I learned about patriarchy and its dangerous hold not only on women, but on men as well.

What I finally understood, some years into the movement, was that what gay men and lesbians really had in common was that we were mutually despised by straight men and for the same reasons: We had eschewed the privilege of either being a man or being chattel of one. There is no place in the patriarchy for lesbians, because women are only genitalia and vessels in the patriarchal construct. There is no place for gay men, either, because they have resisted or denied the role of oppressor of women and have instead taken on a role similar to that of women.

Forty years post-Stonewall, Lesbian Nation may have become a chat-site for discussing the hotness of various celebs, but for me Lesbian Nation will always be a real place, a paradigmatic parallax of the world in which I was forced to live and daily deny my lesbian self before I discovered there was another path to take. My Lesbian Nation may have been a theoretical place, as opposed to the gay male version, which was the drama of the gay bar scene where gay men lived a whole range of experience after dark any and every night of the week, but my Lesbian Nation was no less visceral, even if it was less concrete.

When we reflect on what it takes to build a movement, particularly a civil rights movement, we have to take in all those variant parallax views. When we think about what it takes to write a history of that movement, we have to stoke memory and be unflinching in our retelling of the various tales that make up that history, even if they are not always flattering in the retelling.

My experiences with gay men were not always the best in those years, or even since. I must also acknowledge that the road to Lesbian Nation has not always been smooth, given the conflicts wrought by divergent lesbian politics. Now, of course, I wonder if the women who chat at the new Lesbian Nation have any sense of what it took to get them there, but that part of our history—the assimilationist chapter—has yet to be written, as it is still evolving.

I realize I have lived in Lesbian Nation since that first night I walked into the Radicalesbians meeting. I feel fortunate to have had that experience of being both part of history and building history. The memories of how I entered that world, both bitter and sweet, suffuse me with what it means to actually live history, and later, tell the tale.

Victoria A. Brownworth has been a queer activist for 40 years. She is the author and editor of more than 20 books, including the award-winning Too Queer: Essays from a Radical Life, Coming Out of Cancer: Writings from the Lesbian Cancer Epidemic *and* The Golden Age of Lesbian Erotica: 1920–1940. *She has written for many national publications in both the queer and mainstream press and is a columnist for the* Baltimore Sun, Curve Magazine *and the San Francisco* Bay Area Reporter. *She lives in Philadelphia with her partner, artist Maddy Gold.*

Radical Spirit and Vision

When I attended my first meeting of the Gay Liberation Front in July 1969, I knew immediately that it was what I had been waiting for.

From the time I was a boy in high school, I knew I was gay. I had studied what little literature there was on male love—"homosexuality" or "inversion," as it was then called—John Addington Symonds, Havelock Ellis, André Gide, Donald Webster Cory (Edward Sagarin), Ford and Beach, as well as the writings of psychiatrist numbskulls.

I had attended a few meetings of the Boston Mattachine and the Boston Demophile Society in the early 1960s, and after moving to New York City had gone to a few gatherings of the West Side Discussion Group, a basically social homophile organization. These groups were brave for their time, but the Gay Liberation Front was a quantum leap forward. No more semiclandestine meetings. No more special pleading. No more apologies. Here was a radical organization—wild, woolly and wonderful—ready to fight militantly for freedom.

From this first meeting I remember only a heated debate on whether or not the group, which had not yet decided on a name, should align with the antiwar movement or only work for gay rights. Since I'd been in the antiwar movement since 1965 and had my own battle scars (literally) from that movement, I sided immediately with those who favored a multi-issue approach. We prevailed: The name we chose, Gay Liberation Front (GLF), was deliberately taken from the National Liberation Front (NLF) of Vietnam.

The first year in GLF was the most intense of my life. Not all of my memories are pleasant. There was a lot of dissension. Good people made mistakes, and a few bad people caused trouble. However, there would be no point in rehashing old squabbles, as most of the adversaries are dead, and the issues involved are no longer of interest, so I'll just describe a few of my happy memories.

In the first couple of months, a handful of us went to the Silver

Dollar restaurant on Christopher Street almost every night to discuss our dreams for gay liberation. It was a decidedly downscale restaurant, and the management didn't mind if we stayed there for hours— talking, and only occasionally ordering a hamburger, piece of pie or cup of coffee. We believed we were creating a movement the world had never seen before, and we wanted it to survive and mature.

I remember building GLF's first demonstration, which was against the *Village Voice,* on September 12, 1969. There were two main issues in the demonstration: the *Voice's* bigotry in its descriptions of gay people, and its censorship of classified ads. We were especially offended by an article covering the Stonewall Riots ("Too Much, My Dear") which appeared in the July 10, 1969, issue. The author, Walter Troy Spencer, referred to "queers" "swishes" and "fags" repeatedly. Spencer was more concerned that the Stonewall uprising had caused a bar in the area to lose money and had made extra work for the police, than he was with the long-overdue rights of gay people.

In addition, the *Voice's* advertising department had rejected an ad for the first GLF dance because it contained the word "gay"— which the *VV* considered to be obscene, comparable to "fuck" and other four-letter words.

I can remember from when we were debating whether or not to demonstrate that some GLF members, despite a lot of radical posturing, were nevertheless afraid to appear in broad daylight on a homosexual picket line. Nevertheless, we built the demonstration, using our experience from the antiwar movement, and it was a great success. There was a large and enthusiastic turnout. With militant signs and chants, the demonstration went far beyond the polite ones the older homophile movement had conducted in Washington. The *Village Voice* management, humiliated at our challenge to its vaunted liberalism, agreed to all of our demands.

Much of my time and energies during the first few months were spent on *ComeOut!*, the first publication of the Gay Liberation Movement. The guiding light of this first issue (November 14, 1969) was Roslyn Bramms, who had been managing editor of *Screw Magazine*, which was founded in 1968 to provide a more candid and outrageous alternative to such publications as *Esquire* and *Playboy*. Roz taught us what we needed to know, including news gathering, copy preparation, legal matters and production. I was the top editor under her and also on the production team. On a fine autumn day, members of the *ComeOut!* staff gathered to-

The iconic ComeOut! *masthead, featuring the contributors as photographed by Roslyn Bramms in New York City, 1969.*

gether by the Morton Street pier so that Roz could photograph us for a logo she had in mind. I took some photos of my own, which turned out rather well. Facsimile reproductions of the first issue of *ComeOut!* and my photos of *ComeOut!* staff are on my personal Web site, paganpressbooks.com/jpl/GAYLIB.HTM.

I can still remember proofreading typeset copy the day before layout. Martha Shelley worked as a typographer, using the IBM Selectric Composer system, which was then state-of-the-art. Her boss agreed that Martha could use the equipment after working hours, and so the two of us worked from early evening until dawn the next day. She typed and I proofed. Although Martha and I later became political opponents, I remember her as a top-notch type-setter and a good worker.

At some time in the fall, the decision was made that GLF should have no structure but rather consist of totally independent cells, and that decisions should never be made by voting but only by consensus. Since GLF kept no membership roster, anyone who attended a meeting could consider himself or herself a member of GLF, and could speak in its name. Anyone could form a cell, of any kind whatsoever, and could act under the GLF banner. What this meant in practice was chaos, the inability to make decisions in an orderly and democratic manner. It also meant that GLF could never be a viable political organization.

Since according to this decision everyone had to belong to a cell, a few like-thinkers and I formed our own cell, a Marxist cell, which we rather whimsically named The Red Butterfly. Although some feared that we were advocates of violence, our activities were more cerebral. In a way, The Red Butterfly constituted a radical intelligentsia within GLF, concerned with developing theory of gay liberation and linking it to other movements for social change. Our members included graduate students, Ivy League graduates, artists, poets, workers and a scientist.

The Red Butterfly produced four mimeographed pamphlets. The first one, *Gay Liberation*, published on February 13, 1970, went through several printings—thousands of copies were sold in only a few months. The second pamphlet was a reprinting of Carl Wittman's *A Gay Manifesto*, with comments by The Red Butterfly. The third was *Gay Oppression: A Radical Analysis*, and the fourth was my translation of a 1928 speech by the German philosopher Kurt Hiller: "Appeal to the Second International Congress for Sexual Reform for the Benefit of an Oppressed Variety of Human Being." My revised translation can be found on my Web site.

The Red Butterfly's greatest achievement was our intervention in a huge antiwar conference. On February 14–15, 1970, more than three thousand student activists met at the Student Mobilization Committee (SMC) conference in Cleveland to plan nationwide campus strikes and rallies on April 15. A few of us drove there and set up a table with the GLF banner, GLF buttons, and our just-published first pamphlet. For two days we were mobbed, as everyone wanted to know about the new movement. We scheduled a gay liberation workshop, and the response was overwhelming. Emotions ran high as dozens of activists came out of the closet. I vividly remember two black men who, close to tears, said that they felt far more oppressed as gay men than they ever had as black men. At the end of the conference our proposal was read, asking for the conference's long overdue support of its gay sisters and brothers. Thousands voted for it and only seven voted against it.

It was not easy to assert our claims for respect within the radical movements. On one occasion, three of us attended an Alternate U forum held by Youth Against War and Fascism (YAWF) in defense of the Panther 21. At this time members of the Black Panther Party were being murdered in their beds and imprisoned on trumped-up charges. We were in sympathy with the brother who was speaking until he started using the word "faggot"—using it again and again as his strongest term of contempt. We were in shock for a few moments, and then knew, as members of GLF, what to do.

We yelled at him: "Cut it out! Don't say faggot! We don't call you nigger; you don't call us faggots! We're gay men, not faggots!" The brother was angry at us, and said he could say faggot if he wanted to. The YAWF organizers were taken aback momentarily, but then did the right thing: They explained to him that the word faggot could not be used in their forum. He finished the talk, still angry, without using the word again. For the three of us, this episode was a milestone in our journey to self-respect: no more silently listening to antigay insults, no more crap!

I am proud to have been on the Christopher Street Liberation Day Committee (CSLDC), which planned the first gay pride march. We put a lot of work into organizing the march, but even so I was afraid that the turnout would be small. I needn't have worried: It was huge. Many, many thousands of people from all over the country dozens of groups with their own banners marched up Sixth Avenue to Sheep's Meadow in Central Park on June 28, 1970. The exuberance of this day will stay in my memory forever. I especially remember the tens of thousands of spectators—on the sidewalk, on balconies, leaning out of windows—who cheered us on. I would guess that for every person who walked in the street, there were 10 who supported us from the sidelines.

In late November 1969, several members split from GLF to form the Gay Activists Alliance (GAA). Fed up with the chaos and bickering in GLF, they wanted a single-issue organization, which would be run in an orderly and democratic way. I agreed with them in many ways but nevertheless remained in GLF, loyal to its radical spirit and vision. Sure, there were plenty of mistakes, but it is GLF that transformed the world for gay people.

John Lauritsen, a retired market research analyst, lives in Dorchester, MA. He's written for leading gay and humanist publications. His nine books include: (co-authored) The Early Homosexual Rights Movement (1864–1935) *(1974),* A Freethinker's Primer of Male Love *(1998) and* The Man Who Wrote Frankenstein *(2001).*

Radicalqueens Manifesto #1, 1973

Whereas we are tired of being the brunt of most straight oppression, including fairy jokes, physical assaults, and snickering stares;

whereas we are tired of the oppression of straight-identified machismo gays, including remarks about the "tacky queens," denial of queens as representative of the gay community, and being looked down upon;

whereas gay liberation movements have often denied our right to be ourselves in public and denied our very existence while in the same breath patting us on the ass and telling us we are equal (as long as we remain Uncle Toms);

whereas we have decided that macho straight identification is psychologically oppressive and destructive, we have banded together in a union of Radical Queens: to shatter myths, ZAP! our oppressor (both straight and gay), and thereby stand up and get out right to be ourselves both in the straight and in the gay communities, including wearing makeup, doing drag, and other femme-identified activity that any queen decides expresses him or herself!!!!

The cover of the second Radical Queen *magazine, 1973*

Radicalqueens Manifesto #2, 1973

Having been born men, having been socialized to be independent, aggressive, competitive, assertive, task-oriented, outward-oriented, innovative, self-disciplined, stoic, active, objective, analytic-minded, courageous, unsentimental, rational, confident, emotionally controlled, having been socialized to be leaders, having been made to consider makeup, dresses, crying, touching other men, kissing other men and other related traits "sissyish" or "faggoty," having been made to play war games as a child and to believe that life is a battle to be fought in Vietnam, and against the communists and against those men who are not "manly," having been made to believe that women are the weaker sex, and frail, passive, unexciting, intuitive, emotional, things which real men are not supposed to be, things which only "faggots" are, having been told as men that real men are not hairdressers, that real men are not artists, actors or female impersonators, having been slapped when we tried on our mother's dresses or jewelry, or when we played with our sister's dolls, having been part of movements that, though liberal, still held onto the definition of man as aggressive, competitive, etc., and still reduced the women in the movement to secretaries and typists, having been part of gangs in school, gangs that taunted effeminate boys, kicking and spitting on them, calling them names, pushing them, stealing their books, sometimes beating them up or forcing them to suck us off, having as men defined ourselves as the creators, the conquerers, the scientists, having as men resisted seeing how ugly these images of men are, how destructive they are!

Radicalqueens are not men, we are non-men. We are not women. We do not accept the attributes of femininity, that is, passivity, non-aggressiveness, fragility, etc., things which our sisters in the Women's Movement see as oppressive and undesirable traits socialized into women. We do not accept the traditional role of women as any alternative to the oppressor role of the male. Both roles are inventions of the oppressor, both are oppressive to those who accept them.

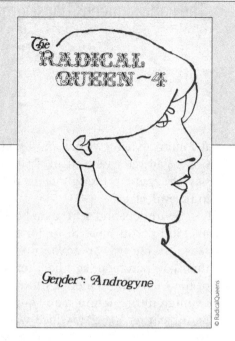

The cover of the fourth Radical Queen *magazine, 1974*

Gender: Androgyne

© RadicalQueens

We of radicalqueens feel it is only by becoming non-men, that is, by throwing off the needs of the machismo man, the need to conquer, to suppress, the need to be like john wayne or any other symbol of strength and "manliness." We feel being sensitive, being compassionate, being able to cry, to touch, to feel, yet without being totally passive, totally non-aggressive, is revolutionary, is Gay. Being homosexual is not the answer to being oppressors. Men have been raised to be the oppressor. All men.

We of radicalqueens will not be the oppressors, we have been working against our own oppressive tendencies. We recommend that all Gay men begin questioning their own feelings. It is only by questioning everything that we can find anything, can find a bit of the truth, by slicing through all of the lies!

The Radicalqueens Trans-formation

Cei Bell

If Tommi Avicolli Mecca and I had been pretty queens or conventional gay men who fit in, RadicalQueens probably would never have happened. Pretty queens didn't spend Saturday nights writing manifestos.

To understand where RadicalQueens fit in with regard to gay liberation, you have to understand the time period. In the early '70s, gay life was an adventure. Today any CPA can be gay. Back then you had to at least be interesting. Gay life was a swirling mix of the Beats and bohemia of the older generation and the hippie/counterculture, feminist and other liberation groups with the whisper of leather BD/SM, which was closeted even among gays. Gays were just beginning to dance in bars. I think the first dance song I heard was "Popcorn" in the Allegro bar, which I had snuck into surrounded by GAA members after a meeting. We started having Gay Dance fundraisers for GAA where we took an enormous space and people paid a small amount to dance. If you didn't have the money, you volunteered. Gay activism had not yet become professional.

In 1972 in Philadelphia, there were maybe 200 people total who were out of the closet. Of those 200 people, about 70 people met once a week for a meeting at Gay Activists Alliance (GAA), a new militant gay civil rights group formed within two years after the Stonewall Riots. GAA was primarily interested in the rights of gay men and was struggling to accept that lesbians were not subservient.

The interests and needs of transsexuals and drag queens ("transgender" had not been coined yet) were not important. Gay activists wanted to establish that gay men were as masculine as straight men. Concerning themselves with the rights and issues of transgender people was contrary to their goals. If queens talked about being discriminated against or physically abused, we were told that if we were more masculine it wouldn't happen.

There were three drag bars in Philadelphia. Miss P's, at 19th and Lombard, was run by a drag queen named Patti Paige and her husband. Miss P's had weekend drag shows that imitated Broadway and Las Vegas routines on a tiny stage. Patti Paige was fond of Carol Channing numbers and tap dance routines. Miss P's had a combination lock on its entrance door. If you didn't know the combination you couldn't gain entrance. This served to keep out homophobes and the police. It seemed like a metaphor for the period. In order to be gay you had to figure out codes and puzzles.

The Forrest Showbar on Quince Street also had drag shows. Then there was the 13 Club on 13th and Locust. It was the most notorious and colorful of the three. The 13 Club didn't have a show. Its customers were the show: Teenage drag queens, transsexuals, sailors, Marines and Mafia men. I remember talking to a guy in a shiny suit who didn't look like a truck driver, who told me he had just driven a truckload of cigarettes from North Carolina. I didn't understand why he would go all the way to North Carolina to get cigarettes. Maybe I was a little green. The 13 Club had a five-foot-five butch dyke doorman named Larry who would easily throw six-foot-three guys out on the street.

There were two lesbian bars that were both named Rusty's (only in Philadelphia). One was located in the downtown theater district, the other in Chinatown. The main white gay male bars were the Allegro at Broad and Spruce Streets (now the Kimmel Center), and the Steps on Delancey Street. Both were known to have carding policies that excluded blacks. Spruce Street was the main gay street, particularly west of Broad. The Ritz was located in a separate black gay area north of Market that has now been developed out of existence by the Convention Center and the Criminal Justice Center.

I came out at the age of 16 in 1971. A year before that, in 1970, a teacher had announced I was gay at the so-called progressive Parkway Program High School. I might have been the first officially "out" student in the Philadelphia public school system. My time in the public school system was spent trying to avoid getting beaten up. I had been beaten up constantly in junior high school, including being beaten by a gym teacher. It almost seemed normal. When I was seven a homophobic adult man tried to kill me. He chased me for two blocks, from 19th to 21st and Fitzwater. Somebody saw me screaming and told my parents and I was punished because nice middle-class black children don't act up in public. Especially before civil rights, acting inappropriately could get you killed, so discipline was a necessity.

Besides being obviously effeminate, I developed small breasts when I was twelve. It's called gynecomastia. I had to endure gym classes with my breasts exposed. Boys would beat me up during classes and teachers would pretend not to notice. The word "homosexual" as a pejorative was hurled at me. I had to guess what it meant because my parents didn't discuss sex with me. I didn't know what sex was, let alone homosexual.

I started reading psychiatry books. That was all that was available on the subject in the library. The books said that only 5 percent of homosexuals were effeminate (another new word). There I was, a middle-class Negro homosexual (I hadn't heard of transsexuals yet) who was effeminate. A minority within a minority within a minority within a minority. I also learned that a favored treatment for homosexuality was electroshock therapy.

The beatings at school left me depressed and suicidal. To make matters worse, my half-brother, who was 19 years older, would come into my parents' house when they weren't there and beat up my brother and me. He would threaten to kill me, yet no one would believe me. When my tonsils were taken out at Children's Hospital, I woke up at 5 a.m. with an orderly on top of me— wrestling, I thought. I didn't tell anyone because I knew I would be blamed for getting beaten up. No one would do anything about it anyway. It only occurred to me recently that he wasn't trying to beat me up.

The public school solution to my getting beaten up was to suggest to my parents that I be sent to a psychiatrist. The psychiatrist was a nice enough young doctor who showed me pictures of boys who also had breasts. For three years, he asked me why I thought other boys beat me up. I saved up my money, bought a copy of *Playboy* and brought it to counseling to convince him I was straight. I was deathly afraid that if I didn't, they would remove my breasts or electrocute me straight via shock treatments. Martial arts classes would have been a better use of time and money.

Eventually, the sessions ended and he told my parents I was a perfectly normal boy. I should have won a Tony or at least an Obie: Best Live Performance by a Transsexual Pretending to be Straight.

The high school I attended, The Parkway Program, was a progressive school based on A. S. Neill's Summerhill, the original alternative educational institution. On the first day, teachers said that you could do anything you want so long as you don't hurt anybody. Some of the teachers were hippies. Some of them semi-openly slept with students. There were teachers who came to class speeding and tripping. When I walked into a photography class the male instructor was sitting with two teenage girls discussing sex. One of the girls asked me who I wanted to ball. I heard the same teacher paid for a teenage student's abortion. I had my first joint in a chemistry class, and the teacher lit it. The teacher overseeing the school underground newspaper *The Rancid Roach* (we changed the name weekly) asked me to draw roaches for the cover. I didn't understand that he didn't mean the insects. Another time he seemed to be trying to start an orgy in an English class.

I was in a Brandywine Workshop group exhibition of silk-screens at the Museum of Art when I was 15, but nobody came to see it. There were sensitivity and encounter groups and we were encouraged to be honest with each other. I still got beaten up at Parkway. My solution was to avoid classes. I found a leaflet for gay liberation that proclaimed "Come Out Come Out Wherever You Are!" and went to the Homophile Action League office. It was closed during the day, and I had to be home by 5:30 p.m. The office of the Resistance, the antiwar group, was open during the day. I thought this would be similar. Then, I tried talking to two teachers and a student about it, which was a mistake.

Shortly afterwards, I walked in on the female teacher I had talked to while she was having sex with an underage male teenage student. She stopped me from taking art classes and announced to the school that I was a homosexual. She was also having an interracial extramarital relationship with the administrator of our unit. They thought I knew about their involvement because of a comment I made to her suggesting they looked like a couple. (There was an interracial marriage in my family. We lived in a middle-class white neighborhood. Nobody told me this wasn't normal.) At that point, the administrator started harassing me, and he beat me up. Being teachers and administrators, they could say anything about a student and get away with it. This was before anyone heard of child abuse.

I was being beaten up at home, at school by students, and now by the administrator. I ran away from home and came back. I went back to school, was expelled and ran away. I was reinstated and ran away again. I dropped out on my 17th birthday because they couldn't force me to get beaten up anymore.

In the middle of all this, I met some teenaged drag queens in Rittenhouse Square and found my way out of the closet. In this colorful unisex, post–Sgt. Pepper world, it was difficult for me to recognize them at first, but out of the corner of my eye I saw a tall, skinny, effeminate African American male chasing a light-skinned, equally skinny and tall, African American male through the Square in a pair of clogs. I thought, "What was that?"

Soon after, I met a Puerto Rican drag queen/freak in the Square and I was officially brought out of my transparent closet. In this new world, I came to know a Dickensian group of throwaway/ runaway kids from 14 to about 20 who hung out at the Square, Penn Center Skating Rink in the winter, 13th and Locust and Dewey's, an infamous diner chain popular with queens and gay men. That was Center City before the skyscrapers were built, back when it was a lovely forgotten ruin. The kids came from almost every background you can imagine. They survived any way they could. If you were pretty there was prostitution and the men who would give you money.

I wasn't pretty, which in the long run was a benefit. I had kinky unmanageable hair, brown skin and thick Coke-bottle eyeglasses when the beauty ideal was blue-eyed blonds. I met other teenage queens who had to leave school and run away from home. Many of them were talented but had no way to use their gifts. For example, I knew two young transsexual concert pianists, one black and one white. The white pianist, "Stephanie," was harassed and pursued by "Jack," an older pedophile, while she was still in high school in Delaware. Instead of receiving any sort of protection or help, Stephanie was expelled from high school and kicked out of her home. Having nowhere to go, she moved in with Jack and they moved to 9th and Spruce in Philadelphia, which was a gay slum at the time. Jack was an alcoholic and abusive, but Stephanie was trapped. One time I was over there and he accused me of stealing $5 and forcibly strip-searched me. After all my clothes were off he suddenly remembered where the $5 was. The $5 was never missing, he just wanted to strip search a 16-year-old black kid. He also told everybody I had stolen $5 to justify his strip-searching me. Later when I went to a GAA political meeting at a member's house, the host asked me to leave because he heard I had stolen $5. Even though my middle-class parents had moved into a white neighborhood and I had gone to a mixed high school, I had to come out of the closet to hear someone call me nigger to my face.

The queens made me aware that my problem with violent men was not mine alone. They even had a name for those men, "neshineau" or "nesh," for short. In addition to functioning as a noun, it was also an early alert to start running when fagbashers were nearby. I began to hear about queens and transsexuals being murdered when a drag queen was found murdered in an alley near 13th Street in the fall of 1971.

I had been in GAA for about a year before Tommi Avicolli Mecca and I first spoke to each other. One June evening after a meeting, we shared a table at Day's Jr., a restaurant (now a bank) at 18th and Spruce. Tommi and I had a mutual friend, another femme queen named Michael. Tommi was involved in the sort of organizing work that he was always doing. He had long straightened hair and aviator glasses. I thought he resembled Gloria Steinem. Tommi was dating a friend of mine.

One day in December, Tommi, his boyfriend and I were sitting on Jerry's bed smoking a joint. Jerry was a friend that I sometimes slept with and occasionally lived with. His apartment on Spruce Street was one of two apartments, the other being longtime queer activist Kiyoshi Kuromiya's, that every teenage gay kid and every teenage hippie passed through in Center City. One of the guys made a comment about being butch. Jerry affirmed that he was butch.

"You're butch?" I asked. It was a query rather than a challenge to the veracity of his statement.

"What did you think I am?" replied Jerry.

Actually I didn't think that we had defined it. Tommi and I started questioning what butch and femme were. Was Jerry butch because he took the "dominant" role in sex? What if Tommi wanted to do the inserting, which wouldn't happen with his boyfriend, who was also butch like Jerry.

I had been having feminist thoughts. All of my female friends were feminists and I wanted to be contemporary and modern. But what did that mean that I wanted feminism and yet I was a femme transsexual? I knew that I didn't want a relationship like my mother had where my father controlled everything. Tommi and I started this discussion and soon we had left the guys behind on the bed.

That night, we formed a caucus of GAA. I first came up with the name RadicalQueens, but we thought that was too far out to bring to the meeting so we started out as the Queen's Liberation Caucus.

Queen's Liberation was a consciousness-raising group for queens. We brought up issues that GAA and the gay liberation movement didn't: Primarily, our right to express a nonconforming gender identity and to live without the threat of violence from men. Tommi had grown up with the similar experience of being beaten and harassed at school and in his neighborhood. He couldn't ride his bike in his South Philadelphia neighborhood without men hurling epithets and bottles at him. A few months later, we changed the name to RadicalQueens and became a committee of GAA. We soon had our own distinct identity.

I didn't make it to the announcement of RadicalQueens in GAA. An abusive man I had been involved with drugged me and raped me. Tommi had also survived being raped by a lover. I was violently raped in Fairmount Park a year later. In none of these situations was calling the police a reasonable possibility. Sexual violence against transgender people is rarely, if ever, reported. Years later I took an informal survey at a meeting. Out of about 15 people in the room 14 had been sexually abused in childhood.

Tommi and I started writing manifestos. We actually thought we could have a radical feminist, gender-free revolution. We had a truly motley group. There was no membership requirement. There were no dues. We came up with ideas, and we did things.

We published a magazine, the *Radical Queen*. The first issue was produced on a Gestetner printer. Once upon a time in the olden days of the previous century when you walked five miles in the snow to get to your consciousness-raising group, if you wanted to make multiple copies you would type and draw on a thick stencil and then put it on a Gestetner. It was a printing press found in most schools. It had a big drum filled with ink and a pad that soaked up the ink. You would press the stencil over the ink pad and rotate the drum a few times until the pad stencil soaked through and then you were ready to print.

We printed 500 copies of the first *Radical Queen* that way. The first issue was a collective effort. No one had a byline and we all took responsibility for the magazine. We published a manifesto. We quickly discovered that we didn't want to take responsibility for each other's opinions, so in the next issue our names appeared with our articles.

We also found that there was a better way to print. I was living in a communal house with a former draft dodger who had been recently released from prison. He worked for the leftist Omega Press. For $20 we could get a professionally printed, double-sided sheet of paper that would be cut into the new improved *Radical Queen*. I experimented with writing poetry (who didn't?) and found there is something worse than not being published: publishing bad poetry.

In the third issue, I wrote my first article, a critique of sexism in advertising entitled "The Commercialization of Emily." We had a Pagan Page written by Phillip Janison-Marra. There was a Castration Department where we ran quotes from sexist men. It featured a drawing of a man's genitalia on a guillotine (entrée in a French restaurant). Heather, blond, sleek, beautiful, like that unfortunate girl on the Munsters, drew a cartoon character called SuperQueen who vaguely looked like me in radical drag. SuperQueen introduced "Cecil B. Demented" in a segment about the Bible. I believe John Waters owes us money for copyright infringement.

We had forums on drag. There was a senior drag queen named Rusty who gave drag instruction. Her brother was in the Olympics. She had a bumper sticker on her makeup case that read "United States Drag Team."

When GAA was planning for the 1973 Gay Pride march, all the committees said they would have a float. Our committee and another were the only ones who actually did. We displayed different types of drag. I did radical drag with a dress, boots and a construction helmet I borrowed from Richie, who did butch/SM drag. Our float was built by Jerry and Mark, gay hippies who lived in Powelton Village before it was expensive real estate.

When Henri David, who had a gala drag contest every Halloween, announced a contest where the most beautiful transsexual would receive an all-expenses-paid sex change operation, we protested. Transsexuality wasn't about beauty, and David backed down.

In 1973 RadicalQueens peformed the first benefit for the Gay Community Center that years later in another incarnation became the William Way Community Center. We were infamous for our drag shows. We took tacky and made it an art form. We did the sickest drag shows on Earth. At one of them, Saj, my big brother of color, performed the Who's "Acid Queen." Tommi played the deaf, dumb, blind kid. He wore a toga that Saj designed and nothing else. Everytime Saj lifted him, the audience got quite a show. When the movie version of the rock opera came out, I thought it was tame. Saj was better than Tina Turner.

Saj directed us in a takeoff of the Supremes. I was a Supreme. The surprising part is I was the only black member of the group. Diana Ross was played by blond, willowy Heather. In our consciousness-raising group Heather would talk about being beautiful. She was buying hundred-dollar shoes when a hundred dollars would pay your rent for a month. She would say, "When you're beautiful you don't know if somebody likes you because of you or because you're beautiful. You don't know what it's like when you're beautiful!" We did another act where Tom Jones, played by Heather, lip-synched into a dildo used as a mike and two go-go boys, played by myself and an obese queen (we didn't believe in typecasting), attacked Tom Jones and carried him off the stage.

We performed the last RadicalQueen Revue in 1974 at the first Gay Coffeehouse on 3rd Street between Market and Arch. Today everybody flocks to Old City for First Friday art shows and the hip bars and restaurants. Back then, nobody went there. Not even artists. I had a record that had Dionne Warwick singing Barbra Striesand songs. Tommi had a record of Barbra Streisand singing Dionne Warwick songs. We tried doing a Warwick/Streisand "reading session" for one of the revues. "Reading" was a term queens used to insult each other. I was taught how to "read" by experts but rarely do it because it isn't fair to use against mere mortals. During the performance my wig spun off my head into the audience and was thrown back at me. Memories

I don't remember the year, maybe 1974, a group of us celebrated Christmas Eve together in a cheap Chinese restaurant. Tommi and I have continued celebrating Christmas with each other ever since, though now we do it in spirit because of the distance. The most precious gift RadicalQueens gave me is my best friend since 1972, Tommi.

How could the past be so simultaneously horrible and yet so wonderful and sweet? I was abused and had to run away from home and drop out of school. I was sexually assaulted and raped twice. I didn't think I had any future as a homely queen with Coke-bottle glasses.

Yet, at the worst moment of my life, I met the most wonderful people and saved my life.

Cei Bell is a writer and artist. Her articles have appeared in the Philadelphia Inquirer, Philadelphia Daily News, Philadelphia Gay News, City Paper, Philadelphia Tribune, Au Courant *and* Blackout Magazine. *She was also on the staff of the* Gayzette *and wrote the workshop plans for the Conference on Racism and Sexism in Lesbian and Gay Institutions. She is finishing a children's book.*

Pat Parker: A Woman of Vision

Tommi Avicolli Mecca

They will not come
a mob rolling
through the streets,
but quickly and quietly
move into our homes
and remove the evil,
the queerness,
the faggotry,
the perverseness
from their midst.
. . . Where will you be?

—Excerpt from the poem "Where Will You Be?" in *Movement
in Black* by Pat Parker, published by Crossing Press, 1978

A movement without poets doesn't have much of a soul. The Civil
Rights, antiwar and feminist movements all had their poets, as did
the counterculture. Gay liberation had them too. They read at pride
marches, coffeehouses and any other stage that was available to
them. They made us laugh and cry and yearn for revolution. They
gave music and rhythm to those early post-Stonewall struggles.

One of the most remarkable among them was Pat Parker, who
is credited with being the country's first out African American lesbian poet.

Born to poverty in Houston, Texas, in 1944, Pat Parker (born
Patricia Cooks) came to California in 1962 to attend city college
in Los Angeles and later San Francisco. After two unsuccessful
marriages, she ended up a single mother raising two daughters in
Oakland.

In the late '60s she became involved with the Black Panthers,
feminism and gay liberation. She helped found the Women's Press
Collective, which published lesbian writers. She recorded an album

of readings of her work ("Where Would I be Without You?") on Olivia Records, along with her friend Judy Grahn (author of *Another Mother Tongue*), another amazing lesbian activist and poet.

By 1968, she and Grahn were reading at women's events as out lesbian writers. "It was like pioneering," Parker later said. "We'd go into these places and stand up to read poems. We were talking to women about women, and at the same time letting women know that the experiences they were having were shared by other people. . . . I was being gay, and it made absolute sense to me that that was what I had to write about."

In her tragically short lifetime, Parker produced five volumes of work. The publication of the first, *Child of Myself*, in 1972, brought her the attention of audiences outside of Northern California, where she was already known and loved in feminist and gay liberation circles.

A year later, the title poem of her second book, *Pit Stop*, led Grahn, in her intro to the book, to write that it was "the first poem I know of dealing with the subject of alcoholism among women, a serious debilitator of minority communities."

Parker never shied away from difficult topics. In *Womanslaughter*, her fourth volume (the third, *Movement in Black*, was a compilation of poems from 1961 to 78), the title piece describes the murder of her sister by her former husband, who received a short prison sentence:

One day a quiet man
shot his quiet wife
three times in the back.
He shot her friend as well
His wife died.

Her final volume, *Jonestown and Other Madness*, examined the tragedy created by Jim Jones, religious leader of the People's Temple.

In her preface to the book, Parker said that she wrote the poems "because we have become too quiet. . . . We are a nation in great trouble. It is time for those with vision to speak out loudly before the madness consumes us all."

Pat continued writing and speaking out until her untimely death from breast cancer in 1989. She was 45. Her voice is sorely missed.

Sisters and Brothers: A Writer Hungering for Family Finds GLF

Perry Brass

Bob Kohler's large, smoky baritone called out, "Welcome, brothers and sisters!," opening the first Gay Liberation Front meeting I attended, on a Sunday in November 1969, at Holy Apostles Church in Chelsea.

I had seriously attempted suicide at 15, after a year of high school hazing and harassment. I had survived the public housing project where I lived with my sister and mother, the only Jewish family there, where I could not walk down the streets without redneck kids yelling, "Hey, Jew-queer! Sissy! Fairy!" Then a year at the University of Georgia where I had death threats in my dorm. And the summer of my 17th year, hitchhiking from Savannah to San Francisco ("crawling with queers," I'd heard)—a year of sleeping between parked cars, eating out of back-alley restaurant garbage cans, living in SRO hotels. And now I was in New York: free. Bob Kohler's words revealed a deep truth within me, something I had been wanting for so long even at 22: to be connected to a family, after being so disconnected.

High inside on that liquor of freedom and youth, happy but disconnected from any world except the gay one, that nocturnal continent of pick-ups and nights with strangers, of hitchhiking through the shadows of my own intense romantic sexuality (tumbling in love over and over again as you do at 20; wanting love so much) . . . but this idea that I could have a room full of brothers and sisters: This was a kind of needed, haunting truth that, like religion itself, rises up from within your own depths.

I'd already been exposed somewhat to GLF through the Saturday night dances at Alternate U. on 14th Street, in the big second-floor space of an office building near Sixth Avenue. I'd been living in a Hell's Kitchen walk-up railroad flat, after having moved to New York a month before I turned 19. I'd had menial jobs in advertising, and loathed it; I'd spent three months in Europe living on almost nothing. Then Stonewall happened.

I was in the venerable gay bar Julius's around the corner in the Village, and came out to see riot lights, squads of cops, street kids gathering in corners, hippie allies milling about. I was thrilled: For the first time, we had fought back. The constant crippling passivity and hammered-in loneliness of the bars; the cringing fear and the hunched shoulders just walking in; the arrogant Mafia goons at the door—all had been ripped away. I loved it, ebullient. But some of my preppier Julius's friends were less so.

"It'll blow our cover," one Ivy League graduate pronounced. "Everything was so good for us. We had our bars, our beaches, our restaurants. Now the girls have blown all that."

I didn't want to see him again; that innate Southern rebellious, take-no-shit attitude in me that was balled up inside could finally be released, even as shy as I was. But that Sunday at Holy Apostles, I had "arrived" and loved it: the bewildering radicalism, the creative organic confusion, the lack of structure—still with genuine order in it. Because the *real* structure was that we were no longer hiding. People used real names. Men and women were together, unheard-of in most gay settings then. They came up to me, talked, welcomed me. People kissed and hugged—I could not remember the last time I saw people who kissed and hugged.

After initial business, we broke into small groups to get to know each other. I remember a young Pete Wilson in my group who seemed so assured about his ideas, and Ellen Shumsky, and other faces crystallize. I said almost nothing. I wanted to listen; I wanted to know everything. I knew almost nothing about politics. I had willed myself into apoliticality. Being gay was my priority, my religion and cosmology: and everything "political," from Republicans and Democrats to civil rights, the student movement, to peaceniks, seemed to shout out loud: "Queers don't apply!"

We talked about real politics: class, race, war and peace, sexism, the ruling patriarchy, the way the "hip" counterculture "fucked over" women and gay men, the bald hypocrisy of that very hipness, the counterculture that so many of were now clinging to for dear life, because outside it was only the War Machine, the corporate-strangled, media-pushing Death Culture, and we sure knew what that was.

Even I knew it from working in advertising art departments: That business that always lied, and the images it used to lie with. I had already conceived a private politics of my own survival (where the body trumped money and organized beliefs), but I had never believed that the "personal" could become real, until the end of that first GLF meeting.

By my second meeting, I publicly invited everyone to Thanksgiving at my apartment. My sister Nancy and I prepared a feast for about a dozen people I didn't know. Only a few showed up, but I realized that now I had friends unlike the bar friends I knew and the scared tricks I knew, and, already, I wanted more than anything to be published in GLF's own newspaper, *ComeOut!*, the first newspaper in the world published about the movement for gay liberation.

I had been writing queer poetry and short stories on my own. At 19 I finished a novel about my year on the road—and I had been assured that none of this would ever be published. *ComeOut!* beckoned and I jumped, joining in the middle of its third issue. It was then very much being run by Lois Hart, a strong-willed woman who'd gone from a convent to an all-woman house-painting business, and her partner Suzanne Bevier, a gifted graphic artist. I felt intimidated. The whole rhetoric and political jargon of GLF was still foreign to me.

I published several poems and a woodcut under the name "Mark Shields" (who I later learned became a mystery to subsequent scholars of GLF), but my real name appeared on the masthead. We published out of an apartment in the East Village, when the neighborhood was still '60s cheap, macrobiotic restaurants and old Jewish delis, and the Hell's Angels were down the block. The paper was printed at night on the sly, somewhere in Brooklyn at a small shop that did advertising circulars by day, by long-haired straight movement guys who were in sympathy with our radicalism; a small cadre of us used Lois and Suzanne's van to pick up 3,000 baled copies at 3 a.m. We were hysterically excited just getting it into our hands. Lois told us that the two guys who hand-ran the paper through the press were both doing acid while they worked. I felt like we were smuggling something intensely radical under the noses of the straight world: We were. There had been other papers about the "homosexual agenda," but *ComeOut!* was rife with politics, screeds, positions, calls to action, personalities and viewpoints, the buzzed-out underground artwork of the period, poetry and stories. In it, the Underground met the queer-sexual New Left, and it flowered.

I was crazy about it and got sucked into the vortex of its personalities and politics, in its walk-up East Village "office" (actually the spare bedroom of Ellen Broidy and Linda Rhoades, who also ran a lesbian paperback book service from it), its diffusions of personalities, anchored by an outspoken Lois and a quiet Suzanne, with other voices from Martha Shelley, Bob Kohler, Jim Fouratt, Pat Maxwell (the first person I ever encountered to use the term "gay art," which she said we'd have to "invent," a seeming impossibility to me), Kay Van Deurs, Bernard Lewis, Earl Galvin, Dan Smith and Diana Davies, to mention only some of us. It would be hard to imagine any publication that so totally reflected the people it represented.

The *ComeOut!* cell (or collective) voted on all submissions, although some votes counted more than others, and Lois often had the last word. She was difficult, but passionate about the paper. Every meeting we had turned into a consciousness-raising session about women, lesbianism and patriarchy. As I became more involved, I was either her pet or pariah, roles others found themselves in as well. Some women followed her and others loathed her. She was particularly disdained by drag queens like Sylvia Rivera and Marsha Johnson, who called her "Louie Hard." I remember one meeting where she reduced me to tears by announcing that, as revolutionaries, we should seriously consider blowing up (as "a bastion of male art") the Metropolitan Museum: one of my favorite places in the universe. I started sobbing that the artists and people in the Met had nothing to do with "male art." It wasn't their fault; they were only artists and art lovers doing what they needed to do. "As revolutionaries," Lois affirmed, "we have to consider it. It's part of our commitment to change and oppressed women everywhere."

As you can imagine, after that I started feeling that I needed to work around Lois instead of tremulously hiding behind her. There was no safety there. She announced at the beginning of the fifth issue that she was tired of working on the paper, she and Suzanne were in danger of breaking up because of the tensions involved with the Movement, as we always called it, and the East Village women wanted their spare room back. I agreed then that the paper could be published out of my apartment in Hell's Kitchen.

This was tricky. Many women decided that without Lois leading the paper, they would drop out, but several new women and men came in. The paper was becoming more and more known as one of the voices of the Gay Liberation movement. Several of our pieces, like Steven F. Dansky's "Hey, Man!" about phallocentricism in gay and Movement life, the fabulous group piece "Woman Identified Woman," which rocked feminism by proclaiming that true feminists had either to be lesbians or to identify with them, and, strangely enough, my own piece "From the Men: Games Male Chauvinists Play," which delineated for the first time the politics of gay cruising (and which Lois had retitled, because she felt that my original title, "Games Men Play," did not castigate men enough), were reprinted dozens of times, appeared in numerous other underground papers, anthologies and broadsides, and were discussed at consciousness-raising sessions, in the corners of smoky bars, and of course on pillows and between the sheets all over the country.

It was a time of huge personal contact: something difficult to believe in our current age of impersonal digital networking. But the contents of this newspaper that printed, at most, 3,000 to 4,000 copies, were read by 100,000 people, and then more. Gays and lesbians and Movement people and people just coming out of the closets and the shadows, and people who went to free rock concerts in the parks where the bushes and benches were alive with "weed"—they were all talking about it. I felt that we had to continue with the paper, and would do anything to keep it alive.

Rumors went rampant: Perry was now "ego-tripping" on the paper; I had "ripped it off" and was now running it. Bob Kohler told me that STAR, the street drag queens, wanted to take over the paper themselves, and that I should simply produce it for them, since they could not do it alone: As a revolutionary I must be committed to this. I had no idea how I was going to do this, but as a threat he told me that Sylvia and some of the other girls had told him that if they did not get at least part of the paper under their own control, they would set fire to the newsstands in the Village that carried it.

Another faction, Third World Gay Revolution, also made a similar demand: They would control a section of the newspaper outside the collective that we would produce for them (and also distribute and sell for them—as Third Worlders, they would have nothing to do with the degrading capitalism of selling the paper, as I did on the streets myself), and if we did not, I would be branded and isolated as a racist. Since I had grown up in Georgia, it was *a priori* accepted that I was one: There was no getting around that.

Luckily, I was supported at this time by a newcomer, Steve

Gavin, who had some experience in journalism and writing and was crazy about the paper too; also by longtime movement heavy Martha Shelley; another young woman named Deborah Moldavan; Roy Eddy, a newcomer from Tennessee; and several other people who agreed that we had to keep the paper together, not give in to threats, and still publish it as a collective.

We did for the next four issues. My whole life became involved with it. Every issue brought in new challenges and demands: Dealing with the ongoing Viet Nam war; the "Cuban question" of loyalty to revolutionary Cuba amidst its imprisonment of gay men into special camps as "threats to youth and education"; women, feminism, and the role of gay men among them; sexual role play, such as S&M, and how this affects revolutionary thinking; race and racism; and an emerging gay and lesbian culture that was really coming out of the shadows of corporate sensationalism or government censorship. We would not be sexually exploitative, although we had nudity in it sometimes (that we had to get past our various rock-bottom cheap, bootleg printers). We sold the paper for a quarter a copy (difficult even to imagine today), and we refused to carry advertising. Subscriptions were $7, and a large number of libraries carried it. We usually had just enough money at the end of every issue simply to print the next one. It also featured some of the first queer work of other writers who went on to have literary careers, such as Rita Mae Brown, Dennis Altman, Allen Young and Tony (Nikos) Diaman.

The paper was extremely inflammatory to the authorities; it was avidly radical and made no bones about mixing two of the most incendiary issues in American life: homosexuality and the New Left's militant socialism. It was covered by other papers in Europe, and some of its content was translated into French, Italian, and German. One day I got a call from a man claiming to be with the New York Police Department. Since my phone number was published as the *ComeOut!* "office number," I was used to fielding calls. He asked me if I knew anything about the paper. I told him I did not.

"Do you know where it's printed, and who prints it?"
"No, I don't."
"Do you know where it's sold?"
"No."
"Who edits it?"

"I don't know that either."

He hesitated, then said, "I guess I'm not going to get any-where with you, am I?"

"Yes," I replied. He hung up.

Like a lot of other Movement people during this time of un-rest, police surveillance and plainclothes police plants, I was sure that my phone was being tapped. I used to joke about being en-tertaining on the phone to the third parties listening in, but the tension from this was no joke. I got to meet several people who had "gone underground," on the lam from the cops, and saw what their life was like: not good.

I got other calls, too: From young people just coming out and writers who wanted to submit. Also calls where they'd hang up, or whisper obscenities into the phone. It was unnerving but all part of publishing *ComeOut!* Finally, at the end of the eighth issue, we real-ized that we could no longer go on with the paper. It had outlived GLF, which died in a war of attrition and factionalism: Too many people dropping out or scattering into too many subgroups, includ-ing one that was so orthodox Maoist that it became almost a comic version of young middle-class kids playing Lefties. (I remember one meeting when a woman came in with a Louis Vuitton purse to discuss the Red Book.)

The war in Viet Nam was grinding to an end, I was back in school at NYU, and the big question was what was going to hap-pen next? The Gay Activists Alliance was still collecting steam, and some GLFers simply moved their own alliances over to them. I could not. Like any good convert, I believed to my core every-thing that GLF had taught me: that the Movement and the people had to come first, instead of my own "bourgeois professionalism" (Bob Kohler had harangued me about this once on Christopher Street, the same way that Lois had gone after my loathsome male chauvinism); that all of us were brothers and sisters and problems could only be solved through consensus; that only a radical change might create a world in which gays and lesbians could be equal to straights, and our own needs and sensibilities be taken seriously.

But even more, I was burning out and breaking down. It was hard for me to argue anymore, "rap out my politics" as we used to say, and go through the whole catechism in which patriarchy became seated as the source of all evil in the world. I wasn't even sure if I could believe that anymore; it took me years to understand what a "genitaled" man's true worth in the world was, and how much I was still attached to that, to the depth and density of that worth.

Before GLF, the attitude was that at some point, homosexuals would "adjust" enough that society might actually tolerate us. GLF said that we could look at society ourselves, see it from the lens of our own oppression and galvanize the queer world enough to throw off the chains that held us. We saw the constant homophobia that permeated the very language we speak, and still does; the sexism and racism that we felt binds together capitalism producing a constant class of losers; the white patriarchy behind the sexism and racism; and finally we started looking at each facet of society individually and in concert that promote and promulgate gay oppression: religion, the law, medicine, the arts, the military, business and commerce. Looking at each of these instruments of our oppression and seeing within them the radical "roots" of our own constant, daily queer destruction—this was the work that GLF did.

GLF, and the people in it, did not cook these ideas up from scratch. But our use of them was revolutionary: Instead of the older queer adaptations of constant accommodation, we provided the radical and youthful energy needed to blow accommodation out the water and bring in a new atmosphere of self-invention, acceptance and love.

We did this through ideas and tools that we brought from other parts of the radical movements of this period, namely from the women's movement, the peace movement, the student movement, and the movement for racial equality.

Foremost was consciousness-raising: the very idea that human consciousness creates institutions of oppression, and we can change consciousness by becoming aware of how it forms us and how it is deformed from oppression. This was borrowed from the women's movement and also the peace movement.

Second was collectivism: the idea that together we could do more than we could do individually. This was brought about through the use of consensus rather than voting: The idea being that we would have no "losers" on an issue, but all sides would come to a collective consensus. Sometimes this worked wonderfully; other times it did not. Instead of producing alienated minorities within our own queer minority, it came with the intention that every one of us was important. Many of us also tried to live collectively, or were involved in work collectives—something almost unknown within a gay stereotype that said that queer people could not be trusted to come together for any reason other than sexual gratification.

Third was using the power of the media, especially the radical underground media of this period, as best we could. It also meant inventing the whole idea of gay media, something that older organizations asking for homosexual tolerance could not imagine. Instead of begging *Time* magazine, for instance, to "recognize" our existence and then go about recasting its own lies about us, as *Time* regularly did, we would create our own magazines, newspapers, videos, theater and art. We literally invented the idea of gay art as a positive thing. Before GLF, queer art was always cast as perverse, sexually provocative or exploitative. It was either something that could not be brought out into the open, or was a sideshow in the cultural market. I believe we changed that attitude.

Fourth was dealing with sex itself. We rejected the old sexual role types of top and bottom, hustler and john, butch and femme, maricón and macho, man/boy, S&M. We felt that within the context of the times, these were exploitative and had to be looked at as such, the idea being that within each of these roles someone is acceptable and someone is less acceptable. Someone can "pass" as non-"queer" and someone is cast as "queer." We wanted to blow these roles up and have an open, sexually egalitarian society. This was one of GLF's most controversial stances, and it often led to derision from non-GLF parts of the LGBT movement, but it allowed us to examine sex roles, see them in the light of oppression and exploitation, and if necessary reform and revitalize our thinking about them. In doing this, GLF radicalized sex roles enough to bring about much of the academic thinking we now think of as "post," as in "post-Gay," or "post-Queer." We could look at sex roles and then change them, instead of simply marching lockstep in them.

We did all of this within a space of about three years, from 1969 to 1972. GLF had no dues, no Robert's Rules of Order or membership lists. Meetings were free to anyone who came in. Some people remember them as free-for-alls, and the disorderliness of some of them became legendary. All work was done by cells or affinity groups, and some of those groups went on to become separate organizations like Radical Lesbians, Gay Youth, Third World Gay Revolution, Street Transvestites Action Revolution or STAR, the Red Butterfly Group, and the Come Out! cell that published the GLF newspaper *ComeOut!* We also organized a speaker's bureau, and for many people this was their first connection to the Gay Movement through GLF speakers. There were also work cells, such as the 28th of June Cell that put on dances or organized demonstrations we called "actions," and which later put on the Christopher Street Liberation Day March, which later became New York's Gay Pride Parade. The thing that characterized GLF to me was the sense of freedom, support and affinity. GLF literally invented the idea of a gay community with our "gay community dances," the first open dances held outside of bars, our constant calls for community actions and our feeling that we were all each other's sisters and brothers.

That to me is the lasting legacy of the Gay Liberation Front, that we could think of each other as brothers and sisters. I can still hear Bob Kohler using those words at the first Sunday night meeting I went to. I can still hear him saying that, and all of us saying it, and believing it.

Perry Brass, a poet/novelist and "pioneer of gay literature" (ForeWord magazine), has published 14 books, including How to Survive Your Own Gay Life, The Lover of My Soul, The Harvest, Angel Lust, Warlock, *and* The Substance of God. *His newest is* Carnal Sacraments: A Historical Novel of the Future. *A finalist six times for Lambda Literary Awards, he had been given IPPY Awards from Independent Publisher for* Warlock, A Novel of Possession *(2002) and* Carnal Sacraments *(2008) which was also named a ForeWord Book of the Year Award finalist. He has had 50 poems set to music by such composers as Chris De-Blasio, Ricky Ian Gordon, Christopher Berg, Mary Carol Warwick and Paula Kimper and has been included in 25 anthologies, including the ground-breaking* Male Muse, *edited by Ian Young, and* The Columbia Anthology of Gay Literature, *edited by Byrne Fone. He lives in the Bronx, where he reads, writes and watches the Hudson River. He can be reached through his Web site, www.perrybrass.com, at MySpace/PerryBrassbooks or through http://urbanmolecule.wordpress.com*

DYKETACTICS!:
Electrifying the Imaginations of the Gay and Women's Communities

Barbara Ruth

In fine anarchist tradition there isn't even consensus as to who was a member of DYKETACTICS! I offer this retrospective as one truth among many—my current memory and framing of events that filled the air with revolution and changed my life.

In 1975, I worked at the University of Pennsylvania Women's Center, a hangout for many feminists and lesbians. Some of us met there the night of December 3rd and decided to turn up the heat at a demonstration planned at City Hall the next day, where Bill 1275, the gay rights ordinance, would almost certainly be denied a vote by the full City Council yet again. If tabled, the long-sequestered bill would die. Some of the women who were there that night—I hadn't even known one was a lesbian—coalesced, along with others, into DYKETACTICS! (The name came from a film by Barbara Hammer.)

We were dykes who resisted assimilation. I don't believe we would have fought for the rights of gays and lesbians to serve in the armed forces or to marry. We wanted to abolish military and matrimony and create a world with different dreams, different aspirations. From our inception, DYKETACTICS! worked both within and against the system, often at the same time. We thrived on contradiction. I hated 1275's mystifying, desexualized term for queers: "Affectional preference." Still, it enraged me that any group, regardless of whether I belonged to it, could be brushed aside so callously and casually, without even a vote. I believed that taking action on the extreme Left benefited liberals; pushing the Left further out created more space for reforms to blossom. But what I truly wanted to bloom were the flowers of anarchism. I wanted what our first DYKETACTICS! press release announced as our goal: to "raise public consciousness and electrify the imaginations of the gay and women's communities."

That night we never discussed being met with violence. The closest we came was asking the one law student among us what would happen if we chained ourselves to the most butch woman

137

on City Council, a strong supporter of the bill. The law student advised against it; we were likely to be roughly separated from the council butch on our way to jail. We also thought we'd likely alienate her, and we abandoned that idea. (From the beginning we were great brainstormers. My own limits were repeatedly expanded by the brilliant, wild, impractical and unexpectedly perfect ideas of my sister dyketacticians.)

The Coalition for Bill 1275 advocated dressing conservatively and unobtrusively mourning the bill's death. The women of DYKETACTICS! were inspired by the testimony of a lesbian before City Council when they considered the bill the year before. She told them, "You will never have the comfort of our silence again." DYKETACTICS! resolved not to be a silent, comfortable presence. We made signs, asked the law student a million "what if we" questions, and borrowed a friend's 10-foot witch puppet. The next morning in City Hall, before City Council convened, I slipped into the puppet and in my best witch voice proclaimed to the people waiting in the hall for the room to open, and to anyone else passing by: "I am the lesbian suppressed in every woman. I am the woman in every male crucified on the cross of manhood." Then I stashed the puppet and entered City Council chambers where dyketacticians were positioned around the room.

At that time Philly had a Civil Disobedience (CD) squad, young men who could supposedly pass for hip and had been trained to negotiate with radicals, maintain their cool when called names by demonstrators, and blend into a crowd. That day in City Hall they wore suits, like the gay men in the Coalition. Three public school classes were there to see local government in action: fourth graders, eighth graders and high school seniors.

We raised our clenched fists during the opening prayer. When the bill was tabled and therefore killed, some of us demonstrated "affectional preference" by kissing each other, with tongues. Some of us chanted: "Free 1275." The CD squad lost it.

Things blew up so quickly. The president banged his gavel. A gay male activist jumped up to the podium and threw the president's papers onto the floor. Someone said to clear the room, but I never heard that in the melee that erupted. The CD Squad pushed past the gay men to attack the dykes.

A man in a suit hurdled over the row in front of me and grabbed me. Reflexively I fell back on the passive resistance training I learned from my days in the civil rights movement and went limp. This did not go well for me. I was dragged to a doorway by my long hair (which I buzzed within the week). People were forced to walk over me as cops herded them out the door. I was kicked in the breasts, belly and vulva. I tried to grab one of those shoes, as evidence of who the kicker was, but my arms were pinned.

The butch Councilwoman shouted from the chambers floor, "Stop beating that woman!" I think "that woman" was me.

After we were all forcibly evicted, I was thrown into a room off the hallway. It was then I realized I was hurting, although that didn't seem like sufficient reason to stop demonstrating.

Other activists ended up in the same room. Dyketacticians went back into the hall, chanting and singing outside Council Chambers. As we prepared to leave, we realized all the other queers were already gone. Members of the CD squad suddenly appeared again. They started pulling on gates I hadn't even realized were there; in their "open" position they were flush against the wall. The gates ratcheted, grinding into the lock position. Some of the high school students, all African Americans, came around a corner, witnesses to whatever was going to happen next. An African American dyketactician first was herded over with the students. Then the CD goon realized his mistake. "No, get her," he said. "She's one of them." That night in televised coverage of the show-down at City Council, her picture was shown with her name and DYKETACTICS! beneath it. This was the woman I hadn't known was a lesbian. She came out in a big way. Other stations said they couldn't use the name of our group because it might offend law-abiding lesbians.

We told the CD cops we were leaving. They corralled us through the only exit, closed that gate as well, and shoved, kicked and punched us down four flights of marble spiral stairs. As we were being assaulted, dyketactician Sherrie looked up at the students and cried out, "You see what they do to gay people when we try to get our rights? It's the same thing that happens to Blacks when they stand up for theirs." Picking herself up off the steps, she made eye contact with the students and continued, "We need to unite!" I was so proud of her. This was how I wanted to live: seizing the moment for political action wherever I found it, regardless of what damage was being wrought on my body. This was a dyke tactic.

Over the next several months we struggled and played together, many of us in collective households. Everything was open to examination: income sharing; polyfidelity; "the Man" in all his guises, including the internalized oppression we called "the prick inside your head."

A month after the beatings in City Hall, my lover and fellow dyketactician Kathy was kidnapped at gunpoint, taken to an abandoned house in Camden, N.J., assaulted, repeatedly drugged, interrogated and dumped barefoot in the snow, her jacket slashed up the back. I never thought I adequately responded to what happened to her, but I still don't know what an "adequate response" would have been. Dyketacticians started getting death threats in the mail, on the phone and attached to a brick thrown through the window of Alexandria, the feminist bookstore where some of us worked. The extremity of the violence against us, especially what happened to Kathy, was impossible for me to fully take in. I thought we were an exciting, funny, high-energy bunch of dykes, so obviously on the side of justice. We tried to set up our own security, keeping track of each other's whereabouts, and we refused to stop our radical actions. We had the right combination of defiance, courage, rage and righteousness to act as though we thought we were invincible.

We tried to live our evolving practice and theory with practice in the lead. Someone would call a meeting (well, it often wasn't as formal as all that) and convey her excitement about an action she thought we should take. I usually found her excitement contagious. We brainstormed, decided who would do what, and our theory grew out of that action, formalized in the press release we wrote when it was over. We were funny, in your face—each of us able to take the initiative. We egged each other on, bringing out audacity, outrageousness and laughter that thrilled me. These dykes were the closest thing I've ever found to comrades, compañeras. I fought with them and loved them. I wish I'd told them how very much I loved them.

"In trouble? Need Lesbian-Feminist help? Call DYKETACTICS!" We graffitied this take-off on an antichoice group's billboards and put it in subways and on campuses, in bars and on telephone poles. Women called us to help them fight lesbophobia in high school, stand guard when their dangerous ex-husbands had court-sanctioned visits with their children, and heal illnesses of the body and mind with our music and poetry.

In late January 1976, we got a call from a member of the National Organization For Women (NOW), because she was fed up with NOW's decision on the movie *Snuff*. NOW considered picketing, but voted it down because the majority thought the First Amendment rights of the men making money from this venture overrode any other issues.

Snuff films, reported to be made in Argentina and screened in secret for wealthy men by organized crime syndicates, showed the actual murder and often dismemberment of porn actresses. We knew this wasn't a real snuff film. But it lured its audience by advertisements which suggested that it was. And given the advertising ("The movie they said could never be made" "Filmed in Argentina, where life is cheap") we weren't about to let this movie, regardless of its content, have its world premiere in Center City, Philadelphia. Inspired by a dyketactician who had been a girl gang member, we insisted, "Not on our turf."

First we contacted the theater manager, who said, "Come on out and demonstrate. Pickets bring tickets." No way would we contribute to his profits. We meant to stop *Snuff*, whatever it took. One idea was to pour honey into the projector.

At a community meeting of about 20 women the night before the film opened, we asked who could risk arrest. I was one of eight who said yes. Like Emma Goldman, I always carried a book with me to demonstrations, so I could use my time productively if I got busted. Many could not risk arrest, for the same reasons they weren't on the DYKETACTICS! first string. The first string dyketacticians all had movement jobs or ones we didn't really care if we lost. At 27 I was the oldest; the youngest was 19. None of us had children. And we were all able-bodied, a fact I didn't even notice at the time.

As the clicks (an old sign of wiretapping) on our phones indicated, we would face the cops again at the *Snuff* action. We had filed a federal suit against the CD cops, the City of Philadelphia and the City Council Sergeants at Arms for use of excessive force and quelling a legal demonstration. We hoped our suit might buy us a modicum of safety from public police assault while it was pending.

Thirty-five protesters met at 10 a.m. in front of the theater. Police and rent-a-cops already blocked the doors.

The larger-than-life puppets made another appearance. Inside them, demonstrators leaned into the windows of stopped buses, talking to passengers about *Snuff* and violence against women.

About 12:30, one dyke shimmied up a lamp pole in front of the theater and started yelling. All the cops rushed over to get her down and five dyketacticians walked right in the theater doors. As planned, we dispersed inside the theater, headed for the screen, the projection booth and the bathrooms. Outside, a dyketactician who taught dirty street fighting at the Free Women's School was clubbed by a cop. She kicked him in the balls. As other police came to arrest her, about 50 supporters locked arms and encircled her. These included women who the night before had said they could not risk arrest. Police backed off and no one was busted.

Back in the theater the five of us were rounded up in the aisles, where we screamed, "Brown women die, white men profit!" and "The murder of women is not entertainment!" Dyketactician Kathy stood quietly. The theater manager said, "All right. I'll negotiate with one person. You!" and pointed to her. Another dyke tactic: While your sisters are screaming their rage, look so innocent and reasonable that the Man will think he can walk all over you. Political aikido.

Communications with lawyers—theirs and ours—began after a temporary injunction limited how close we could get to potential ticket buyers, but did not stop the demonstrations. The theater hired more rent-a-cops. Kathy went in and out of the theater, wearing her leather jacket with DYKETACTICS! emblazoned on the back in studs, keeping the demonstrators abreast of every development and getting our input for her next move.

Only a handful of people purchased tickets during the day. About 40 demonstrators threatened: "Close the movie or lose your theater." Management capitulated, canceling the evening shows. The North American distributor vented his astonishment to the press: "When protesters start dictating what a movie theater can show . . . this country is in bad shape. These dykes are vicious. They're militant."

But local people felt we were on the side of justice. The daily papers refused to carry advertisements for the next day's showings. More than a hundred people signed our petitions condemning real and simulated snuff films, and demanding this one be shut down. All who signed, including those who objected as Christians, saw that something called DYKETACTICS! wrote the statement and called the demonstration. I watched them hesitate and imagined them thinking: "*Snuff* is a bad thing and these DYKETACTICS! girls seem so earnest." Some shook their heads and walked away, but most signed the petition and some spontaneously joined our picket line.

During their breaks, middle-aged waitresses from the Horn

and Hardart restaurant on the block brought free coffee to demonstrators, saying, "I know you must be cold out here." "Keep up the good work." "That movie is terrible." Their solicitude and solidarity thrilled us.

When we arrived at the theater the next morning, the marquee announced, "Final Showing Today." We stayed till the box office closed, entreating potential moviegoers not to cross our picket line. At no time were more than 10 percent of the theater's 1,200 seats filled.

Some men joined us throughout the demonstration. DYKE-TACTICS! was establishing a tradition of women-only energy circles at the beginning and close of each action. When we explained, the men graciously stepped aside, and about 15 women formed a circle in front of the theater, blessing each other and our supporters and hexing all who profited from any snuff film, sending them bad dreams.

Kathy and I returned to our bed blissful and exhausted. A passerby had given me a piece of paper with the distributor's home phone number. Not sure it was for real, we called the number. He answered the phone, acknowledged who he was and said, "I was there today. I saw you." I asked him, "How are you going to make any profits? Lesbians work in post offices all over the country. They're going to destroy any film from you that goes through the mail." He seemed to misunderstand why we objected to *Snuff*, thinking we opposed the portrayal of heterosexual sex. He whined to Kathy how hard it was to make a buck in porn. "You've gotta have something extra, people are bored with the same old stuff." He explained that he needed the "something extra" to send his daughters through college. Kathy suggested he try selling shoes.

In fact, dykes did protest *Snuff* all over the country, doing considerable property damage to theaters that showed it in Southern California. *Hera*, the Philadelphia feminist newspaper with national distribution, published the *Snuff* guy's name and number. DYKETACTICS! was extraordinary in many ways, but we weren't the only radical lesbian activists in the mid-'70s.

In September came the trial. Twelve groups before us had unsuccessfully sued Philly police for excessive force, but somehow even our radical lawyers thought we might win. I figured we might get injunctive relief, meaning the cops would go back to beating dykes in private places, such as paddy wagons, and not in City Council.

We had documentation: Five of us had gone to the hospital

December 3rd due to injuries sustained in City Council and on the four flights of steps the cops kicked us down. We had witnesses: other demonstrators who were there that day and those high school seniors.

The defense attorney quickly established that each defendant was married, with children and membership in civic organizations. He asked us if we were lesbians. Watching the reaction of the judge and jury, we could tell these conflicting core identities trumped all our documentation and witnesses.

So we used the trial as guerrilla theater. When our lawyer questioned him, one of our attackers explained the extremity of the provocation, which caused him to administer "rough justice." (This was their basic defense: The defendants did what was necessary, given the threat we posed to public safety. Their lawyer said we were lucky they didn't use billy clubs on us.) The attacker produced a card one of us had given him that day: "You have insulted a woman. This card is chemically treated. In three days your prick will fall off."

After having the card read into the record our lawyer asked him, "And have you had any reason to believe the card did in fact contain chemicals with this result?"

The cops' lawyer asked dyketactician Paola if she believed in violence. With classic anarchist subversiveness, she truthfully answered, "I'm a vegetarian." Another dyke tactic: Move outside the Man's categories and tell your truth from there.

At every break our lawyers—straight National Lawyers' Guild feminists who represented us for no pay, and refused to state their sexual preferences as they were frequently harassed by male lawyers in the months leading up to the trial—went into the hallway to tell us what had been said out of our hearing and discuss with us what to do next. This demystified the legal process and made me feel we could at least participate in the trial on our own terms.

One witness, a public school teacher, was asked by the defense attorney if she was a lesbian. She knew that telling the truth would jeopardize her job, which brought us back to the now dead bill, which would have changed that. As she hesitated, the judge threatened to hold her in jail overnight for contempt of court. We were the ones on trial, and so by extension was anyone who supported us.

Before the verdict was announced, cops stationed themselves around the courtroom, with a phalanx next to the jury. After the

**YOU HAVE INSULTED A WOMAN
THIS CARD IS CHEMICALLY TREATED
IN 3 DAYS YOUR PRICK WILL FALL OFF**

DYKETACTICS!

This card was created and handed out by the radical lesbians of DYKETACTICS!

judge read the decision—all defendants not guilty on all counts—the police escorted the jury to a secure elevator, where they wouldn't have to risk whoever might be lurking in a public one.

We wrote a press release indicting the City and the named Civil Disobedience cops. *Hera* printed a picture of many of them, taken outside the courtroom, with the caption, "Caution! These men are dangerous." We graffitied "Lesbians arm yourselves" in the usual places. Alexandria prominently displayed the *Women's Gun Pamphlet.*

The verdict officially sanctioned open season on dykes, specifically DYKETACTICS!, and the anonymous death treats continued. I found myself at the edge of a huge leap, which included picking up the gun and going underground. That fall, while I danced on that edge, catastrophe came from a whole other direction.

During the summer, Kathy's sister Theresa had given sanctuary to a friend whose boyfriend was battering her. Inspired by Kathy's activism, Theresa went with her friend to press charges against him. In November, Theresa was raped and murdered, the night before the batterer's trial. (A serial rapist, the batterer was subsequently found guilty of Theresa's murder.) Theresa was 21 years old, with a seven-month-old baby, and she loved her life. I knew and liked her. She and Kathy were very close. Her death probably had nothing to do with DYKETACTICS!, but her death was completely political.

I wasn't dancing on any edges anymore, just getting through the next night, the next day.

It was time to get out of town. Kathy and I took to the road, performing music and poetry and facilitating workshops at women's, gay and radical venues all over the United States for a year and a half. In our travels we told DYKETACTICS! stories and heard tales of lesbian activism happening in most of the places we stayed. Mid-'70s radical lesbian actions are not documented in movement herstories/histories in nearly the abundance I experienced them. I am glad for this opportunity to set the record queer.

I can't tell at this distance if I realized at the time how extraordinary it was, living my life in the whirlwind of a movement for social change. I know when I've approached that intensity again with activist groups, my point of reference has always been DYKETACTICS!

It has taken me decades to realize, despite the rage and terror we experienced, how lucky I was to live in anarcha-dyke extremity, with women who inspired and challenged me to move farther, faster, than I dreamed I could.

Barbara Ruth continues to be an anarcha-lesbian-feminist with wide-ranging passions. Following the 2000 presidential theft by Bush and subsequent events, those passions include election integrity, the 9/11 Truth Movement, prisoners' rights here and abroad, and indictment of Bush/Cheney et al. As she is severely disabled, most of her activism now takes place from home. For over 20 years, creating disabled women's culture and increasing accessibility have engaged her mind and heart. She is currently the resident poet of Fabled Asp, a San Francisco Bay Area disabled lesbians' storytelling project. She hopes to continue and to strengthen her ongoing friendship with sister dyketacticians.

Simeon White:
A Life of Seeing Connections

Tommi Avicolli Mecca

Simeon Meadows White, a longtime gay, black, civil rights and anti-war activist, took Martin Luther King Jr.'s words to heart, especially when the famed civil rights leader said, "We know through painful experience that freedom is never voluntarily given by the oppressor; it must be demanded by the oppressed."

Born in Kinston, North Carolina in 1944, Simeon, like King, faced segregation everywhere during his childhood—in separate public bathrooms ("whites" and "coloreds"), in restaurants, theaters, and drinking fountains.

Inspired by a sit-in organized by college students in nearby Greensboro, Simeon formed his own chapter of the NAACP (National Association for the Advancement of Colored People) and recruited his fellow high school students to protest at the lunch counter of a local drugstore. He later brought together students and adults in a series of demonstrations aimed at segregated stores, movie theaters and even a public pool where his father, an all-state swimmer, couldn't swim. Simeon's mobilizing eventually led to the desegregation of Kinston.

Simeon's nephew, Khary Lazarre-White, who heads a New York group for African American and Latino youth, wrote in an article that his uncle was so "enraged at the injustice of it all" that he simply "felt the urgent need to act." And act he did.

His efforts attracted the attention of a local TV and radio commentator by the name of Jesse Helms (who would go on to become a five-term senator from North Carolina and one of Congress's most outspoken bigots). Helms denounced Simeon as "a little colored boy leading a movement down in Kinston, causing trouble, and bringing in outside agitators." He also described him as the "local Communist nigra boy." It didn't discourage Simeon.

After college, Simeon attended the Martin Luther King Jr. School of Social Change in Chester, near Philadelphia. When drafted for the Vietnam War, Simeon refused to go. He convinced a local black church to provide him sanctuary in order to frustrate the FBI agents who were sent to arrest him. He also joined the American Friends Service Committee (AFSC), a Quaker organization whose mission it is to carry out "service, development, social justice and peace programs throughout the world."

Simeon was eventually indicted for refusing to fight in a war he didn't believe in. He avoided prison on a technicality. But the experience cemented his commitment to pacifism and nonviolent struggle.

Simeon moved to San Francisco in the early '70s and became involved in the city's early gay liberation movement. He fought alongside Harvey Milk in the campaign to defeat the Briggs Initiative, which would have banned queers from being teachers in the state of California. He was a founding member of the Harvey Milk LGBT Democratic Club, which was started by Milk as the Gay Democratic Club. It was renamed after his assassination in 1978.

Though he emerged as a very public gay activist, Simeon remained committed to many other causes as well, for he always saw the connection between all oppressions. He was elected president of Service Employees International Union 535, his union when he worked at the city's welfare department. He served on many boards, including the AFSC and the Names Project (which gathered together the AIDS quilt).

He was appointed to several committees of the Human Rights Commission and the San Francisco Unified School District. He served two terms as the first African American elected to public office on the Democratic County Central Committee. At the time of his death

Simeon White

from AIDS in March 1994, he was planning a run for the San Francisco Board of Supervisors "to address the issues of all San Franciscans, including and especially those most disenfranchised." He died surrounded by friends and comrades, never tired of the struggle that he fought hard all his life to win.

Fopping It Up: Former Cockette Rumi's story

Interview by Tommi Avicolli Mecca

Note from the editor: Rumi Missabu is a survivor of that fabulous era of gay and sexual liberation in San Francisco when men in radical drag (also known as genderfuck) lived in communes, paraded on the streets and took to the stage. The sexual revolution that started in the Haight Ashbury had spread throughout the city. Years before Harvey Milk strived to be elected to public office, the mostly gay male troupe the Cockettes was producing musical reviews that took the art form far from where it had ever dared to go. Videos such as "Tricia's Wedding" (a spoof of the wedding of the daughter of then president Richard Nixon) placed the troupe in the vanguard of alternative art in the United States. The troupe even had members who went on to international fame, including disco singer Sylvester and actor/actress Divine.

Rumi, too, has achieved international attention. He chose the name Rumi Missabu, as he explains it, "in 1969 when my spiritual transformation was complete. I picked Rumi as my first name in honor of the Sufi poet. At the time he wasn't well known or hardly translated, but today outsells Emily Dickinson in sales in America. Missabu is the name of a messenger or angel of the God Arcan, the ruler of Monday in Celtic mythology."

A member of the original Cockettes and later the Angels of Light (a split-off of the Cockettes), he now travels around the world keeping alive the memory of those performance groups. He has amassed a large collection of Cockettes and Angels of Light memorabilia. His story is in many ways the story of a lot of queers who left their families and hometowns in the mid to late '60s to answer the call of the sexual and political revolution that was happening in America's big cities.

What follows is the excerpted transcript of an interview I conducted with Rumi in June 2008 in my Castro apartment. Rumi was warm and funny and opened up immediately. He kept me engrossed with his story, which flowed like a monologue.

BORN IN A TRUNK

I was born in Hollywood. My parents were kind of on the fringe of show business. They never quite got their act together. My father was an auto body mechanic and had a gas station/body shop on Santa Monica Boulevard on Sunset Strip. He played steel guitar. He never played professionally, but he would jam with famous people like Tex Ritter at Tex's home when I was a kid. So I used to play with Tex Ritter's son, John. I was raised in the San Fernando Valley. I went to a six-year public school. It was a senior high/junior high combined, and all the stars' children went there. Dick Van Dyke was the president of the PTA.

I was an art major at first, then switched to drama in senior high and did all my high school plays with people like Sally Field. She was queen of the drama department and I was king. I first took LSD with Cindy Williams, who became Shirley on *Laverne and Shirley*. When I was 16 my family decided to move to Idaho. They said that they were going to follow the white people. My grandmom had land up there. I said, "What about my career?" They said, "There's a little theater in Lewistown." I actually visited there twice one summer. They were so archaic. They would do vaudeville shows. I said, "Have you ever heard of Tennessee Williams?" "Who?" Eugene O'Neill? Who? Edward Albee? Who? No, they didn't know any of those people, it was foreign to them.

So I decided not to go. I fought like hell just to finish high school. I got to go to junior college in Los Angeles with the stipulation that I sign up with the Selective Service when I turned 18. Of course, I signed up, but my draft board was the Hollywood draft board and I don't think they ever took anybody from there. They must've sent me a notice, but I moved so many times they could never find me, so I became like a draft resister.

BERKELEY CALLS

I went to Los Angeles City College and majored in theater there. Then I realized that I just didn't want to do that type of theater. I didn't want to get involved in the whole Hollywood scene. It wasn't for me. I was taking a lot of psychedelics at the time. I was 19. I was living with Cindy Williams before she became an actress. She was an actress, but hadn't done anything major yet. One day in 1967 I went to Hollywood Boulevard and saw a film called *She Freaks*. This film changed my life and it put me where I am. The day after I saw that film I went back to our apartment and wrote her a note: "Dear Cindy, I can't take it anymore." I got on a Greyhound bus and I moved to Berkeley.

I had the addresses of two girls I went to high school with and another woman I had known in L.A. I was sure one of them would be able to put me up. One of them said, "Here's the address of a poetess I know on San Pablo Avenue." She lived in a water tower behind a free store run by these bikers. She took me in for the winter. We just had enough room for our bed and a table we fashioned out of an old door in between to make our crafts. All winter we did crafts and sold them in Berkeley and S.F.

At that point we participated in Stop the Draft Week at the Oakland Induction Center. It was 1968. We were to be arrested, our bail had been pre-posted. We were going to perform this act of civil disobedience. Instead, they just arrested the celebrities like Allen Ginsberg, Ira Cohen, Joan Baez and the rest of the crowd they billy-clubbed and maced in the face and made disperse. That was one of my last times demonstrating and protesting. I did it one more time in the Haight Ashbury in the Panhandle in a demonstration against the Vietnam War. Vanessa Redgrave was the speaker and her Trotskyite rhetoric or whatever she was spewing that day turned me off. I ended up walking away and I never actively protested again. I've done a lot of charity work and have donated as much as I can. As far as protests, that was the end of it.

FOPPING IT UP

I hadn't realized I was queer yet. People in high school told me I was. My high school drama teacher told me he was going to have trouble casting me because I was slightly effeminate. The dean of the college told me the same thing. He said that his wife could come in and give me walking lessons. His wife! He said that all I was capable of playing were fops and dandies. At the time I didn't know what a fop or a dandy was. I had to go home and look it up. And when I looked it up I realized, OK! I'm going to turn this around. You want a fop, you want a dandy? I'm gonna fop it up. I took a straight part in *The Madwoman of Chaillot*. It was the part of the prospector who discovers oil under the streets of Paris. I made him so gay, everyone just roared. I got the plaque that year for best actor from Sally Field.

COCKETTES

In Berkeley, I really wanted to be in this group called Floating Lotus Magic Opera Company. They were like the Angels of Light—they were very spiritual, unlike the Cockettes. They did plays with the goddess Kali and Krishna, temple dancers and all that. The director, Daniel Moore, wouldn't permit me to be in the production. He would never cast me. I was living with them and sleeping with half the cast, the boys and the girls. I was able to have meals with them and meditate with them, but he wouldn't let me in the damn play. He didn't like me or whatever. So I said OK, I'm going to start my own thing. I tried to direct a group that was similar to them and came up with a play called *To Kingdom Come*. It went nowhere. Then the Living Theatre came to town. It was this wonderful in-your-face type of agitprop theatre that actually would bring the audience into the play. They did two performances of a play called *Paradise Now* and I got to be in both of them.

In 1969 I wondered what there was for gay people in Berkeley. I still had three girlfriends. I discovered that there was a group of young gay men meeting at a church called Sherwood Forest. What I saw at those gay liberation meetings were circles, or semi-circles, of young gay men having to face the facts of coming out to their parents. I never had to have that experience. As I said, my parents moved away to Idaho. The last thing they knew I was running around with loose married women. I never had to come out to them. They never found out.

I would go to these meetings and find them kind of sad and miserable. I really wanted to enlighten those people, but I wasn't sure how to go about it. So every time I'd go back I would bring a band with me. I made a movie at Land's End [a beach area on San Francisco's Pacific coast] called *Tree Your Sap Beats Gently Against Mine*, a silent film with a Rossini score. This was shot in 1969 at the peak of sexual revolution. The only requisite was that actors had to appear naked in it and with no contemporary jewelry, to give it a vintage or old faery feeling to it. There were all the Cockettes before we were Cockettes in that tree movie. We met at the Capri Bar on Grant Avenue in North Beach, and we met at the Palace Theater that started doing midnight movies, also in North Beach. That theater was a meeting place where we could go at midnight and smoke dope and take our shoes off and have an orgy in the balcony. We could do anything we wanted.

Then the Cockettes kind of morphed into those midnight

movies. We became like a filler. Our first show was at midnight on New Year's Eve 1969–70. All we did was put the Rolling Stones' "Honky Tonk Woman" on an old phonograph record on the stage, then cranked it up and came out and danced and lost our clothing. The crowd roared and wanted more. We put the same record on and did it again. We were asked back the following week. The following month it was the same thing, except to a Martha and the Vandellas record, "Dancing in the Streets."

The name came from Cockette Ralph, who was only in the first show. He just died. He named us Cockettes after the Rockettes because it was always on our minds anyway. It was easy to be a Cockette. All you had to do was show up for a rehearsal. If you were a guy, it was especially easy because there was a shortage of guys. All the guys wanted to play girls. Originally we were a commune of 13 that included 10 men, three women and an infant. Within six months and after a lot of publicity, there were 65 people onstage for the first Halloween show. Now, as archivist, I count 168 people who were in one show or another.

TRICIA'S WEDDING

It was thought up overnight. I thought it was mean-spirited that they were trashing the real Tricia Nixon. There was no script. I was supposed to be Jackie Kennedy. I didn't get along with the manager. I sent my boyfriend Johnny, who was my boyfriend in the Cockettes, to be Jackie Kennedy. I was busy doing *Elevator Girls* at the time. People regard *Elevator Girls* as a Cockette movie, but I made the film after I quit the Cockettes and took a lot of them with me. I put them all in it.

AND THE DRUG OF CHOICE

In *Elevator Girls,* the drug of choice was angel dust. The producers had the formula. That's how they financed the film, through the making of angel dust. I made another film and the drug of choice was heroin. I was on cocaine; that was my drug of choice. And I was in circles where I could get it for free. The cocaine really made me conceited or arrogant or stuff like that.

LAST CALL

After the Palace Theater, the shows started getting a little struc-
tured. We would do reviews. We would each pick a musical number and use any kind of musical accompaniment we could get. That
morphed into more structure, more sets, scripts, stuff like that. I
was in the group the first year and then I quit. I was in the original group. I quit because I felt extremely exploited by our manager, who happened to be Bill Graham's accountant at the time, his
bookkeeper. I just didn't think it was fair the way the monies were
trickling down. They were only charging $2.50 at the door or maybe
it was $2. The theater seated 1,500 people and we would sell out
all the time. We were never really hassled for using obscenities, but
we were by the fire marshal for letting people sit in the aisles. By
the time the money was dispersed, I'd only have enough to buy a
pair of false eyelashes for the next show. We were so angry about
it. During the board meetings, Hibiscus and I would go and make
homemade bread. As the bread came out of the oven, he would
glaze it with his cum and serve it to the Cockettes and the manager
unbeknownst to them.

So I quit the Cockettes after the first year. Hisbiscus went back
to New York. One day I was making love to my boyfriend in the
Cockettes, Johnny, whom we called our beauty, on the rooftop of
the old gay center at 330 Grove [in San Francisco] and I noticed
that his nipples were enlarged and his breasts were hard. I freaked
and I said what is it? He said that he and Bobby, the two youngest
members of the Cockettes, were going to a place called the Society for Special Problems. They were taking hormones pills. They
were getting hormone therapy to become women. I was shocked.
I screamed and I fled the country. I couldn't take it. As liberated
as we were, I couldn't take the fact that my boyfriend, my lover,
was going to become a woman. I fled the country and I moved to
Montreal.

THE COCKETTES LIVE ON

We didn't realize how political we were back then or what the
ramifications were or what it would all become or what it would
spawn. We had no idea that a couple years ago they would do a 32-
page tribute to us in the Italian *Vogue* and one film after another.
The shows were just vehicles to find boyfriends. We were just out
to party and to have a good time.

Gay Raiders

Mark Segal

Years ago, I helped leaflet for the first gay pride march organized by the Christopher Street Liberation Day Committee—though that first one wasn't called gay pride, but rather "March and Gay-In." We didn't know then that we were making history. I didn't know what would happen next to any of us. Or where what we were doing would lead.

In 1970, it was all about gay rights. At the time, that meant assuring that gay people could come out without losing their jobs, apartments, family or more. In 1970, anyone, anywhere in the United States, could be fired simply for being gay. In 1970, it was still illegal for a bartender in New York to sell a drink to a known gay man.

In Los Angeles, a gay man or woman couldn't even get a job as a sanitation worker. You could be arrested for being gay, kissing or holding hands. In mental hospitals all over the nation, doctors were experimenting on gay men and women with drugs, electroshock therapy and even water and sleep deprivation to "cure" their homosexuality.

In May 1969, Marty Robinson recruited me into the "action group," a subgroup of Mattachine NY. If there were organizers of the demonstrations on the nights following the "Stonewall Riots" at the end of June, it was us. After the first incident in which cops raided the bar, Marty had the brilliant idea to have us write in chalk on Christopher Street: "Stonewall tomorrow night." For three more nights, we gathered and protested. We quickly realized there was strength in numbers.

After the riots, our action group merged with the Gay Liberation Front. From 18 to 21, this involvement was my coming of age.

For me, GLF was an education on how to change the world: I learned how to win, survive and bring about consensus and coalition. It also taught me to contribute and achieve. But never did

I expect that those contributions would change the world. And those of us from that era—and before—changed the world.

At 18, my first contribution to the creation of a gay community was the formation of Gay Youth as a caucus of NYC's GLF in 1970. Gay Youth was the first LGBT organization to look out for the needs of our children. We went on TV and radio, spoke in high schools, held dances, had a gay youth hotline and even published a newsletter.

With our partner, the Street Transvestite Action Revolutionaries (STAR), members of Gay Youth would debate into the night about what we needed to do to serve our special constituencies: youth, street kids and transpeople (the term hadn't been coined yet). We also partnered frequently with the women of GLF in their battle against sexism. We cut our teeth on survival issues, making such important decisions as whether to support the Black Panthers or Jane Fonda and her "Free the Army" road show. GLF taught me how to survive those battles. To the early activists, the battles in the community today are mere child's play.

Those GLF/Gay Activists Alliance years in NYC also saw my first arrest. I don't even remember what the demonstration was for, we had so many. All I recall is being handcuffed to a heating pipe at the 10th Street police station. It was revolutionary at the time to be arrested in a gay demonstration. I'm proud to say that I have been arrested many times for nonviolent civil disobedience.

Early on, I learned about aversion therapy—an attempt to change sexuality using drugs or electroshock treatment. The latter was done mostly with electrodes strapped to the genitals. The father of this idea was a Dr. Goldstein, who hailed from apartheid South Africa and practiced at Eastern Pennsylvania Psychiatric Institute, part of Temple University, which got its funding from the state of Pennsylvania.

Using the tactics learned in GLF, and a few of the more theatrical ones I picked up elsewhere, I led a group to pressure the Pennsylvania legislature to review the state budget and suggested to the president of Temple that this practice should end. Through the efforts of a number of us, Temple eventually cut off funding to Dr. Goldstein's project.

In 1972, I had the pleasure of debating Dr. Green of the American Psychiatric Association (APA) on the *Phil Donahue Show* regarding his characterization of homosexuality as an illness. It was the first such public debate about the APA's nomenclature, a few years before Dr. Anonymous (a gay shrink) made his infamous appearance at the APA convention and helped the group make its monumental decision in 1973 to stop classifying gays as sick.

Next came the Gay Raiders, the nation's first gay organization to take on homophobia in the mainstream media. At that time, there were no gay characters on TV, not a one. The word wasn't even used. TV news seldom touched the subject. I realized that media and publicity was the way to change minds: We had to sell gay rights like toothpaste.

Americans, at that point, didn't know gay people. Very few were out. I ended up being that out person. I introduced America to their new gay boy next door: me. Since the networks wouldn't send me an invitation, I invited myself onto their sets and into their studios. From 1971 to 1973, you could see me pop up on many a live show. *Variety* once stated that I had caused the networks $750,000 in tape delays and lost income. I visited the *Today Show,* the *Tonight Show*, the *Mike Douglas Show* and, most notably, *CBS Evening News with Walter Cronkite.*

An estimated 60 percent of America was watching the *CBS Evening News* when Mark Segal, the Gay Raider, walked onto the live broadcast and sat on Cronkite's desk holding a sign and yelling "Gays protest CBS' discrimination." The CBS national network went black for three minutes as the production staff in the studio wrestled me to the floor and wrapped me in wires. The next morning it got front-page coverage in almost every newspaper in the country, another first. I was now America's No. 1 gay radical. At this point, the talk show was coming into its own and I was invited to appear on many of them. In every city I traveled to, there were newspaper and magazine articles on gay rights.

The Gays Raiders' "Campaign Against the Networks" resulted in agreements with NBC, ABC and CBS to end bias in news and programming years before Gay and Lesbian Alliance Against Defamation came into existence.

I was a founder and president of the National Gay Press Association and the National Gay Newspaper Association. In 1976, we set out to do something that had never been done before: We sent questionnaires to all the presidential candidates about their stand on gay rights. Most thought it was a joke, and didn't answer. A few did. One was a peanut farmer from Plains, Georgia. That letter—still hanging on my wall—was the first letter from a presidential candidate (later president) affirming support for gay rights. (Thank you, President Jimmy Carter.)

We also decided to poll governors (23 responded) and major city police chiefs from around the nation. That information led to numerous new relations between gay activists and state governments and police around the nation.

As gay liberation activists, we changed the world.

Over the years I've signed my name in many ways—chairman, president, commissioner, producer, executive committee, board member and publisher—but this is the first time in that 40 years that I sign it Mark Segal, Gay Activist.

Mark Segal is the dean of the gay press, having been the publisher of the Philadelphia Gay News *for 32 years. He's a founder and former president of both the National Gay Press Association and the National Gay Newspaper Guild. He's been on the Board of Directors of the Pennsylvania Newspaper association and is on the editorial committee of the Suburban Newspapers of America (SNA). He coordinates the Gay History Project, which unites local LGBT publications each October to celebrate gay history. Mark is also known as the baby of gay pioneers, which he writes about here.*

Puerto Rican contingent in New York's 1972 Gay Pride march.

REVOLUTION AROUND EVERY CORNER

Between Bohemia and Revolution

Flavia Rando

In the current political climate, there has been a resurgence of interest in the liberation movements of the 1960s and 70s, of histories and activists that have been alternately embraced and forgotten. The year 2009 marks the 40th anniversary of the Stonewall rebellion. As with many other activists and academics, my imagination has turned back to those decades with renewed urgency.

In 1961, I had just completed my first year at Brooklyn College. I loved to read, and I was reading in the public library, the refuge of a first-generation daughter of Sicilian immigrant parents. I sat in the faded but still imposing reading room of the New York Public Library's main branch. I was 17 years old, and I had just come out. In the absence of even the possibility of an adult mentor, I had come here to read Radclyffe Hall's *The Well of Loneliness*. Would this be the text of my new identity? I read all day.

As I read, I willed Radclyffe Hall to teach me. Who was I now that I had come out? As I finished the book, I felt affection, sorrow and then an unexpected skepticism that tainted the identification I had hoped would occur. Instead, I thought, it does not have to be that way—that was then, this is now. I was very young.

Even in the midst of the virulent homophobia of 1961, a moment Samuel Delaney characterizes as "still . . . part of the fifties" ("It's even hard to speak of that world," he adds), I believed in books, education, as a means to the self. Having found my desire, I now had to find its meaning and my place in the world.

My lover and I met when we were both first-year students at Brooklyn College, the same institution where I now teach Women's and Sexualities Studies. Six months later, I packed a suitcase and took the subway from Brooklyn to live with her on the Lower East Side.

Now the East Village, the Lower East Side was then a village traced by an always present past of political activism, immigration and poverty. Some of the streets between Avenues C and D were still unpaved. Avenue C was lined with pushcarts selling food and unidentifiable secondhand goods. The air was thick and dark from the smokestacks of the nearby Con Edison plant. Immigrants—Jewish, Puerto Rican, Polish and Italian—and kids like us, downwardly mobile, looked for apartments rented, no questions asked, at $36.50 a month.

My lover and I settled into poverty, in an apartment in which there was no cold water in the summer, and water froze in the winter. On the streets, we were harassed, called names, stoned. Forced to a margin I had been unaware existed, I now became a marker of that location. In rapid succession, I who had been a cloistered, working-class, Sicilian American girl, became an artist, a beatnik, a lesbian, an outcast—queer. We lived our queer life, at a price. "Having escaped" as Monique Wittig has written, "one by one" from compulsory heterosexuality, we shared an often brutalizing poverty with previous waves of refugees. Happy to find the right place, to find any place at all.

Eventually we learned we had been preceded by others who offered alternate models, other ways to be lesbian: Pearl, who ran an antique store and improvised salon, and the artist Helen De Mott, whom I saw walking with her two dogs for a decade before we met. When Helen and I finally talked, she would tell me about what it meant for a woman, for a lesbian, to try to survive as an artist, to be part of the 10th Street gallery scene. Later, I would read Audre Lorde's biomythography, *Zami: A New Spelling of My Name*, and learn that she had left the neighborhood only shortly before I arrived. It gave me solace to think we had shared the same walk to the subway, the same coffee shop.

In addition to harboring those of us who sought domestic refuge, the East Village was a site of outlawed public sexuality and queer cultural resistance from the gay drag clubs that in the 1960s lined East Fourth Street street to Mickey Ruskin's poetry cafés and the 10th Street galleries. I began attending performances of the Ridiculous Theatrical Company. They insisted on outrageous presence and outrageous art. I saw in exuberant perversity a queer political act.

My lover and I continued to travel to Brooklyn College, where I studied painting with Ad Reinhardt and Philip Pearlstein. Here, even in the studios and classrooms of an art department that prided itself on its bohemian and counterculture atmosphere, the words *lesbian* and *homosexual* were not uttered except in negative assessment of one of numerous students' inescapable identification. We were fortunate to find the "artists and gay table" in the College cafeteria, where students nurtured each other. In the Brooklyn College library, we discovered little-known works by Gertrude Stein and Virginia Woolf. But Stein's more explicitly lesbian auto-biographical work, *Q.E.D.*, like Djuna Barnes's *A Ladies Almanac*, were out of print and could only be found in the Rare Book Room of the 42nd Street New York Public Library. To gain access to these books, we fabricated elaborate identities and research projects.

Three years later, the apartment my lover and I shared was devastated by neighbors turned thieves. Even the front door was destroyed, and we were forced to flee. The societal violence common against "unprotected" young women was linked in our minds inescapably to the ever present violence of homophobia.

In the summer of 1969, shortly after the Stonewall Rebellion set the West Village aflame, we learned of a meeting of the newly established Gay Liberation Front. After a decade of soul-destroying homophobia, my response was "I have been waiting for this all my life."

The Lesbian/Gay Liberation Movement exploded into being and we began to change the way in which we knew/understood ourselves. The Movement was the expression of a remarkable shift—of rage and hope nurtured by the liberation struggles that had come before—that allowed/demanded that we challenge received knowledge. The editorial for the first issue of *ComeOut!*, the newspaper of the Gay Liberation Front, November 14, 1969, concluded with the extraordinary declaration "We are going to transform the society at large through the open realization of our own consciousness." We began to re/write our history, to give ourselves lineage, family, community. We had experienced the costs and now we were beginning to develop the insights of breaking free/the margin.

We began to learn lesbian, to understand and to declare that we had a unique way of learning—through rap sessions, consciousness-raising, consensus—that we had something to contribute beyond the accumulation of historical details. We became our own teachers, creating our own classrooms, libraries, texts—the materials we needed for psychic survival. We formed support groups and researched and self-published studies such as *Lesbians and the Health Care System*. The Lesbian/Gay Movement taught and sustained me, imbuing me with a lasting belief in the ability of communal political activity to restructure the manner in which one understands the self and one's place in the world.

The following year, many of the women of Gay Liberation Front joined disenfranchised lesbians from the feminist movement to form Radicalesbians. On May 1, 1970, members of Radicalesbians wrote, published and distributed, "The Woman Identified Woman," the essay that has become a manifesto of and for the right to lesbian self-definition within a political (feminist) context. On February 24, 1971, a Romaine Brooks retrospective, curated by Adelyn D. Breeskin, opened at the National Museum of American Art including Brooks's "lesbian portraits," among them her iconic 1923 *Self Portrait/Portrait of an Artist,* certifying lesbian presence in the institutional art world. In 1971, Fran Winant, a member of the Gay Liberation Front and Radicalesbians, established Violet Press and collected material for the first anthology of lesbian art and poetry to be published in the United States and in the world. That anthology, *We Are All Lesbians*, was published in 1973.

A Lesbian Art Collective grew out of Radicalesbians—our goal was to create a context for ourselves as artists in a collective political process. Our strategy was one of maximum visibility in the lesbian community and on the streets. Everyday intimacies—the markers of lesbian life—were viewed as political, and used as the raw materials for agitprop. Linking identity to art-making and both to politics, our first action was to poster subways, streets, especially near lesbian bars, and midtown offices, the site of our day jobs, with fliers of our work stamped "lesbian art." Art shows were mounted in provisional art galleries such as Fort Dyke, where the work was shown by candlelight.

Our reference point was liberation. We attempted to create a community survival network, an urban back-to-the-land movement, and for a glorious moment we succeeded. We needed communal space and in 1970, women occupied a derelict city building, the Fifth Street Women's Building, where meetings were held and classes taught. In 1972, the Lesbian Food Conspiracy, a food coop open to all, was begun. The St. Marks Women's Clinic, community-run and nonprofit, was established in 1974, pioneering lesbian health care. All Crafts opened on St. Marks Place teaching women construction skills. Medusa's Revenge was a performance space and the place to dance—often to lesbian big bands. If Medusa's

Revenge is, as Hélène Cixous believes, women's pleasure—then, this was the place.

I was now living in another East Village, one in which the other inhabitants were lesbians taking public space to remap the geography of the self. My experience of the street was transformed. When I met friends, we kissed each other slowly on the mouth, lingering in order to distinguish our kisses from those of relatives— are you two sisters?—from the greetings of straight women. Our queer performance inscribed the streets with our desire—social, political, erotic. Lesbians with queer ideas re/imagining their world as a utopia between bohemia and revolution.

Sections of this essay appeared in another format in "The Next Generation: Lesbian Learning/Learning Lesbian" published in *From Our Voices: Art Educators and Artists Speak Out About LGBT Issues,* edited by Laurel Lampela and Ed Check (Kendall Hunt Publishing, 2003).

Flavia Rando, a lesbian (art) activist since 1969, was a member of the Gay Liberation Front and Radicalesbians. She is an art historian who currently teaches Women's and LGBTQ Studies at Brooklyn College, City University of New York. As an academic activist, she has organized and served on numerous diversity, feminist and LGBTQ task forces, committees, and panels. She is the founding member of the Astraea Lesbian Foundation for Justice Visual Arts Program and is the co-editor of the Special Issue of the Art Journal *Gay and Lesbian Presence in Art and Art History.*

Gay Liberation Front: Report from London

Richard Bolingbroke

This is a personal recollection of events, dates and names. The author welcomes any information that would correct his highly subjective memory. After all, it was 35 years ago and I took no notes!

I guess I was fortunate to have arrived in London in July 1970 to attend London University at the tender age of 18, right at the beginning of the contemporary gay movement in the U.K.

I had just come out at the neighborhood bar, the King William IV in Hampstead, conveniently located at the end of the street where I had lodgings. Little did I know that within months I would be swept up in the outpouring of energy created by the budding gay rights movement and find myself marching, demonstrating and answering phone banks, all in the name of Gay Lib.

Gay bars in England were probably safer havens than they were in the United States. There was an unstated social rule that what you did in private was OK. But if you dared to flaunt it, as Oscar Wilde found out, then the law hit hard and you became an outcast. All this to say that there were no "gay" bars, just bars where men met men, fags, drags and even leather men.

So when Aubrey Walter and David Fernbach, two gay monogamous Maoists, arrived back from the United States, (probably from New York City) with the news that Gay Liberation was happening, and organized the first GLF meetings, the social rule was first cracked and then smashed, and all hell broke loose.

To be honest, I don't remember how I found out about GLF—probably a flier. I remember arriving at the LSE (London School of Economics) for my first lesson in anarchy and political chaos. Aubrey and David were old-school Maoists (capital M), and they very much had it in mind that this would be a tightly controlled, left-wing proletariat movement. That's not what happened. While the details have been erased from my then teenage brain, I do remember that all hell broke loose as the twin currents of sexual liberation and political correctness collided. Needless to say, the

168

drag queens and shop girls had louder voices, and poor Aubrey and David soon found that GLF was not to be the neat collective they envisioned.

Soon, meetings were being held at the Church Hall in Notting Hill Gate. Committees were formed, meetings were chaired by acclamation, demonstrations were organized and magazines were created. GLF had found itself a funky basement office near Kings Cross Station, had a phone line and a never-ending supply of eager queer volunteers to pass out fliers, buttons and rags, hold demos, picket bars and create all kinds of in-your-face nuisance that the British found highly annoying.

The first major event was the Gay Pride March of 1971. I believe it was funneled down Park Lane (but it could have been Oxford Street) with the goal of congregating at Speakers' Corner for an afternoon of rabble-rousing speeches and genderfuck drag.

I had recently joined a Street Theater Collective that was started by Peter Bourne, Stuart Feather and Michael Lyneham, amongst others. We actively engaged in spontaneous street actions and, after a year, squatted in an old abandoned film studio as a real commune (more on that later). That day a number of us were dressed in nuns' habits, fishnet tights and high heels, and carried large cucumbers—the English variety! This was way before anyone conceived of the Sisters of Perpetual Indulgence, and we were doing this in a sincere attempt to mock the church and the establishment. In that regard, we succeeded wonderfully, as we were all arrested and thrown into Hyde Park jail. That didn't last long as several of us had concealed joints in out tights and we became so rowdy and unruly that the cops let us out. We were charged, however, with that wonderful catch-all British law "behavior that is liable to cause a breach of the peace," which we couldn't argue with, since that was what we were trying to do. The judge found that our salacious wielding of the very large cucumbers, which included pushing them in between our legs, was indeed a violation of that law and we were all fined 15 pounds—well worth it by all accounts!

The meetings at the Notting Hill Church hall continued monthly and produced many actions and demonstrations. We regularly picketed notorious gay bars such as the Boltons and the Coleherne, and succeeded in pissing off the undercover gay establishment as well as the straight world.

We were getting noticed, which was what we wanted. Our

goal was to crack open the unspoken code that allowed gay men and lesbians private freedoms as long as they were not public about their desires. We wanted openness and acceptance from society, and from ourselves, but to do this you had to come out of the closet and go public so that not only straight folks but gay ones too knew we were there. The later chant "we're here, we're queer, get used to it" could well have applied, though at that time we were not bold enough to take back the word *queer*. However, the power of being out and open began to be undeniably demonstrated. We got the ball rolling.

This was the time when David Bowie was recording "Ziggy Stardust" and featured himself in a dress on an earlier record. We considered him one of us and attempted to get him to play for a benefit concert. It turned out that Bowie was just riding the wave of social trends, and this never materialized, though his music is still among the anthems of the era.

Very soon, the familiarity of the members of the Street Theater Collective became such that we decided that we had to find a place to all live communally. We lucked out when we discovered, very close by, a small abandoned film studio. It was at the end of a small cul-de-sac, quiet and out of the way. It consisted of a small entry room, a kitchen, an upstairs space that became the makeup room, a very large main space and in the rear a bathroom and another room that became our closet.

Around 20 of us moved into this space, which was termed a "squat," as we weren't paying rent. The main room was furnished with wall-to-wall mattresses, a wonderful stereo system and on the main shelf above the stereo Clarice, the magic teapot. Clarice was actually a genuine art deco teapot by the renowned '20s designer Clarice Cliff, and she was the source of our genuine experiment in social living. When anyone had money, they put it in Clarice. When anyone needed money they took it out of Clarice. If she was empty, we went to work! We ran a stall on Portobello Road (the far cheap end!!) selling antique clothing and deco pottery, a flair for which Peter Bourne helped instill in us. We would buy wonderful "drag." It would live in our closet for a while, then we would sell it. Or not. But it helped feed and clothe us.

We became very close as a group. I wish I could remember more names, but Peter, Stuart and Michael stand out, as does Rex Lay, Peter's artist boyfriend (who pointed out to me the young David Hockney, walking in the neighborhood with his first boyfriend, Peter), and actor John Church. Most collective members were in their 30s or 40s, John being ancient at 52, and myself, at 19, the youngest. We all assumed theater names and personas for our street actions, though I don't recall us ever wanting to be cross-dressers full time. It was a way to let out our feminine side and to draw attention to the cause. And we used to have weekly LSD parties where we all imbibed sugar cubes laced with the best acid. This not only fueled the intensity of our bond, but ultimately flung us all apart again.

After nearly a year of intense communal living, the squat was discovered and we were evicted. By this time, my stint at London University was over, my government salary as a student had come to an end, and I needed a job.I started a business cooking for weekend consciousness-raising groups. I decided that I had done enough LSD, and started meditating. Within four years I was living in India, and by 1981, the United States.

However, the gay movement in England had begun with a vengeance, never to look back. The rag *Gay News* was started, bars opened, parades happened regularly and despite Thatcher's wet blanket, England became a hive of gay activity. In 1971, we used to go to Amsterdam for fun. By 1991, the trend had reversed, and now London is one of the most gay-friendly cities.

When my participation in Gay Lib was over, I felt a strong bond with the movement I helped create. It has affected, and continues to affect, many lives, and I truly believe we changed the world. For that, I feel blessed—for this was a rare opportunity that we used to the fullest.

Richard Bolingbroke was born in Portsmouth, England, in 1952. He was sent to boarding school at the age of 7 until the age of 17. He went on to complete a pre-Diploma in Art at Winchester College, and a Bsc in Geography at Bedford College, London University, graduating in 1973. It was during these years in London that he was active in GLF. After living in Holland and then India, he arrived in the United States in 1981. He now resides in San Francisco, where he lives with his husband of 17 years. He is well known both locally and nationally as an artist and watercolor painter, and his work has been shown in museums around the country.

Sylvia Rivera: A Woman Before Her Time

Liz Highleyman

Sylvia Rivera, a veteran of the Stonewall Riots and the early gay liberation movement, dedicated her life to fighting for the rights of gay and transgender people, people of color and the down-and-out, especially queer youth.

In many ways, Rivera was a woman before her time. While she has been credited with planting the seeds of transgender liberation—GenderPAC's Riki Wilchins called her "the Rosa Parks of the modern transgender movement"—Rivera's unapologetic flamboyance and uncompromising politics often were not well received within a movement beset by gender, race and class divisions, and she felt increasingly marginalized as the gay movement sought mainstream acceptance. Though her issues were pushed to the back burner, they never went away, and successive generations of radical queer activists continued to raise them in the ensuing decades.

Originally named Ray Rivera Mendoza, Sylvia Rivera was born in the Bronx on July 2, 1951, reputedly in the backseat of a taxicab. When Rivera was 3 years old and already abandoned by her father, her mother committed suicide, and she went to live with her grandmother.

As a child, Rivera was bullied for being effeminate. By the time she was 11, she had dropped out of school, left home, adopted a new name and begun to work as a transvestite prostitute in Times Square. She also began using hard drugs and was repeatedly arrested for infractions such as loitering, prostitution and heroin possession.

"The early '60s was not a good time for drag queens, effeminate boys or boys that wore makeup like we did," she later recalled. "Back then we were beat up by the police, by everybody."

In June 1969, at age 17, Rivera was among the drag queens and local street youth who took part in the riots following a police raid at the Stonewall Inn in Greenwich Village—the event popularly regarded as sparking the gay liberation movement. Although some accounts of the events credited Rivera with throwing the first brick (others said it was a high-heeled shoe), she herself once claimed to have thrown the second missile, a Molotov cocktail. "I'm not missing a minute of this—it's the revolution!" she shouted at the time. Years later she would reflect, "that's when I saw the world change for me and my people."

Rivera immersed herself in activism on behalf of gay people, transvestites, sex workers and street youth, as well as antiwar and civil rights struggles, working with groups such as the Young Lords. She joined the Gay Liberation Front and later the Gay Activists Alliance, but with her brash manners and frequent intoxication, the teenage Puerto Rican drag queen often clashed with other activists.

In 1970, Rivera and another Stonewall participant, Marsha P. "Pay It No Mind" Johnson, formed Street Transvestite Action Revolutionaries (STAR), thought to be the first transgender activist group. The two opened STAR House, a shelter for homeless queer and transgender youth in an abandoned building on the Lower East Side, supporting the effort by hustling for food and rent money.

Rivera took an active role in GAA's fight to pass a New York City gay antidiscrimination bill in the early 1970s. Arthur Evans recalled that activists took petitions supporting the measure to a meeting of the Village Independent Democrats, and when Greenwich Village councilwoman Carol Greitzer refused to accept them, Rivera hit her over the head with a clipboard.

In an attempt to improve the bill's chances, GAA dropped protections for transvestites—a move echoed some 30 years later when the Human Rights Campaign (HRC) supported a version of the Employment Non-Discrimination Act (ENDA) that excluded protection on the basis of gender identity.

In the early 1970s, as rifts emerged between men and women in the gay liberation movement, a backlash began to develop against drag queens. Some activists believed transvestites interfered with efforts to present a more mainstream image, and some lesbian feminists condemned drag as a mockery of women. The tension came to a head at a rally in Washington Square Park following the 1973 Christopher Street Liberation Day march, when Rivera stormed the stage, grabbed the microphone from emcee Vito Russo and confronted members of a lesbian feminist group protesting drag performers.

Feeling betrayed by these developments, Rivera pulled back

from gay activism. In the late 1970s, she moved to Tarrytown, in Westchester County, where she worked as a food services manager for the Marriott Corporation and bought a home with her partner Frank.

After a decade of stability, however, Rivera began using crack cocaine. By the early 1990s, she had lost her job and was once again homeless in New York City, living on the Hudson River piers and acting as surrogate mother to a community of transgender and queer street youth.

Despite these hardships, Rivera once again immersed herself in political activism, working with groups such as ACT UP and Queer Nation. Facing the devastation of the AIDS epidemic, an indifferent government and a resurgent religious right, a new generation of activists reclaimed the radical ideology and tactics of the early gay liberation movement.

"I was a radical, a revolutionist," Rivera told Leslie Feinberg in a 1999 interview. "I am still a revolutionist."

By the mid-1990s, Rivera began to receive the recognition she felt she deserved. She was among the Stonewall veterans who led the New York City march commemorating the 25th anniversary of the riots in 1994, and in 2000 she was honored at World Pride in Rome. She was featured in Martin Duberman's book *Stonewall* and provided inspiration for "La Miranda" in a fictionalized movie of the same name. Profiled in the June 27, 1999, *New York Times Magazine*, she said, "When I was young, I never thought I was going to be a part of gay history—I didn't even expect that gay history would be in existence. So there's a lot of joy in my heart to see the 30th anniversary of Stonewall."

In 1997, Rivera began living at Transy House in Brooklyn, a successor of sorts to STAR House. She got off drugs and alcohol and began a relationship with Julia Murray, a transsexual woman who would remain Rivera's partner until death. "I've thought about having the operation and becoming a lesbian," Rivera told an interviewer, "but I really like myself the way I am."

Rivera got involved with the Metropolitan Community Church, where she directed a food program and facilitated a transgender spirituality group. She was one of more than 100 people arrested at memorial march for Matthew Shepard in 1998, and following the 2001 murder of transgender prostitute Amanda Milan, she revived STAR, changing "Transvestite" in the acronym to "Transgender."

Members of Street Transvestite Action Revolutionaries, including Sylvia Rivera (seated), 1970

"If we continue to be invisible, people are not going to listen to us," she said. "And if we ourselves don't stand up for ourselves, nobody else will do that for us."

Rivera continued to butt heads with the gay and lesbian establishment, repeatedly confronting HRC over its refusal to include transgender protection in ENDA. Shortly before her death, STAR issued a press release calling the group "a separatist organization devoted to money and power."

Despite failing health, Rivera pursued her fight for transgender inclusion to the end. From her hospital bed just hours before she died in February 2002, she continued to lobby gay leaders—unsuccessfully—to include gender identity in New York's Sexual Orientation Non-Discrimination Act.

After Rivera's death from liver cancer, thousands gathered for a memorial at the Stonewall Inn, followed by a funeral procession in which her ashes were carried through Greenwich Village in a horse-drawn carriage and scattered in the Hudson River, near the piers she had once called home. Although the transgender movement made great advances over the course of Rivera's lifetime, it still has not achieved the civil rights and equality for which she fought.

References

Duberman, Martin. *Stonewall* (Penguin, 1993).

Evans, Arthur. Rivera recalled. *Bay Area Reporter*, February 28, 2002.

Nestle, Joan et al. (eds.). *Genderqueer: Voices from Beyond the Sexual Binary* (Alyson, 2002).

Shepard, Benjamin. Amanda Milan and the Rebirth of the Street Trans

Action Revolutionaries. In: *From ACT UP to the WTO: Urban Protest and Community-Building in the Era of Globalization*, eds. Benjamin Shepard and Ron Hayduk (Verso, 2002).

Liz Highleyman is a freelance journalist who has written widely on LGBT issues, sexual politics, civil liberties and progressive activism. From 2002 through 2008, she authored Q Syndicate's queer history column Past Out. As a medical writer, she focuses on HIV and hepatitis. A San Francisco resident since 1994, Liz lives with her partner and two beagles.

TWO SONGS

Blackberri

I was born in Buffalo, New York, but traveled around a lot in those days. I moved to Tucson in 1968. I was openly gay and had lived as such for most of my life. A straight friend named Joel gave me the insert from his copy of the *Village Voice*. He was from New York City and wanted to keep abreast of the happenings there. It was the first gay liberation issue. I read that thing from cover to cover! I remember the front page had Carl Wittman's "Refugees from America: A Gay Manifesto." Wittman was a civil rights marcher, labor organizer and leader of the SDS (Students for a Democratic Society) who came out in 1967.

I felt inspired to start a gay liberation group in Tucson. I think it was the summer of 1972. I got permission from some women at the Women's Building to hold the first meeting there. I made some flyers announcing the meeting and posted them everywhere, including the University of Arizona campus. When I passed them out at the bars, some people said that I was looking to get them out of the bars. They saw the group as a threat. I bought doughnuts, made a big pot of coffee and went to one the cruisiest parks in town one night. I passed out doughnuts, coffee and flyers. People congregated and talked to each other, drinking coffee and eating doughnuts. I'm pretty sure some of those guys hooked up with each other.

The first meeting was held on a Sunday afternoon. There were about 35 or so people who showed up. They were White, Latino, Black, and Native American. Women came and men came, too. The name Gay Liberation Arizona Desert (GLAD) emerged from that first meeting. GLAD had a sister group, GLAD II, that formed later in Phoenix, headed by Cleve Jones, who would go on to become well known as a mover and shaker in Harvey Milk's campaign for supervisor. The two groups met once at Picacho Peak State Park, a central point between Tucson and Phoenix, for a picnic, so we could meet and chat with one another.

I was always passionate about activism and music. A friend at the time told me I had to make a choice. Not wanting to give up either one, I chose to marry them. My friend said it would never work. I wonder what he thinks about this marriage today. I often refer to the music as lubricant for the lyrics.

If the music is good then people will listen to the lyrics, and if you can express them both with your heart then magic happens. People often tell me how memorable my music is. A friend in D.C. wrote once in a review for a local Black gay publication, "Ever hear a song one time and remember it? Such is the music of Blackberri."

Music has been very good to me. It's supported, comforted and healed me many times and still continues to do so. Might I add that many times I've woven a spell with a love song and captured the heart of some young man I fancied. Yes, music has been very good to me.

Here are two songs, one from those early days of gay liberation activism, one from a decade later. They were both published by Berri Nice Music.

EAT THE RICH

(written around 1975 and featured on the 1981 LP *Blackberri and Friends*)

When your icebox is bare.
Eat the rich.
Show your stomach you care.
Eat the rich.

CHORUS:
Oh the rich have so much power.
Lord I think it's a shame.
They swear they're not the problem,
but we know who's to blame.
And I'm tired of being manipulized,
by those stupid guys.
Eat the rich.

You got the poverty blues. (I do)
Eat the rich. (Yum yum yeah)

You ain't got nothing to lose. (So go on)
Eat the rich. (Yum yum yeah)

CHORUS

Chemicals in your food.
Eat the rich. (Yum yum yeah)
Because the rich they eat good. (So go on)
Eat the rich. (Yum yum yeah)

CHORUS

Now this is the part of the song,
that I like a lot.
Cause this is where we get to look at the menu.
If we want to know what there is to eat.
We have to look at the menu, don't we.
Mmmmmmmmmm. Mmmmmmmm.
It sure looks good. Make my mouth just water.
It sez here that Melons are always in season.
Yall better git you one. I want a dozen.
They got Gettys and meatballs. (Gettys and meatballs)
I said Gettys and meatballs. (Gettys and meatballs)
Now, some folks they like Oysters Rockefeller. (Oysters
    Rockefeller)
but not me I like to watch TV and eat Hearst
Patty uhah. (Hearst Patty uhah)
They even got something for all of you organic freaks.
    (organic freaks)
They got Rose hip tea and it's hip you see, cause Rose is a
Kennedy.

CHORUS

Now this is the part of the song where I get to eat a little bit.
When I was growing up my Mama told me don't smack your
    lips, but this taste so good. Say buddy can you spare a rib.
    That's a mighty tender rump you got there, you better
    watch out.

180

(rhythmic chewing)

Hey Berri! . . . HEY BERRI! Hey git up off that rib sucka!!!

Not now, I'm in the middle of a Rothschild.

CHORUS

BEAUTIFUL BLACKMAN

(written in the mid-'80s and featured in the movie *Looking for Langston*)

Beautiful blackman I'm just like you.
You know I face discrimination too.
Got here about ten,
when I walked in that place,
hardly nobody here would
look me in the face.

CHORUS:
You're such a beautiful blackman
but somehow you've been made to feel
that your beauty's not real.
You're such a beautiful blackman
but you walk with your head bending low.
Don't do that no mo'.

Beautiful blackman did they ask for ID?
Did they want two with picture
or did they want three?
I know it's hard, but sometimes we must
just walk away,
shake our heads in disgust.

CHORUS

I saw you cruise that white guy over there.
The one with the wavy hair (yeah).
I cruised him, too, but I couldn't get through.
It's not that you're ugly

You see he might have a problem
He may never, ever notice you
or me for that fact too

CHORUS

Beautiful blackman I'm glad you looked my way.
Let's go home together what more can I say.
You say you don't see what I see in you.
Well I see the beauty I wish that you knew.

You're such a beautiful blackman
but somehow you've been made to feel
that your beauty's not real.
You're such a beautiful blackman
Come on put a smile on your face
Be proud of your race.

Come on be proud of it. (repeat)

Honey, We Unshrunk the Shrinks!

Pam Mitchell

The presentation was already in progress when Phillip, Jim and I found seats together in the back row of the midsize meeting room in downtown Los Angeles. Speaking into a mic at a movable podium at the front of the room stood a bespectacled, jittery fellow who reminded me of the English comic actor Peter Sellers, with an accent I took for British and an appreciable stutter. He was lecturing about his program of "aversion therapy" for "h-h-homosexual" men, explaining in clipped academic King's English that applying electrode shocks to these "volunteers" was a humane alternative to allowing them to live their sexually maladjusted lives.

I quickly scanned the room. Several dozen mental health professionals and academics sat attentively in rows of movable wooden chairs. Intermingled with them I spotted 20 or so h-h-homosexual activists. Although in keeping with the relaxed dress code in the autumn of 1970, where even the docs and grad students had an abundance of hair creeping down over their necktie-free collars, the activists could easily be distinguished from the regular conference attendees by their relative youth, patched jeans and ratty ponytails. My friends and I—first-year students at a junior college 20 miles away—were the youngest people present. I was one of only a handful of women in the room.

I wasn't entirely sure why I was there that day. All I'd known when my wild new friend Phillip and his pal Jim pulled up in front of my low-rent "garden apartment" complex to pick me up that morning was that we were headed to a gay rights protest, one that might involve a "zap," a style of brash, creative, in-your-face guerrilla theatrics first popularized by anti–Vietnam War activists. (Needless to say, I'd arranged to meet them out front so as not to have to introduce them to my mother.)

While I rode shotgun in Jim's powder-blue Karmann Ghia convertible, with Jim taking the curves of the Pasadena Freeway a little faster than I might have preferred, Philip filled me in on the basics. We were headed to the campus of the University of

Southern California for a national conference of psychiatrists. A new group called the Gay Liberation Front L.A. had negotiated a deal with someone at the registration desk: Individuals identifying themselves as gay activists could get into the workshop on "aversion therapy" for free in exchange for a promise not to organize a protest outside the conference or otherwise create a media circus. Earlier that year, in San Francisco and the Midwest, GLF and feminist demonstrators had wreaked havoc on American Psychiatric Association gatherings with outraged outrageousness; the shocked shrinks were averse to a repeat performance.

"You're going to have to tell them you're gay in order to get in, Pam," Phillip teased me, poker-faced, as we approached U.S.C. "Think you can handle it?"

I gulped. At that time, I hadn't quite gotten around to telling *myself* I was gay. He flashed me a dimpled grin and kissed my cheek.

Phillip Pratt (a pseudonym) was the first acknowledged gay person I'd ever met. We had found each other just a few weeks before at our work-study jobs in the library at Pasadena City College, a conservative working-class backwater during that period of cultural revolution and political tumult at most other college campuses across the country. What little I knew then about the emerging gay and feminist movements I'd gleaned from radical radio station KPFK and the *L.A. Free Press*, an underground newspaper whose back pages daringly featured gay and bisexual ("AC/DC") classifieds. Although Stonewall was not yet the iconic symbol it was later to become, I must have learned through KPFK and the Freep about how on the night of Judy Garland's funeral the previous summer, the New York cops had raided the wrong gay bar at the wrong time, setting off a riot in Greenwich Village that continued for three days. I'm sure I cheered, as I was in the habit then of cheering every act of resistance. My world was divided back then not along lines of gender or sexual preference but between rebel freaks of whatever stripe on the one hand and "the Establishment" on the other.

Phillip and I had spent hours in intense conversation about poetry and politics as we did the mindless tasks of alphabetizing cards and shelving books. I developed a chaste crush on him, the type that many young pre-lesbians develop on gay guys—our "transitional objects" on the journey from what we were taught we should desire to figuring out what we really want. I loved him for his red high-tops and his sapphire turtlenecks that matched the color of his eyes, for the tickle of his laughter and the way he tossed his black silk hair out of his eyes. He was literate, hilarious, radical, irreverent and totally unthreatening.

In the musty library basement he would regale me with blush-inducing, sordid tales of his adventures with his various boyfriends, and of all the places—including a crotch of branches high up in an ancient oak on his high school campus—they found in which to, as he smirkingly called it, "do the nasty-nasty."

Looking back on it, I wonder if he took me and my best friend Nancy for a lesbian couple. We dressed like twins, in worn jeans and work shirts embroidered in the same places with the same threads, matching ponchos, similarly bared feet when weather permitted or lace-up tan work boots from the same store when it didn't. We went everywhere together. I knew all the lyrics to the songs she strummed on her guitar—Baez, Joni Mitchell, Phil Ochs—and sang them lustily. Maybe he just figured.

He was doing his damnedest to call me out of my closet. He'd made his first attempt a week before the USC "Behavioral Modification" conference. No doubt aware that I was of a mind to follow him anywhere, he'd proposed that we take LSD and hitchhike the 20 miles into L.A.

And so, my first acid trip: "Orange barrel," Phillip called the stuff. We washed the little bullet-shaped pills down with an orange soda as we stood at the freeway ramp, our thumbs thrust out. Just as I began to feel the effects of the drug, a van pulled over. The passenger door was broken, so the driver had to get out to let us in. At first I thought I was already hallucinating. Halloween was still a month away, yet the guy was dressed up as a sea captain, complete with pirate's eye patch. "Got a great deal on the outfit," he explained in response to my stare. "Sale of old costumes over at the MGM movie studios." He motioned behind the Indian bedspread print that hung behind the seat of his old VW bus. (I noticed he had a mattress set up in the back—one of those hippie vans our friend Nancy's mother persisted in calling "roving whore wagons.") "There's more costumes in the back if you want to try them on," he added. While I lost myself in the rock music pulsing from his enormous speakers, Phillip climbed over the seat to play dress-up.

By the time we got dropped off somewhere near Vermont Avenue, the acid was really kicking in. I was no longer in constant contact with planet earth.

But Phillip managed to navigate, perhaps because he had known all along where he was leading us: to a down-at-the-heels old Victorian off Wilshire Boulevard that was serving as a rudimentary gay meeting center. (Years later I would learn that the rundown Victorian morphed shortly thereafter into the Gay Services Center—from which the lesbians, fed up with invisibility and sexism, soon seceded to form a center of their own. The Gay Services Center eventually became the Gay and Lesbian Services Center, now the largest queer community center in the world.) That day, some teenagers sat around a circle on the floor in the would-be living room telling stories (one of the first support groups for gay youth anywhere) and I was saying, in my mind and maybe out loud, too, but probably not: Phillip, I am tripping my brains out and why on earth would you bring me here on acid? I remember men—boys, really, of high school age mostly, scruffily dressed kids even skinnier and gawkier than Phillip—and one girl. My first sighting of an avowed lesbian and I couldn't begin to tell you what she looked like. The LSD was fracturing her into a multitude of different heads with light brown ponytails spoking out of each of them, her acned face spinning circles around itself. I got lost for a while in the intricate tooling on her brown leather cowboy boots, which she had on even though there was a sign by the door asking people to remove their shoes. I can't even remember whether she said anything, whether hers was one of the harrowing stories I heard that day: "My dad broke my nose when he found out about me." "Mine tossed me out in the rain at 1:30 in the morning." Although I couldn't concentrate, I'm pretty sure the stories got worse as people got warmed up. I think there was some talk of sexual abuse.

Whatever was being said, I reached the point where I could no longer bear another word of it—what could their pain possibly have to do with me? I fled down the narrow staircase to the landing where we had left our shoes and tried for what may have been hours or might have been only seconds to figure out which of the tangled piles of shoes like fish in a net could possibly belong on my feet, which were pulsating and seemed to be changing sizes. How was I supposed to know whether the size 6 tennis shoes were mine or the size 11 sandals? One of each? I couldn't run away without finding my shoes. The kids, some of them had been talking about running away and I wanted to run away from them and from this haunted house and from Phillip, from beautiful, demonic

Phillip, but I couldn't because I couldn't find my shoes. Closer to home I might have darted out to the street in my bare feet, but the unfamiliar streets of downtown L.A. seemed far more daunting than Colorado Boulevard.

Phillip found my boots for me, sat me down on the stairs and helped me lace them up. I ran down the wooden steps to the street and he came tumbling after. "Why didn't you say something up there?" Phillip asked. "You never say anything. Why didn't you tell your story?" I had no ready answer, no story I yet knew to tell. At that moment I was too stoned to form words, so how could I even try to explain to him why I never spoke when I couldn't speak?

A week later, I found myself squished between two gay guys in that little blue sports car, circling the streets of L.A. just a mile or two from the Gay Community Center. My gay pied piper was giving me another chance.

"You're going to have to tell them you're gay in order to get in, Pam. Think you can handle it?"

In the event, wild-haired teenager that I was, with my rolled-up denim shirtsleeves and work boots, my usual bad-ass working-class attitude and a fairy on either arm, I didn't have to call myself out at the registration desk. Only a shrink, a shrink-in-training or a queer (or queer-in-training such as myself) would have been aiming to gain admission to this gig. They drew their own conclusions about me.

The dude in the front of the conference room who brought to mind Peter Sellers was nattering on. Despite the fact that the GLFers had thus far been on their best behavior, the speaker appeared to be unnerved by their presence, by an undercurrent of tension in the room. He couldn't seem to say the word "homosexual" without stuttering.

Each time he stumbled over that potent little word, I could tell that Phillip was having a hard time suppressing his mirth. I chewed on the inside of my cheek, staving off my own case of the giggles, feeling that to laugh in a roomfull of shrinks would be tantamount to laughing in church or a courtroom. It wasn't that we respected these Big Three citadels of the social order, these enforcers of conformity and definers of "normal." But we knew enough to fear them. In fact, in my own young life and from what I knew of Phillip's, so-called "mental health" had played the role of primary enforcer. We hadn't been in serious trouble with the law, nor did we come from families who had much truck with religion.

(Phillip's foster dad at the moment was an Episcopal priest, but of the liberal, hippie-bead sort who didn't impose his belief system on others.) But we had both faced our share of decidedly unhelpful "helping" professionals, me as a tomboy misfit and deeply discombobulated, disembodied incest survivor, Phillip as a gay teenage runaway. Streams of guidance counselors and psychiatrists had allied themselves staunchly with our parents' and our society's power to mistreat us, blaming us for our own misery, intent on molding us into the upstanding "gender-appropriate" worker drone bees that were supposed to emerge from the working-class families we'd been born to.

As a consequence of extensive sexual abuse, a fog had descended between myself and my body and sexuality. Consciousness-raising had not found its way to Pasadena. *Our Bodies, Ourselves* had not yet been published. The first issue of *Ms. Magazine* was still a year in the future. It wouldn't be long before the power of women telling the truth to one another changed all that and helped me cut through the haze—with no help from the mental health profession. Well into the 1970s, psychology textbooks were still getting away with claiming incest was a rare occurrence—if they mentioned it at all. A year younger than I was, Phillip was still legally a minor, a throwaway kid from the Northeast who had washed ashore in Southern California. On his own he'd found a decent family to take him in and gotten permission to jump to junior college without having completed high school.

At the podium in the USC meeting room, the speaker—whose name, I found out later, was Dr. Feldman—introduced the movie he was about to show us about his aversion-therapy clinic in northern England, where he and his colleagues had been attempting to switch gay men into straight men by means of an aggressive behavior modification program. He claimed an initial "cure" rate of close to 50 percent, which brought derisive snorts from some in the audience. Defensively, he admitted there was a significant rate of recidivism within a year of "treatment" and hastened to get the projector rolling.

On a small pull-down screen, we viewed black-and-white rats running through black-and-white mazes while a deep-throated masculine voiceover explained how aversive conditioning works to modify behavior.

Then with an abrupt fade-out/fade-in, the camera moved to Dr. Feldman's clinic for members of our own species. We watched as the bodies of young human males were wired with electrodes. In the darkened room at USC, I heard coughs, the rustle of trousered legs crossing and uncrossing. Somebody gasped. It might have been me. On the screen a scientist in a white smock was telling us how these research subjects wanted to change, how they'd come asking for help, had volunteered to participate in the study. Speaking with no emotion, he went on to explain that after being hooked up, the subjects—the young men whose blurred images were still visible behind him, young men who could have been our friends, classmates, coworkers—would be asked to look at photographs of attractive males; if they responded sexually, they would be given electric shocks strong enough to cause physical pain.

Suddenly the lights in the USC meeting room came on. The screen went blank. From different directions, GLF activists strode up to the microphone at the unattended podium. "This isn't treatment, it's torture," said one, "and it has to stop!" Another denounced the folly of trying to "cure" people who weren't sick. Being gay is not a mental illness, he proclaimed. Fear and loathing of gay people is. My friends and I cheered and applauded. Several others, not all of them GLFers, joined in.

An uproar ensued. One of the activists began reading from a list of demands, foremost among them that homosexuality be removed from the list of official psychiatric "disorders," that the use of shock aversion therapy against gay people be denounced by the psychiatric profession and that mental health providers help educate everyone, gay and straight alike, to accept homosexuality as a normal human variable. Somebody seated in front of me demanded that the film resume. Someone else threatened to call the cops. Then a voice of reason—the event organizer? a man who spoke with authority, at any rate—said, "No, no. Maybe we should listen to what they've got to say."

And they did. One of the GLFers at the microphone announced that everyone was to break into small discussion groups, each group to be led by a GLF activist. The assembled shrinks blinked in alarm. A handful of them turned red in the face and stomped out of the room. The remainder milled around in confusion, some grimacing, others grinning affably, and gradually began to cluster and coalesce. Finally we all settled into groups, and the participants spent the remainder of the session in serious dialogue.

Almost exactly three years later, in a red-letter day in the history of queer liberation, the American Psychiatric Association voted to remove homosexuality once and for all from its diagnostic list of mental illnesses. At that time, spokespeople for the organization made it clear that the change had come about in response to on-going confrontations like the one that occurred at USC that day. The "healing" professions would no longer stand as a solid bearing wall in the structure of contempt and bigotry and misinformation that held GLBT oppression in place. In our small way, Phillip and Jim and I had helped create fissures in the edifice of homophobia.

When I arrived home on the afternoon of the zap, I immediately encountered my mother. (She was hard to miss in our three-room place.) Impulsively, I decided to tell her what I'd been up to recently (leaving out the part about the LSD). Mom was into liberation struggles. By the time *she* was 18, she'd already been a street-fighting, card-carrying Communist revolutionary for years. The only behaviors that she, a devout atheist, recognized as sins were the greed and avarice of "the bosses." Although her own political fire had been doused by McCarthyism and she had been reduced to expressing her views solely by yelling invectives at the TV nightly news, she'd been proud of me (if a little anxious for my safety and future) when I'd demonstrated for civil rights and protested the Vietnam War. Naïvely, I expected a similar reaction to gay liberation.

Instead, she welcomed the news with about as much enthusiasm as she greeted the cockroaches who scurried across the counters of our tiny kitchen. Mom clung tight to the last refuge of secular humanists who couldn't let go of the societal prejudice against homosexuality: the conviction that being queer was sick. She was still falling for that lie, but that day a couple of dozen brazen, gutsy, revolutionary queers had convinced me and a roomful of shrinks otherwise.

"Gay!" she spat. "And does this mean *you're* gay, Pam?"

"Maybe I am," I retorted, challenging not only her but myself to deny it. "Maybe I am."

Pam Mitchell is a longtime activist for social and economic justice and against child abuse. She is former associate editor of the feminist monthly Sojourner *and staff writer for the cosexual, leftist newsweekly* Gay Community News *(may both publications rest in peace upon their laurels) and editor of the 1980 Alyson Press anthology* Pink Triangles: Radical Perspectives in Gay Liberation. *She lives in the San Francisco Bay Area, where she writes fiction and memoirs and has a day job at a public interest law firm dedicated to workers' rights.*

The Radicalesbian Story:
An Evolution of Consciousness

Ellen Shumsky

Note from the author: The first half of this article originally appeared in the December–January 1970 issue of ComeOut! *The second half was to have been published in a 1972 issue of* ComeOut! *Sometime before production, the print shop that housed the galleys was raided (perpetrators unknown—at least to me) and the galleys were destroyed. The latter half of this article, tracing the rise and fall of Radicalesbians, never made it to press. This is the first publication of this herstory in its entirety.*

Radicalesbians began during the dreary months of the dying winter of 1970. A nucleus of Gay Liberation Front women, with a growing women's consciousness, began to feel the need for an all-women's GLF dance.

They had previously been working on and attending GLF dances, which were overwhelmingly attended by males. The oppressive atmosphere was a simulated gay men's bar—an overcrowded, dimly lit room where most human contact was limited to groping and dryfucking, packed together subway rush-hour style.

Earlier attempts by women and some men to create an ambience that encouraged group dancing and space for conversation were nullified by the "pack-'em-in" attitude of the GLF men running the dances. There were so many men at each event that the women felt lost to each other. It was intolerable to many, but the women put up with it, hoping it would change. Finally when it became obvious it was only growing worse as the weather grew warmer, GLF women decided to have an all-women's dance.

This first dance was a great success: an environment of women—rapping, drinking, dancing, relating with fluidity and grace—was a new and beautiful phenomenon. That dance was followed by several more. Besides enjoying the events, the women had to meet and work together. Weekly meetings of GLF women became routine. This provided a fine opportunity to work collectively and to get to know one another.

At the same time, something else was happening. Some GLF women, together with feminists from the Women's Liberation Movement, had formed a consciousness-raising group. Out of these meetings two major accomplishments materialized: the writing of the lesbian feminist manifesto, "The Woman Identified Woman"; and a plan to confront the issue of lesbianism at the NOW (National Organization for Women)-sponsored 2nd Congress to Unite Women.

At the Congress, on May 1, 1970, 20 women wearing lavender T-shirts stenciled with LAVENDER MENACE liberated the microphone from the line-up of planned speakers and initiated a forum on why lesbianism was the most threatening and most avoided issue in the Women's Movement. The entire audience of 400 women related to the topic of lesbianism through their own personal experiences and feelings. This was followed by two days of workshops attended by more than 200 women. The paper "The Woman Identified Woman" was distributed. Our resolutions (we hope) became part of the report of the conference: "WOMEN'S LIBERATION IS A LESBIAN PLOT. WE ARE ALL LESBIAN." Instead of purging lesbians from the Women's Movement, we will proudly own and assert the woman-identified woman in all of us.

The aftermath of the congress coup is not so well known. We called for consciousness-raising groups and 50 interested women met the call. Four groups were set up—with new women from the NOW Congress and Lavender Menace lesbians participating in each group. Many of the women in these groups were straight-identified women who wanted to confront the issue of lesbianism and perhaps the lesbian in themselves. A very large majority turned out to be active lesbians, latent lesbians, closeted lesbians, one-beautiful-experience lesbians, freaked-out lesbians, spaced-out lesbians. From the ranks of the Women's Liberation Movement they responded.

After having related for months and years to the broader women's issues at the sacrifice of their own sexual identities, these women were ready now to come out—to use their energies to create a lesbian community and to make sure that the concepts of primary value and commitment between women, developed in the paper "Woman Identified Woman," were taken on by the Women's Liberation Movement. These sisters started coming to our weekly GLF women's meetings, and as word spread through the grapevine, more and more unaffiliated women started attending those meetings.

At that point, the various groups of women had so thoroughly merged that the name GLF Women seemed inappropriate; it was obvious we were an independent, autonomous group and while there were some women who continued to relate to GLF, there were many feminists who felt they could not affiliate with a male-dominated organization that was in large part sexist. We decided to drop the name GLF Women and create a treasury to relate to our own needs and the needs of other gay women. The money was taken from the GLF community center fund—that portion that had been contributed by the women who had been attending GLF dances. It was enough to fund our first independent dance under our new name, Radicalesbians.

In this way, a movement of radical/revolutionary gay women organically coalesced—not artificially out of some theoretical political necessity, but through the natural flow of our experiences and changes in consciousness. Difficulties were anticipated because priorities differed. Some women felt themselves to be an arm of the Women's Liberation Movement. They viewed the struggle as one waged by women against male supremacy. They experienced their primary identity as women (with a difference). Others felt themselves to be in close affiliation with GLF; they continued to relate to GLF and viewed the struggle as one primarily between heterosexuals and homosexuals. Still others saw their situation as unique—a struggle against sexism through the prism of a gay woman's consciousness. Some women had not shaped or articulated their politics. They only knew that they liked to be with their sisters and wanted to help. With these differences we began meeting and working together, respecting if not loving each other.

Because of our past experiences in the Gay Liberation Front and other movement groups, we came together committed to finding an organizational form that would avoid the pitfalls of entrenched leadership hierarchies. We did not want a situation in which a few leaders represent and run an organization in the interests of an apathetic community and ultimately in their own self-interest, as their community abandons a boring, non-growth situation. A marathon weekend was planned, during which randomly arranged small groups of women talked about the issues they felt a gay women's organization should address. The 50 or so topics that emerged from this marathon weekend were written up on poster boards that became our scrolls. These were ceremonially unrolled at meetings each week and became known as our "agenda." In the course of discussing each item on the agenda it was hoped that the shape of our organization would emerge. It was not to be pre-defined but to assume the shape of our collective needs.

Immediately adopted was the lot system for randomly select-ing women to write up minutes, speak at colleges and attend to the variety of tasks that are ordinarily dealt with by an election or a volunteer system. The lot system ideally would involve every woman in all the tasks of the organization and protect the group from domination by strong women with better-developed skills to the detriment of everyone else's growth. Our discussions fol-lowed the procedure of each woman who spoke calling on the next woman to her left who wished to speak. Thus we avoided a chairwoman and the kinds of manipulation that are possible when one person becomes the center of an organizational universe.

However, in spite of all our efforts to keep a leadership syn-drome from establishing itself, it became clear that one was emerg-ing. Women with organizational experience and clearly articulated political ideas tended to dominate the discussions. They had the most to say and spoke every time during the circle go-arounds. They became vortices around which other women's vague, ill-defined or scarcely felt political inclinations flowed. And while their ideas were needed, women grew to resent them because it was felt that somehow they were responsible for this failing attempt at a truly participatory form.

When some of the most committed and articulate women de-cided to leave New York and stopped coming to the meetings, it became clear how much of the group energy had centered on their seeming political clarity. Their organizational experience, well-developed feminist consciousness, commitment and dedication to the necessity of constructing a viable large group political form had fed and directed the group. In their absence the group floundered.

For a while, one woman, clearly committed to large group poli-tics, functioned as an unacknowledged leader, but that caused con-flict with the basic premise of the necessity for a nonleader, nonhi-erarchical form. A fundamental contradiction in the situation was brought into sharp focus. On one level the group took responsibility and understood that a leader was created and indulged out of fears and weakness. On another gut level, it was felt that this situation inhibited our growth and kept us locked into old oppressive forms.

Instead of dealing with these contradictions, the group began to direct its frustration and resentment at its most visible target—the leader.

During this time, attendance at the meetings began to rapidly decline. Perhaps some women were disgusted at what seemed like an obvious hypocrisy. Perhaps they were disappointed and not committed enough to struggle. Perhaps they simply did not know what to do. But the fact was that numbers and energy were diminishing. Then the scapegoated leader, feeling frustrated and alienated in the face of group resentment, believing that she had clarified her priorities for herself and they were not being supported by the group, left to begin new work.

Meetings became more directionless, awkward and unfulfilling. Radicalesbians gradually abandoned all the forms the agenda so gloriously extolled. Each week, instead of 50 or 60 women, only 15 or 20 would appear, many of these new women coming for the first time, never to be seen again—they probably wondered what the desultory, unfocused meeting was all about. It was impossible to re-create the group history for these women. There was always some business to attend to that had practical currency and it seemed impossible to explain all the twists and turns of our group process. It had been a process to be lived, not one to be described or prescribed.

At this time, some members were very much locked into the need for weekly meetings because they perceived Radicalesbians as an organization whose membership came together once a week and could be counted. There was also empathy for the women who were coming for the first time and trying to connect—lonely women, women with urgent needs for community and half-formed visions of a new lifestyle. It was felt that Radicalesbians had to provide a connecting point, a way of opening our embryonic community. Frantic efforts were made to keep the organization together despite the obvious absence of creative spontaneity. Trapped in an organizational mindset, unable to see any alternatives, some women became obsessed with revitalizing the weekly meetings that seemed to constitute the essence of Radicalesbians. Efforts were made to get the "dropouts" to return to meetings, and when that didn't work, anger, resentment and self-righteous denunciations were directed at these sisters for their apparent abandonment of the struggle.

During this time, the so-called dropouts, disheartened and devitalized by the alienating atmosphere of the large group rhetoric, had not just stopped attending meetings but had recentered themselves in their consciousness-raising groups, where there were feelings of warmth and trust. These women also began to move out into other groups and activities that spoke to their political needs: squatters actions, print-shop media centers, the Women's Center, the now woman-controlled underground newspaper *RAT*, a newly formed Radicalesbian group in Philadelphia, campus groups. Because of their negative experiences in the Radicalesbian weekly meetings, they carried the awareness that a dynamic of engagement and affinity was essential to their work. More and more, in addition to doing actions, groups began focusing on their relationships as an area of primary concern for political struggle.

When dialogue was reestablished between "dropouts" and "hold-outs" what we came to realize was that old conceptions of organization had blinded us to the evolutionary process moving through us. A new gestalt had formed in the shape of our own needs and the connections we were making with each other that no organization could contain. Radicalesbians had been trying to fit a life force into an arbitrary form. There was a new realization that Radicalesbians was not a thing but a process, a flow, a way of looking at life from our own centers and trying to live in accordance with that self-knowledge. We saw the flow all around us in the changes we made in our lives: quitting alienating, deadening, humiliating jobs; telling our parents and friends about our gay selves; moving into collectives to create chosen families; working on projects and activities that are alive and meaningful. Perhaps the voyage was launched from the weekly meetings, but the reality had become that women were leaving home and moving into new affinity and interest groups.

This is the herstory of the process that Radicalesbians underwent from 1970 to 1971 in New York City. During that time, spontaneously, lesbian feminist groups formed all over the country, each undergoing its own evolutionary process. This explosion confirms that we were not an organization but a movement—a consciousness that continues to live and grow whenever it awakens in the hearts and minds of gay women.

Ellen Shumsky was a young, closeted Brooklyn-born schoolteacher studying photography in France when the Gay Liberation Front was formed in the summer of 1969. She immediately returned from France and spent the next three years immersed in GLF and Radicalesbian activism under the name Ellen Bedoz. Her photos appeared in the GLF newspaper ComeOut! *as well as in numerous counterculture anthologies of the time, including Jerry Rubin's* We Are Everywhere. *She was one of the authors of the lesbian feminist manifesto "The Woman Identified Woman" and a founding member of Radicalesbians. For the past 30 years, she has been a psychotherapist in private practice. She writes about and teaches postmodern psychoanalysis. Her Greenwich Village office is around the corner from the Stonewall.*

The Woman Identified Woman Manifesto

This paper was first issued by the Radicalesbians in 1970 during the "Lavender Menace" protest at the Second Congress to Unite Women in New York City. The principal authors were Artemis March, Lois Hart, Rita Mae Brown, Ellen Shumsky, Cynthia Funk and Barbara XX.

What is a lesbian? A lesbian is the rage of all women condensed to the point of explosion. She is the woman who, often beginning at an extremely early age, acts in accordance with her inner compulsion to be a more complete and freer human being than her society—perhaps then, but certainly later—cares to allow her. These needs and actions, over a period of years, bring her into painful conflict with people, situations, the accepted ways of thinking, feeling and behaving, until she is in a state of continual war with everything around her, and usually with her self. She may not be fully conscious of the political implications of what for her began as personal necessity, but on some level she has not been able to accept the limitations and oppression laid on her by the most basic role of her society—the female role. The turmoil she experiences tends to induce guilt proportional to the degree to which she feels she is not meeting social expectations, and/or eventually drives her to question and analyze what the rest of her society more or less accepts. She is forced to evolve her own life pattern, often living much of her life alone, learning usually much earlier than her "straight" (heterosexual) sisters about the essential aloneness of life (which the myth of marriage obscures) and about the reality of illusions. To the extent that she cannot expel the heavy socialization that goes with being female, she can never truly find peace with herself. For she is caught somewhere between accepting society's view of her—in which case she cannot accept herself—and coming to understand what this sexist society has done to her and why it is functional and necessary for it to do so. Those of us who work that through find ourselves on the other side of a tortuous journey through a night that may have been decades long. The perspective gained from that journey, the liberation of self, the inner peace, the real love of self and of all women, is something to be shared with all women—because we are all women.

It should first be understood that lesbianism, like male homosexuality, is a category of behavior possible only in a sexist society characterized by rigid sex roles and dominated by male supremacy. Those sex roles dehumanize women by defining us as a supportive/serving caste in relation to the master caste of men, and emotionally cripple men by demanding that they be alienated from their own bodies and emotions in order to perform their economic/political/military functions effectively. Homosexuality is a by-product of a particular way of setting up roles (or approved patterns of behavior) on the basis of sex; as such it is an inauthentic (not consonant with "reality") category. In a society in which men do not oppress women, and sexual expression is allowed to follow feelings, the categories of homosexuality and heterosexuality would disappear.

But lesbianism is also different from male homosexuality, and serves a different function in the society. "Dyke" is a different kind of put-down from "faggot," although both imply you are not playing your socially assigned sex role . . . are not therefore a "real woman" or a "real man." The grudging admiration felt for the tomboy, and the queasiness felt around a sissy boy point to the same thing: the contempt in which women—or those who play a female role—are held. And the investment in keeping women in that contemptuous role is very great. Lesbian is a word, the label, the condition that holds women in line. When a woman hears this word tossed her way, she knows she is stepping out of line. She knows that she has crossed the terrible boundary of her sex role. She recoils, she protests, she reshapes her actions to gain approval. Lesbian is a label invented by the Man to throw at any woman who dares to be his equal, who dares to challenge his prerogatives (including that of all women as part of the exchange medium among men), who dares to assert the primacy of her own needs. To have the label applied to people active in women's liberation is just the most recent instance of a long history; older women will recall that not so long ago, any woman who was successful, independent, not orienting her whole life about a man, would hear this word. For in this sexist society, for a woman to be independent means she can't be a woman—she must be a dyke. That in itself should tell us where women are at. It says as clearly as can be said: women and person are contradictory terms. For a lesbian is not considered a "real woman. " And yet, in popular thinking, there is really only one essential difference between a lesbian and other women: that of sexual orientation—which is to say, when you strip off all the packaging, you must finally realize that the essence of being a "woman" is to get fucked by men.

"Lesbian" is one of the sexual categories by which men have divided up humanity. While all women are dehumanized as sex objects, as the objects of men they are given certain compensations: identification with his power, his ego, his status, his protection (from other males), feeling like a "real woman," finding social acceptance by adhering to her role, etc. Should a woman confront herself by confronting another woman, there are fewer rationalizations, fewer buffers by which to avoid the stark horror of her dehumanized condition. Herein we find the overriding fear of many women toward being used as a sexual object by a woman, which not only will bring her no male-connected compensations, but also will reveal the void which is woman's real situation. This dehumanization is expressed when a straight woman learns that a sister is a lesbian; she begins to relate to her lesbian sister as her potential sex object, laying a surrogate male role on the lesbian. This reveals her heterosexual conditioning to make herself into an object when sex is potentially involved in a relationship, and it denies the lesbian her full humanity. For women, especially those in the movement, to perceive their lesbian sisters through this male grid of role definitions is to accept this male cultural conditioning and to oppress their sisters much as they themselves have been oppressed by men. Are we going to continue the male classification system of defining all females in sexual relation to some other category of people? Affixing the label lesbian not only to a woman who aspires to be a person, but also to any situation of real love, real solidarity, real primacy among women, is a primary form of divisiveness among women: it is the condition which keeps women within the confines of the feminine role, and it is the debunking/scare term that keeps women from forming any primary attachments, groups, or associations among ourselves.

Women in the movement have in most cases gone to great lengths to avoid discussion and confrontation with the issue of lesbianism. It puts people up-tight. They are hostile, evasive, or try to incorporate it into some "broader issue." They would rather not talk about it. If they have to, they try to dismiss it as a "lavender herring." But it is no side issue. It is absolutely essential to the success and fulfillment of the women's liberation movement that this issue be dealt with. As long as the label "dyke" can be used to frighten women into a less militant stand, keep her separate from her sisters, keep her from giving primacy to anything other than men and family—then to that extent she is controlled by the male culture. Until women see in each other the possibility of a primal commitment which includes sexual love, they will be denying themselves the love and value they readily accord to men, thus affirming their second-class status. As long as male acceptability is primary—both to individual women and to the movement as a whole—the term lesbian will be used effectively against women. Insofar as women want only more privileges within the system, they do not want to antagonize male power. They instead seek acceptability for women's liberation, and the most crucial aspect of the acceptability is to deny lesbianism—i.e., to deny any fundamental challenge to the basis of the female. It should also be said that some younger, more radical women have honestly begun to discuss lesbianism, but so far it has been primarily as a sexual "alternative" to men. This, however, is still giving primacy to men, both because the idea of relating more completely to women occurs as a negative reaction to men, and because the lesbian relationship is being characterized simply by sex, which is divisive and sexist. On one level, which is both personal and political, women may withdraw emotional and sexual energies from men, and work out various alternatives for those energies in their own lives. On a different political/psychological level, it must be understood that what is crucial is that women begin disengaging from male-defined response patterns. In the privacy of our own psyches, we must cut those cords to the core. For irrespective of where our love and sexual energies flow, if we are male-identified in our heads, we cannot realize our autonomy as human beings.

But why is it that women have related to and through men? By virtue of having been brought up in a male society, we have internalized the male culture's definition of ourselves. That definition consigns us to sexual and family functions, and excludes us from defining and shaping the terms of our lives. In exchange for our psychic servicing and for performing society's non-profit-making functions, the man confers on us just one thing: the slave status which makes us legitimate in the eyes of the society in which we live. This is called "femininity" or "being a real woman" in our cultural lingo. We are authentic, legitimate, real to the extent that we are the property of some man whose name we bear. To be a woman who belongs to no man is to be invisible, pathetic, inauthentic, unreal. He confirms his image of us—of what we have to be in order to be acceptable by him—but not our real selves; he confirms our womanhood—as he defines it, in relation to him—but cannot confirm our personhood, our own selves as absolutes. As long as we are dependent on the male culture for this definition, for this approval, we cannot be free.

The consequence of internalizing this role is an enormous reservoir of self-hate. This is not to say the self-hate is recognized or accepted as such; indeed most women would deny it. It may be experienced as discomfort with her role, as feeling empty, as numbness, as restlessness, as a paralyzing anxiety at the center. Alternatively, it may be expressed in shrill defensiveness of the glory and destiny of her role. But it does exist, often beneath the edge of her consciousness, poisoning her existence, keeping her alienated from herself, her own needs, and rendering her a stranger to other women. They try to escape by identifying with the oppressor, living through him, gaining status and identity from his ego, his power, his accomplishments. And by not identifying with other "empty vessels" like themselves. Women resist relating on all levels to other women who will reflect their own oppression, their own secondary status, their own self-hate. For to confront another woman is finally to confront one's self—the self we have gone to such lengths to avoid. And in that mirror we know we cannot really respect and love that which we have been made to be.

As the source of self-hate and the lack of real self are rooted in our male-given identity, we must create a new sense of self. As long as we cling to the idea of "being a woman," we will sense some conflict with that incipient self, that sense of I, that sense of a whole person. It is very difficult to realize and accept that being "feminine" and being a whole person are irreconcilable. Only women can give to each other a new sense of self. That identity we have to develop with reference to ourselves, and not in relation to men. This consciousness is the revolutionary force from which all else will follow, for ours is an organic revolution. For this we must be available and supportive to one another, give our commitment and our love, give the emotional support necessary to sustain this movement. Our energies must flow toward our sisters, not backward toward our oppressors. As long as woman's liberation tries to free women without facing the basic heterosexual structure that binds us in one-to-one relationship with our oppressors, tremendous energies will continue to flow into trying to straighten up each particular relationship with a man, into finding how to get better sex, how to turn his head around—into trying to make the "new man" out of him, in the delusion that this will allow us to be the "new woman." This obviously splits our energies and commitments, leaving us unable to be committed to the construction of the new patterns which will liberate us.

It is the primacy of women relating to women, of women creating a new consciousness of and with each other, which is at the heart of women's liberation, and the basis for the cultural revolution. Together we must find, reinforce, and validate our authentic selves. As we do this, we confirm in each other that struggling, incipient sense of pride and strength, the divisive barriers begin to melt, we feel this growing solidarity with our sisters. We see ourselves as prime, find our centers inside of ourselves. We find receding the sense of alienation, of being cut off, of being behind a locked window, of being unable to get out what we know is inside. We feel a real-ness, feel at last we are coinciding with ourselves. With that real self, with that consciousness, we begin a revolution to end the imposition of all coercive identifications, and to achieve maximum autonomy in human expression.

Berkeley & the Fight for an Effeminist, Socially Transformative Gay Identity

Nick Benton

My personal gay revolution began in Berkeley, California, in the tumultuous year leading up to the Stonewall Riots.

Until I moved from a small California coastal town to Berkeley to enter postgraduate seminary in 1966, I was convinced my primary struggle through life was to carry the secret of my gay orientation to the grave. But the civil rights and antiwar ferment I found in Berkeley changed all that.

It motivated me to do the last thing I had expected to do: not only to come out, but to become the first-ever openly gay person seeking ordination in a major Protestant denomination; to cofound the Berkeley Gay Liberation Front; to become the first openly gay speaker officially included at an antiwar rally in San Francisco; and to become a prolific writer on universal gay liberation themes for numerous alternative weeklies in the Bay Area.

Little did I anticipate the social ferment that escalated in Berkeley shortly after I arrived there. The civil rights and anti–Vietnam War movements began spilling over into the streets. Marches and demonstrations more than once turned violent. From the Pacific School of Religion's location on a hill above the University of California, we watched from our classrooms as helicopters dropped tear gas on demonstrators. Often I was a demonstrator on Telegraph Avenue myself. I drove daily from my Oakland home to my classes past long rows of National Guard troops lining the streets.

My seminary colleagues and I, as with growing legions of the general public, were deeply moved and inspired by the influence of Dr. Martin Luther King Jr. As seminarians, we were particularly struck by his role as a religious leader, inspiring and motivating a huge mass movement for civil rights. Dr. King's assassination in April 1968 had a profound effect on us all.

It was compounded by the assassination only two months later of Democratic Presidential candidate Bobby Kennedy in Los Angeles. Late that night, I saw on live television the unfolding of pandemonium at the Ambassador Hotel as the news of the Kennedy shooting spread in the hall, and someone went to the microphone to shout, "Is there a doctor in the house?"

That summer of 1968, I attended a session at the seminary attached to Northwestern University, just north of Chicago, where the Democratic National Convention in August drew thousands of angry antiwar demonstrators who were frustrated by the war and the King and Kennedy assassinations, and where an ugly police riot ensued that the entire nation watched.

In response to all this, I didn't necessarily think to myself, "I have got to come out," as my personal contribution to the spirit of the antiwar, pro–civil rights revolution. But when I returned for my third year in seminary that fall, I responded to a flier posted on a bulletin board offering seminarians a few days of exposure to discussions by gay leaders and to the gay scene in San Francisco, just over the Bay Bridge. It was sponsored by the Council for Church and the Homosexual.

I signed up, braced for questions from faculty and fellow students about why I would do that. I can't imagine anyone suspected I was gay, because I had the misfortune, I think, of being able to hide behind a pretty straight image, having gone through undergraduate college on an athletic scholarship and even getting married. We separated just prior to the summer of 1968, as my desire to turn a new page in my life was becoming stronger and stronger.

At the seminar, I pulled off my "curious seminarian" routine pretty well, I thought. I expressed concern for the usual Biblical prohibitions and so forth. But I think the gaydar of some experienced gay leaders knew better. I met the legendary Del Martin and Phyllis Lyon, and other San Francisco gay leaders that I would consort with for years after that, once I came out.

Sadly, that seminar marked the first time I ever knowingly encountered another gay person. The biggest single impact it had on me was not only to see gays as real, intelligent people, but to notice that many were darned cute. More than anything, I confess, that sealed my determination to come out, though cautiously, over the next few months.

Filled with paranoia and dread, I staked out some gay bars in San Francisco's Tenderloin District before getting up the courage to slip inside for the very first time in March 1969. Once I finally entered the gay world, I was traveling over to the City almost every night.

Graduating seminary with honors in May 1969, I moved to a small efficiency overlooking Powell Street in downtown San Francisco, a half block from Union Square. I watched and heard cable cars pass below my window every night and day. A few yards away, hustlers, most of them runaways, hung out under the canopy of the St. Francis hotel at Powell and Geary. Up on Sutter Street, the liveliest gay bar in town, the Rendezvous, was packed with stunning young guys every night. There was dancing, but in those days, no touching. The final song played nightly, as the dance floor undulated, was Diana Ross's "Ain't No Mountain High Enough."

Across the continent, in New York City, the Stonewall Riots began on June 28, 1969, marking the recognized launch of the gay rights movement.

Over the next year, while in postgraduate study at the seminary, I began coming out to a wider and wider circle of friends and classmates, as well as gay activists in Berkeley and San Francisco. My thoughts progressed toward melding the notion of gay liberation, my own liberation included, with the "bigger picture," the one informed by my theological education.

By the summer of 1970, some friends and I officially formed the Berkeley chapter of the Gay Liberation Front, and I worked with a collective that was starting the *Gay Sunshine* newspaper. I had the honor of writing the first editorial ever for that newspaper, published in August 1970, titled, "Who Needs It?"

It sounded what was my signature theme at the time, that indeed, gay liberation was part of the larger struggle of human beings for liberation, in solidarity with the civil rights, antiwar, feminist and Third World liberation struggles. *Gay Sunshine* will represent, I wrote, "those who understand themselves as oppressed—politically oppressed by an oppressor that not only is down on homosexuality, but equally down on all things that are not white, straight, middle class, pro-establishment. . . . It should harken to a greater cause—the cause of human liberation, of which homosexual liberation is just one aspect—and on that level take its stand."

"If homosexuality is really nothing different than something like left-handedness, then the creation of a paper for homosexuals makes no more sense than a newspaper for left-handers." I acknowledged that "a gay newspaper would be a powerful tool in the homosexual fight for equal rights, as it would be a catalyst that could call forth . . . political potential."

In proposing the sociocultural revolution imbedded in the

very notion of gay liberation, I wrote in the October 1970 edition of *Gay Sunshine*: "Sex between persons of the same sex is the cultural antithesis to the most fundamental proposition of the whole Western capitalistic mentality, which is derived from one fundamental act, the 'missionary position' (male atop female) sexual intercourse."

"The 'missionary position,' penis in vagina for the explicit purpose of the creation of offspring, is the first presupposition of everything Western culture represents. From it are derived the concepts of purposeful existence, patriarchy, capitalism, nationalism, imperialism, fascism. From it come the thought patterns of active/passive, dominant/submissive, I/you, we/they, top/bottom, greater/lesser, win/lose and on and on and on. . . . An absolute antithesis of this presupposition is an orgasmic sexual act between persons of the same sex."

That fall, a surprise financial gift from an aunt enabled me to rent an apartment directly across Berkeley's Telegraph Avenue from the White Horse Inn, which was the only gay bar in Berkeley, and was very low-key. A picket line had been thrown up in front of the bar by some gay radical brothers and sisters, protesting the fact that long-haired, hippie-type gays were not welcome in the bar and that touching was, naturally in that day, also prohibited.

With help from friends, I had the idea to turn my $130-a-month apartment into what I called "The People's Alternative," and it became just that. Demonstrators in the picket line across the street were invited in. There was virtually no furniture but lots of cheap wine and a boom box.

For over two months in the fall of 1970, my "People's Alternative" became a magnet for fun gay organizing activities of all types. Often it was filled far beyond capacity, including one night when everyone who'd attended the first-ever officially sanctioned gay dance at the university, a half mile away, poured in after the dance ended. Gay religious services were held there. I was ordained into an obscure sect there. Famous older gay icons held forth there, too. But mostly people came for a good time. It was no Studio 54, but pretty damn lively. In mid-November, the landlord found out about all this, and I was swiftly and unceremoniously evicted.

In November 1970, I and and another openly gay seminarian were invited onto a panel with two faculty members, one conservative and one more liberal, to discuss the new gay movement at the Pacific School of Religion (PSR). More than 400 students from

PSR and other neighboring seminaries turned it into a standing-room-only event, one of the best-attended general assemblies ever held at the school. I brought the house down with my declaration that the Bible commands us to be "both fruitful and to multiply."

One of my fellow seminarians, Bill Johnson, chose the occasion to stand up and "come out" in the middle of the meeting. He was met with wild applause and numerous group hugs. Sadly, I looked out and saw another seminarian, with whom I'd had a brief relationship months earlier, who chose to remain in his closet, and perhaps has to this day.

One Sunday, at a United Church of Christ church in San Francisco, a sermon was delivered by its pastor, an older man who'd confessed to me that he was gay. The sermon was intended to be compassionate, but with the title "People Unlike Ourselves" it was offensive. During the coffee-hour discussion afterward, I went to the microphone and angrily denounced the apologetic tone of the sermon. While not "outing" the minister, I declared my resignation from the church and the termination of my ordination process.

(The United Church of Christ went on later, in 1972, to ordain my seminary classmate, Bill Johnson, making him the first openly gay person to be ordained by a mainstream Protestant denomination. I've long since rejoined the UCC, whose history dates to the Mayflower, the Abolitionist movement, the Underground Railroad and the founding of scores of institutions of higher education for freed slaves after the Civil War. In 2005 its ruling national body became the first representing a major Protestant denomination to vote to fully support gay marriage.)

Also in the fall of 1970, I began writing for the *Berkeley Barb*. I came with a lot of journalistic experience, having been the editor of my high school and college papers and a full-time writer for my hometown paper before entering the seminary. I began writing mostly about gay issues at first, but later I became, on and off, virtually its principal writer, covering stories on all topics until January 1973. I wrote articles on gay events and themes almost every week. During one stretch, I wrote a seven-part series on "The Gay Scene in San Francisco," which described bar life and street life with a lot of not-so-pretty accounts of alienation and discrimination based on age, attractiveness and so forth. Two of them, "The Same Old Game" and "David," were later published among a compendium of essays in Len Richmond and Gary Noguera's *The Gay Liberation Book* (Ramparts Press, 1973). A third essay of mine published in that book critiqued the so-called "men's liberation move-ment" and was called "Don't Call Me Brother."

The barely adequate income derived from writing and doing page layout for the *Barb* came under fire at one point from some of my gay radical counterparts, who showed up one day to challenge me to leave. They didn't like that I had a job and many of them didn't. Some of them felt that true radicalism involved making the state pay for your livelihood by qualifying for welfare. I told my boss, *Barb* founder and owner Max Scherr, that I had no intention of bending to their pressure.

By the summer of 1971, a friend, Jim Rankin, and I developed the notion of the social paradigm shift that we felt gay liberation represented. We saw the movement allied with radical feminism as an effort to end war and oppression by transforming male-dominated society. To this end, we argued against those who saw gay liberation as only sexual freedom, or even as strictly a fight for legal rights. Many of my articles in the *Berkeley Barb* promoted the notion that, fully actualized, gay liberation had the potential to be socially transformative. We had exchanges with the likes of San Francisco's legendary Harvey Milk and Berkeley's gay poet-in-residence, Allen Ginsberg.

My friend and I decided to launch our own newspaper to fur-ther advance this perspective. We called it *The Effeminist*. We de-signed, wrote, printed and distributed it, including hawking it on street corners on Telegraph Avenue and off Union Square in San Francisco. We wound up producing two slender editions, and I've never seen one since those days.

With copies of *The Effeminist* and specially prepared statements on fliers, a small circle of us leafleted a number of San Francisco gay community meetings where Milk began launching his career to become an openly gay member of the San Francisco Board of Supervisors.

We who were *The Effeminist* challenged his "equal rights only" focus with our cultural paradigm–shift theme. He wouldn't take up our challenge to help transform the movement, but repeatedly affirmed our right to our views while steadfastly maintaining his own narrow focus.

In the case of Ginsberg, *The Effeminist* took him on for hav-ing confessed in print to masturbatory fantasies involving really young guys. We leafleted at one of his readings in Berkeley, call-ing his confession "sexism, homosexual oppression that makes it impossible for us to be gay." He became my polemical punching bag on more than a few occasions in the effort to differentiate his typical notion of "gay" as merely lusty sexual attraction from our view of "gay" as the basis for a profound social paradigm shift.

But in the fall of 1972, I said good-bye to that intense phase of my life at a three-day gay issues confab, the Southwest Regional Conference on Gay Organizations, in Sacramento. I had a major role in a number of seminars where I tried to get across my effeminist way of looking at things.

Ten days later, George McGovern was defeated in the landslide reelection of Richard Nixon. Burned out, I quit my job at the *Berkeley Barb* in January 1973, and I decided to be more of a socialist activist than a gay liberationist. I wrote a more-or-less exit essay for a San Francisco gay publication titled "Socialism or Homosexuality," denouncing what I saw as the prevalent understanding of homosexuality as "predatory" in nature, mirroring the values of the dominant American culture, and not transformative as I'd felt it should be.

The incredible thing about those days was the sense that one's ideas and activism were at the cutting edge of a new direction that the overall culture was taking. We felt that sense, and it was certainly not unfounded.

Nicholas F. (Nick) Benton, an honor graduate of the Pacific School of Religion in 1969, was the cofounder of the Berkeley Gay Liberation Front in 1970. In 1991, he founded the weekly Falls Church News-Press *(ww.fcnp.com) in the northern Virginia suburbs of Washington, D.C., and after 18 years it is widely recognized as the most progressive newspaper in Virginia. As its openly gay owner and editor, Benton has served twice as president of the local Chamber of Commerce, been named Falls Church's "Pillar of the Community" twice and "Business Person of the Year" once, and had his newspaper named "Business of the Year" twice.*

TWO POEMS

Dajenya

In 1970, at 16 years old, Dajenya was the youngest member of GLF in New York City. As a multi-ethnic, African American and Jewish, pansexual red-diaper baby who had been raised on civil rights and peace marches, she was drawn to the way GLF applied radical politics to sexuality. Gay (LGBT) liberation seemed a natural extension of the struggle for freedom for all.

After moving to the San Francisco Bay Area in 1973, Dajenya raised two sons while attending school, eventually attaining a master's degree in social work in 1996. She has remained active in many struggles throughout her life. Today, at 55, she is a social worker living in California with her life partner, Lois.

Dajenya's poetry has been published in *Women's Peace Journal, Anything That Moves, Sinister Wisdom, Rites of Passage, Women's Recovery Network, Current Magazine,* various newsletters, and four anthologies: *Bi Any Other Name: Bisexual People Speak Out; Sister/Stranger: Lesbians Loving Across the Lines; Bisexual Politics: Theories, Queries & Visions;* and *What I Want From You: Voices of East Bay Lesbian Poets.*

My heritage
(1975)

my heritage is black
my heritage is rebel
my heritage is soul
my heritage is love
my heritage is flesh
my heritage is gay
my heritage is proud
of what I am no matter *who* may say
my heritage is drums
my heritage is flutes
my heritage is dance

my heritage is fight
for being free
for being female
for being black and gay and proud
for being here
now
alive
in the flesh
and ready

LGBT Supermarket

(1994)

Rainbow rings
twenty-nine ninety five.
A lesbian cruise to Greece
if you have
three thousand dollars . . .
lie in the sun and tell yourself
you have arrived.
Are we a movement
        or a market?

If you've got the T-cells
we've got the beer
And let's be sure to make it clear
to all the world
what good citizens we are,
what good soldiers,
good consumers,
We'll respect the status quo
if they let us buy in.
Are we a movement
        or a market?

Remember
we bring lots of tourist dollars
to the city every year with our parade.
Food vendors wait at the end of each march
to cater to our thirsty throats

and rainbow dollars.
Where does the money go on our very own day?
Are we a movement
        or a market?

While gay youth still jump out of windows
and prisoners suffer torture for their love
and mothers lose their babies to grandmothers
and thousands keep dying of cancer and AIDS . . .
we celebrate how far we've come
with merchandise and yearly parades.

Look around.
Is this all we wanted?
Is this enough?
Time's running out.
We must decide.
Are we a movement
or a market?

The Effeminist Moment

Steven F. Dansky

There is nothing in this world that does not have a decisive moment.
—Henri Cartier-Bresson

The year 1970 was crucial for the women's movement with the publication of three essential feminist works: Shulamith Firestone's *Dialectic of Sex* (Morrow, 1970), Robin Morgan's *Sisterhood Is Powerful* (Vintage, 1970) and Kate Millet's *Sexual Politics* (Doubleday, 1970). The feminist challenge to the patriarchy was cataclysmic and universal. During that year following the Stonewall Rebellion in Greenwich Village—universally accepted as the catalyst for the emergence of the modern gay liberation movement—several clusters of antisexist men, mostly in New York City and Berkeley, began to formulate pro-feminist theory that they termed effeminism.

Analogous to Cartier-Bresson's *decisive moment*, the effeminist movement of antisexist men was more accurately a moment in a historical frame than a political movement. A moment, as opposed to a movement, because effeminism was often dismissed as "extremist" or "violence-prone," and effeminists were characterized as making "frothing denunciations" (*Gay Sunshine Newspaper*, 1973). As a result, effeminism attracted controversy rather than magnetizing followers. Many of our essays named names, publicly attacking and harming former colleagues and friends, particularly gay liberationists.

The term effeminism had a twofold function. First, it designated those men who supported the women's movement. Second, the term effeminism connoted the societal ostracizing of men considered to be effeminate. The "Effeminist Manifesto" decreed, "All effeminate men are oppressed by the patriarchy's systematic enforcement of masculinist standards, whether these standards are expressed as physical, mental, emotional, or sexual stereotypes of what is desirable in a man."

During the summer of 1971, Nick Benton and Jim Rankin

213

published two editions of *The Effeminist* newspaper in Berkeley, selling it on Telegraph Avenue and distributing it to independent bookstores. Of effeminism, Benton later said the following:

> Our concept of *effeminism* was not so much to flaunt ef-feminate behavior, but to affirm our solidarity as gay men with the feminist movement. We saw ourselves creating a *flank* of the feminist movement among males, especially gay males, seeing that oppressive features of the male chauvinist and dominated society that the most progressive feminists were seeking to undermine and redefine were also at the root of the oppression of gay men.

An emergent schism within gay liberation also became apparent during 1970 with the publication of two major works questioning the commonality of lesbians and gay men. First, Daughters of Bilitis founder Del Martin wrote in the *Ladder*:

> Goodbye to the male chauvinists of the homophile movement . . . and to gay liberationists whose liberation would only further enslave us. . . . It is a revelation to find acceptance, equality, love and friendship everything we sought in the homophile community—not there, but in the women's movement.

Then, Radicalesbians released "The Woman Identified Woman":

> But lesbianism is also different from male homosexuality, and serves a different function in the society. . . . It is the primacy of women relating to women, of women creating a new consciousness of and with each other, which is at the heart of women's liberation, and the basis for the cultural revolution.

The passionate debate about sexism extended from gay liberation into the mainstream media. jill johnston wrote in 1972, in the *Village Voice*: "Effeminists are the first western male revolutionaries. The first men to confess the inappropriateness of their manhood and to withdraw from the classic male demand of support from the female." Martin Duberman reviewed effeminist writing in a 1972

New York Times Book Review: "While Revolutionary Effeminism may seem 'adventurist,' violence prone and opaque . . . it is formulating basic questions on gender."

In 1973, the New York effeminists published the "Effeminist Manifesto" in *Double-F: A Magazine of Effeminism.* The Manifesto generated feverish controversy, setting forth in the first four (of 13) principles that all women are oppressed by all men; sexism is the root of all oppression; and men must accept women's leadership in the struggle for social change. Of course, the Manifesto had a strong correlation to "The Redstockings Manifesto," which states, "All men have oppressed women. No male can claim innocence of the crime."

Other principles in the Manifesto defined the oppression of effeminate men—regardless of sexual orientation—by the systematic imposition of masculinist values, took a position against sado-masculinity and discussed male transvestism. The effeminists strongly opposed any notion that transgenderism was anything but a manifestation and promotion of the oppression of women. We never considered it an authentic sexual identity. For instance, Benton maintained:

> We were critics of men who mimicked and oppressed women, or sought to internalize their behavior, and asserted that almost all role-dominated behavior, including the use of uniforms for various stereotyped social functions, were all forms of oppression and therefore were "drag."

In the "Effeminist Manifesto" we linked what we termed *eonism* (that is, male transvestitism) to masochism or *masoch-eonism* with the following assertion:

> Just as sadism and masculinism, by merging into one identity, tend to become indistinguishable one from the other, so masochism and eonism are born of an identical impulse toward mock subservience in men, as a way to project intense anti-woman feelings and also to pressure women into conformity by providing those degrading stereotypes most appealing to the sado-masculinist.

During 2002–03, I joined a private psychotherapy practice whose director, Arlene Istar Lev, is a nationally known expert focusing on understanding the needs of the transgender community. This was the first time in my psychotherapeutic career that I worked with a transgender population despite my postgraduate education at a psychotherapy center and training institute that offered professional services to the lesbian, gay, bisexual, transgender and queer (LGBTQ) community. My principal role in private practice was to assess the mental stability of transgenders who wanted either hormone or surgical therapy. This "gatekeeper" role forced me to rethink earlier effeminist views. I've reversed my position to one that accepts the authenticity of transgenders. I found their narratives compelling and challenged the social construction of an immutable binary gendered world. On rethinking transgender these decades later, it's evident that we, as effeminists, had a very elementary understanding of the construction of gender.

Outlaw sodomy!, the sign proclaimed from a farm off Interstate 80 near Kearney, Nebraska, in 2008. I reflected that it's merely five years since the 2003 ruling by the Supreme Court in Lawrence v. Texas that found that a Texas law prohibiting oral or anal sex between couples of the same sex was unconstitutional—the dramatic reversal of the 1986 Bowers v. Hardwick ruling.

Hippocrates said, "Healing is a matter of time, but it is sometimes also a matter of opportunity." This cross-country trip with my husband provided the juncture for reconciliation-reunions taking place from La Jolla to Las Vegas, from Greenwich Village, Chelsea, and Rockefeller Plaza to the foothills of the Taconic Mountains, from Turtle Bay to Orange, Massachusetts. Climactic, even if tentative, third-act reunions, restoring fragile connections, making amends to those harmed, affirming our commonality as members of GLF who have not seen each other for more than three and a half decades. Bruce Gottfried called it a pilgrimage:

> I'm quite amazed by this GLF pilgrimage you've just made. It seems in a way like the kind of thing everyone should do in their early 60s. But I'm amazed that you have actually done it. . . . So the process, I think, involves finally putting certain issues—issues that were at one time big preoccupations—to rest.

Each encounter began with fixed intensity as we gazed into each other's eyes to locate recognition. Former members of GLF, the 12th Street, 17th Street, 95th Street and Baltic Street Collectives, members of Femmes Against Sexism, the Venceremos Brigade, Gay Guerrilla Group, someone from the People's Coffee Grounds, a Flaming Faggot, an editor of *Double-F: A Magazine of Effeminism* and a member of the *ComeOut!* newspaper collective. There were reunions in a rural octagonal house in the forest; in a Turtle Bay high-rise; in the baggage claim at McCarrin Airport, Las Vegas; a French restaurant in Chelsea, one in Rockefeller Plaza overlooking the Prometheus fountain, another in La Jolla overlooking the Pacific Ocean and in a Greenwich Village bistro on Avenue of the Americas. Effeminism perseveres for me—though imperfect in some choices and tactics, the vision stands as a decisive moment guided by life-giving, creativity and mutuality.

Steven F. Dansky, a longtime political activist and writer, was a formative member of the modern gay liberation movement in 1969. His writing spans nearly four decades and has been cited in nearly every early book on gay liberation. His political writing has been reviewed in the New York Times *and the* Village Voice. *The Steven F. Dansky Papers is archived at the M.E. Grenander Department of Special Collections and Archives, at the University at Albany, State University of New York (SUNY). He is the author of two books,* Now Dare Everything: Tales of HIV-Related Psychotherapy *(Haworth Press, 1994) and* Nobody's Children: Orphans of the HIV Epidemic *(Haworth Press, 1997).* Broken Gender and Other Stories *is in preparation—the title story of the collection was published in* Gertrude: A Journal of Voice and Vision *(2007).*

DYKETACTICS! Notes Towards an Un-Silencing

Paola Bacchetta

What can one say about the mid-1970s in the United States except that it was a particularly turbulent and exciting time for many of us who lived it?

Throughout that period I was deeply involved with DYKETACTICS!, a lesbian political group formed in Philadelphia. DYKETACTICS! membership was fluid, with no clear borders, though it crystallized here and there during certain actions. We came together from many backgrounds: African American, Chinese, Latina, mixed race, Native American and ethnicities generally arranged under the rubric of White such as Irish, Italian and Jewish of several national origins. There were many religious backgrounds: Baptist, Buddhist, Catholic, Jewish and Protestant. We spanned several classes: mainly working class and middle class, but also very poor and upper middle class.

Most of us were born in the United States but some were immigrants. Our ages spanned from the teens to the late 20s. Most of us worked together at Alexandria Books, the city's feminist and lesbian bookstore. A few of us were students. A few of us were unemployed. Together we were committed to lesbian struggles. Most of us had come from and remained within other movements: for national liberation, Black liberation and civil rights, anarchist and socialist movements, and so on. As a group we saw our liberation as inseparably encompassing struggles against lesbophobia, sexism, racism, poverty, neocolonialism, capitalism and the destruction of the environment.

What I remember most about DYKETACTICS! is how together, over time, we constructed a way of life, deep affective-emotional relations and a common, inclusive politics of daily engagement in constructive political battle. These three aspects of our lives were inseparable.

Before we realized that we had come together as a political group, and even had decided upon the group's name, most of us had lived together collectively, mainly in two houses just blocks apart in a low-income, predominantly Black but also mixed area of Philadelphia. I was the youngest member and was given the nickname Tyke Dyke (as in "Hey Tyke Dyke, where are you?"). Sherrie, who was closest to my age, also soon came to be called Tyke Dyke. With time, as our friendship deepened and we ended up configuring many political actions together, Sherrie and I decided to name ourselves The Invincible Tyke Dyke Duo (as in "Ah-hem, hey everyone, listen, The Invincible Tyke Dyke Duo has decided to organize a graffiti zap"). These terms of endearment, of course, were also terms of relationality that we constructed together.

While DYKETACTICS! was very far from separatism *politically*, the collective home space I lived in with other DYKETACTICS! members began as separatist space before opening up. Initially, in 1975, no men were allowed to enter. Not even the gas meter readers. Every month whoever answered the meter man's knock at the front door sent him packing. For the longest time we received, month after month by mail, written warnings from the city about the inaccessibility of our gas meter. One day, one of our housemates got fed up with all the notices. She called the City and demanded that they send us a woman meter reader. Sherrie and I were convinced that this action, if multiplied in other households, would help women get jobs. Instead, the City decided to shut off our gas. After that, we had to let the male gas reader in every month.

Perhaps the biggest change in our home space came, however, when we decided to do something about our landlord, who was also the slumlord of most of our neighborhood. We eventually opened our doors wide in order to organize against him. It began after we formed community with our neighbors. Most were single working mothers. We encountered them while walking past each other's front porches, on the streets, in the corner store. We started talking together regularly about everything and anything: the weather, the trees, food prices, children dodging cars, flowers, stray animals, music, the news. And finally, our houses. Most were rather dilapidated, even falling apart. Some had little or no heat in winter. In one, the plumbing didn't work.

Among our neighbors there were two elderly Latina lesbians. They were butch/femme identified and had been together for most of their lives. They were known, respected and liked in the neighborhood. At one point the butch lost her job and they fell behind on rent. Soon our slumlord threatened to evict them. When I found out, I went home, told everyone and suggested we invite them to live with us until the butch found a job. At our dinner table there were mixed reactions. There was a bit of grumbling about reproductions of hetero-normativity and monogamy-conformity. Some felt that lesbian monogamy was about reproducing the relational modes of hetero-normative marriage, which was historically based in the appropriation of women. We desired to live and relate differently, outside this oppressive mold. Some felt that the constant acting out of dominant, alienating relationalities under our own roof would become an energy drain. But very soon our discussion gave way to a dialogue about basic lesbian, race and class solidarities. Everyone agreed they could move in.

Once the two came to live with us I realized we had a similar rhythm. I got up early for the revolution (as I was convinced it would arrive any morning sometime soon). They got up early out of habit. We ended up having breakfast together often. I was unfamiliar with their generation of "nonpoliticized" lesbians, but still felt they were family. One of the first things I noticed was that the butch liked to do work the rest of us considered femme (she cooked, made coffee, washed clothes), while the femme was very skilled at work we all considered butch (she repaired loose wooden planks on our steps, fixed our old TV, and so on). They fit very well into our heterogeneous home and they contributed to our collectivity in every way possible. I learned quite a bit from listening to them talk about their lives. Eventually the butch got a job and they moved to another block within the neighborhood. Today my strongest memory of them is that they were truly very deeply in love.

One winter, most of the children of a neighbor, a single mother, got constantly ill with colds and flu. One caught pneumonia. Our neighbor, the children's mother, had no health insurance, could not afford a baby sitter and could not afford to take off from work to stay with them. The situation completely drained her. Many neighbors pitched in to help out. One day, in exasperation, we decided we should take some organized collective action. We called a meeting at our home to discuss housing rights and suing our slumlord for neglect. About 15 neighbors came, including a few men. Everyone was on board. Though we had no money for a lawyer, we began to build a collective case and we let our slumlord know about it. We never got to court, but that was fine with us. Under duress, the slumlord made some dramatic improvements to avoid getting sued. We felt we'd won at least a small victory.

I am not sure how to communicate the excitement I felt every day during that period. I lived as though the revolution would arrive any minute, preferably at 8 o'clock in the morning. Even though it didn't, something new was always going on. We were an activist home and we put into practice whatever ideas we were convinced of at the time. For example, across our disparate cultures and racialized positionalities, each of us had been taught, albeit often differently, a whole range of types of shame for our bodies. How could we analyze it together? Move through it, get past it? We tried out many ways of living within our bodies fully. Bodies that come in all shapes and sizes. All colors. All ages. Bodies from which liquids flow: menstruation, perspiration, sexual fluids. Bodies that feel. We tried sitting together in the nude to get comfortable with ourselves and each other. We tried using natural sponges, which was all the rave in many lesbian milieux at the time, instead of pads or tampons for menstruation. The sponges were infinitely more comfortable.

One day, Barbara used her blood-saturated sponge to paint a poem on the tiles of our bathroom wall. After that, I painted my bedroom and the bathroom walls white so we could write and draw on them with our blood-saturated sponges and see the work very clearly. We all began to look forward to every new period: It meant new poetry, art, imaginings, life.

Sponges aside, our home was in general full of poetry, music and theater. Julie Blackwomon and Barbara Ruth both wrote and published brilliant poetry. Both shared their work at readings, on alternative radio and in print. Kathy Fire, Linda, Mojo and I wrote and played music. We animated many an evening at home and many a demonstration in the streets. I wrote the music for Julie's "Revolutionary Blues" and for Barbara's "Powers Are Around" poem. And once Julie and I did a show together on lesbians of color on our local feminist radio station in which she read, I played, and finally I sang her poem "Revolutionary Blues." We also experimented with music and the power of vibrations and energies. With Mojo on flute and me on guitar, we explored healing tones. We were sure we'd found the perfect formula. When anyone in or connected to DYKETACTICS! fell ill, we played for her until she was well again. Monica was an actress in the theater group Rites of Women. The group wrote its own plays and performed them widely.

DYKETACTICS! and our allies in Philadelphia were deeply

involved as lesbians in our own liberation, which, given the heterogeneity of subjects under the rubric "lesbian," we conceptualized in the widest of terms. DYKETACTICS! actions ranged from court cases to daily creative public work across the very local to national and transnational scales. For example, to get messages into the public space in Philly, there were "graffiti zaps" on billboards, subway walls, and buildings.

DYKETACTICS! organized a citywide women's general strike to protest working women's double work day, unequal pay and high rates of unemployment. We demonstrated in front of a local high school where a student was harassed and threatened for being an out lesbian. When a local porn theater scheduled two weeks of films similar to snuff films (in which women of color are tortured and killed onscreen), DYKETACTICS! protested with a constant presence, banners, poster boards and bullhorns in front of the theater door. Soon many other groups joined the protest. The mainstream press covered this amply, and in less than 48 hours the theater stopped showing the films.

We issued statements in solidarity with SEPTA (SouthEast Pennsylvania Transportation Authority) workers striking for better pay and working conditions. We worked to defend prostitutes from persecution by the State. We were engaged in struggles against prisons. We worked in coalitions to free political prisoners Assata Shakur (of the Black Liberation movement) and Susan Saxe (of the movement against the Vietnam War). As out lesbians we supported national liberation movements, including AIM (American Indian Movement) and the Puerto Rican Independence Movement, and local ones such as MOVE.

Founded in 1972, MOVE was an anarchist collective in which all the members, most of whom were African American, took the last name Africa. In 1978, 200 Philadelphia police surrounded their row house, bulldozed the entranceway, used a crane to bash in windows and hosed water into their basement in an attempt to remove them. In this fracas many MOVE members and children were wounded, one policeman died and nine MOVE members were sentenced to over 30 years in prison for third-degree murder. MOVE relocated to another street. But in 1985 the police bombed their home with C-4 and Tovex, killing the founder, John Africa, six adult members and four of their children. Surviving MOVE adults were hauled off to jail, the children were brought to welfare agencies and the MOVE home was razed to the ground.

Our struggles were so many that I cannot name them all in several pages. Yet I would like to give just a bit of detail about the relationship between DYKETACTICS! analytics and practices through two concrete examples of our local struggles that had a certain national impact: Bill 1275 and our police brutality case, and our Bicentennial protests.

DYKETACTICS! became the first lesbian group in the United States to file a federal suit against police brutality aimed solely against lesbians. The whole episode began in December 1975 when DYKETACTICS!, along with many other LGBT groups, went to a public meeting of Philadelphia City Council to demonstrate in support of Bill 1275. The bill, if passed, would have added "sexual orientation" to the existing Human Rights code, thereby protecting LGBT folks from discrimination in employment, public accommodations and housing.

By way of background I should mention that the struggle around these issues had been going on for years with no results. The evening before the bill was to be considered, I remember getting a call from our gay male ally Tommi, who urged us to attend. Kathy Fire also remembers a call to DYKETACTICS! from Women Organized Against Rape asking us to participate. The bill, if not considered by City Council the next day, would have been killed. Thus there was a certain urgency about all this. We discussed the pros and cons of a mixed LGBT action and decided we would indeed attend. We held a meeting at University of Pennsylvania's women's school, had a lively discussion and set about making banners that read: Dykes Ignite; Dykes Unite; Free Bill 1275, and so on.

The next day, we showed up together at City Hall with our banners. The room was packed with LGBT activists. Some of us took seats and some stood at the edges of the room holding banners. We sat and stood through a number of other bills and waited. Finally, Bill 1275 came up. Immediately, it was announced that it would be tabled once again. When we heard this, a wave of emotion swept through the room. While remaining in our seats, or standing at the sides, we raised our fists and began to chant: "Free Bill 1275." Immediately the city's Civil Affairs Police Unit, the riot police who had been trained by right-wing Mayor Frank Rizzo when he was Chief of Police, entered the room with force.

Though we were relatively dispersed throughout the crowd, the officers singled out DYKETACTICS! members. They were probably familiar with us, as we had a history of very public activism.

Without provocation, they came toward each of us, beat us up and dragged us out of the room. I remember seeing a number of policemen attacking Barbara, who was seated not far from me, and, as I was being punched around, managed to move toward her in an attempt to pull the officers off her. I was then dragged out of the meeting room with much ado and finally dumped in an adjacent room, where I found Barbara and others lying on the floor. Other officers had dragged others of us down City Hall's marble steps to the sidewalk.

Some DYKETACTICS! members and allies started enacting a play inside City Hall with the help of a huge orange witch puppet. In the midst of the confusion a friend came looking for those of us who were still inside, found us, brought us out and helped all of us get to the hospital. While many of us were physically injured and rather traumatized, Barbara would develop permanent health problems as a result of the violence she endured.

When we were released from the hospital, we found that the media, which had been present at the Council meeting, had photographed and filmed some of the police brutality. We relived it all again as we saw ourselves and each other in the mainstream press and on TV. We decided to take action. We contacted lawyers, and with their help, six of us filed a federal suit against members of Civil Affairs, the City of Philadelphia and City Council Sergeants at Arms for use of excessive force and for quelling a legal demonstration.

Our trial, which lasted two weeks, took place many months later, in September 1976. It, too, was highly publicized, in mainstream newspapers, on radio and on TV. Initially we thought we had a reasonable chance to win. After all, we had visual records (photos) taken by journalists of the brutality. We had eyewitnesses who would testify, and hospital reports. And we had our own photos of our injuries taken after our release from the hospital.

In the end, none of the evidence would matter at all. From what I remember of it, there was so much queerphobia in the courtroom and in the media that we felt as though our very humanity was on trial. When the police who had attacked us took the stand, their lawyer asked them, one by one, if they were married, how many children they had fathered and what civic organizations they belonged to, in order to establish their hetero-normativity. When we took the stand, the city's lawyer asked us, the DYKETACTICS! plaintiffs, to state whether or not we were lesbians. In 1976 that simple question was probably the most effective way to discredit our testimony in advance. The media began fairly early on to construct us as insane.

After just a few days of the trial it became clear that the jury was reacting with sympathy for the police and with repulsion for us. We tried to turn this around at first, without success. Very soon it became obvious that we would lose the case. So we decided to use the media's presence in the courtroom to spread as much useful information about lesbians and other queers into the public domain as possible. Thus, for example, when we were asked, one by one, "Are you a lesbian?" we replied with various versions of: "Yes, I am a lesbian and so is 10 percent of the population of Philadelphia and the U.S." Through our answers on the stand and the banners we brought daily to the courthouse, we managed to make public a range of arguments for LGBTTIQ rights. Every evening, we discussed together what message we would try to put forth in the courtroom the following day.

Every day the courtroom was packed. I am not sure how many in the audience were our supporters. Activists from LGBTTIQ and other groups were definitely with us, if only because they supported Bill 1275 and opposed police brutality against lesbians. But we also came under much internal community fire. Some mainstream LGBTTIQ groups disapproved of DYKETACTICS! They did not like the fact that we refused to isolate homophobia as an issue. For us it was inseparably linked with racism, poverty, neocolonialism, capitalism and war. They did not like our dyke tactics; they wanted LGBT acceptance as normative, while we wanted to question and uproot normativity.

Some of the people of color, civil rights and national liberation groups in which we had, as individuals and as a group, been out and active, expressed unease about our hyper-public lesbianism. Some of our lesbian, as well as other queer (such as Faerie and trans) and straight political allies in non-queer movements, attended regularly. We knew they were with us all the way. The reaction of family members was mixed: Some of us had already been disowned for being lesbians, some were disowned for going through with the trial and some had family support. So, while most avoided the trial completely, some family members of two DYKETACTICS! women attended. I remember feeling that we were partially heartily supported by, and partially a source of shame to, those who mattered most to us.

After more than two weeks, the jury took just one hour to drop the charges against the police. When the verdict was pronounced, we and our supporters raised clenched fists and peacefully left the courtroom together. Outside, we six plaintiffs issued the following press release:

> DYKETACTICS!, a lesbian feminist organization, finds the city of Philadelphia and named members of the Civil Affairs Police Unit, and the Sergeants at Arms, GUILTY of oppression as charged.
>
> The actions taken against DYKETACTICS! were in direct violation of our civil rights as guaranteed in the Constitution of the United States. We were deprived of our right to freedom of speech, our right to assemble peacefully, our right to petition our government for redress of our grievances, our right to remain secure in our persons.
>
> By bringing them to trial, we denounce the City of Philadelphia and the officers of the law for breaking the spirit and letter of their own laws. For a change, the oppressors instead of the oppressed appear as the defendants.
>
> Through our presence and our testimony, we have succeeded in reintroducing to the public mind our need for a Gay Rights Bill. Gay rights legislation would prohibit discrimination based on sexual orientation in the areas of employment, public accommodations, and housing.
>
> A constant difficulty we share with other oppressed peoples is gaining public recognition for the validity of our culture and politics. For example, because our organizational structure is collective (members having equal power) rather than hierarchical (members having a chain of command), our very existence as a valid entity was constantly questioned, even ridiculed in the courtroom.
>
> By finding the defendants not guilty, the jurors in this courtroom have found DYKETACTICS! guilty of deviating from the norm. It was our lesbianism, not police brutality, that was on trial. We intend to continue our struggle to secure our basic human rights, as women and as lesbians.
>
> You will never have the comfort of our silence again.

Between the DYKETACTICS! beatings (December 1975) and the trial (September 1976), we remained ever active. 1976 was of

course the year of the Bicentennial. It was officially celebrated with
great enthusiasm in Philadelphia. It was also intensely protested by
a number of left, liberation and civil rights groups. DYKETACTICS!
participated in mass protests but also planned some of our own.
Many of us wanted to organize a mass demonstration against the
dominant Church and State's colluding positions against homosexuality. In August, the 41st International Eucharist Congress,
a convention of Catholic nuns, priests, cardinals and bishops,
would inspire about a million Catholics to make a pilgrimage to
Philadelphia.

We were denied a permit to protest. By that time, because of
the upcoming trial, DYKETACTICS! was well known to police officials, and it was unlikely we'd ever be granted permission for a
demonstration.

To get around this little matter, we created a subgroup of
DYKETACTICS!, which we called DAR, or Dykes for an Amerikan
Revolution. It was our own subalternly positioned reformulation
of the dominant Daughters of the American Revolution. Eventually (such impatient dykes!) we moved the date for our bicentennial action up to July 4, 1976, Independence Day itself. We decided
on a threefold protest and wrote a Lesbian Feminist Declaration of
1976 for the occasion.

Our Declaration stated clearly: "We, the Dykes for an Amerikan Revolution, in order to address the mainstream of Amerikan
society and begin to articulate our own lesbian-feminist vision,
seize this moment of history to create herstory. . . . The Amerikan nation has been founded on the genocide of Native American
peoples, financed through the slavery of African and Third World
peoples and sustained through the oppression of all women. All of
these atrocities have been sanctioned by men's religion."

The Declaration then went on to denounce sexism, homophobia, poverty, racism, forced sterilization of women of color, colonialism, the "global system of imperialism," war and the profits reaped
by the rich, the destruction of the environment and hunting animals for sport. It also included some remarkably timely words denouncing "The Man" (those in power in the United States): "He
develops a global system of imperialism which enslaves much of
humanity and threatens the entire world. Under the guise of making the world 'safe for democracy,' he imposes his culture, his government and his religions on other nations. He steals their natural

and human resources to make the United States the richest land on earth." The entire Declaration was published in the summer 1976 issue of *Hera: A Philadelphia Feminist Publication* and later in *Off Our Backs* and elsewhere.

The first target in our threefold protest was Cardinal Krol, Archbishop of the Archdiocese of Philadelphia. Very early in the morning of July 4, we loaded into vans and went to his residence. We formed a circle outside his iron-gated mansion, and one by one each of us voiced our critique of the Church's collusion with the State around homophobia and all other oppressions. When we finished we posted copies of our Declaration on the spikes of the gate and left.

We then scurried off to the second target, the First Presbyterian Church in one of Philadelphia's wealthiest suburbs. As planned, we got there just as church members were arriving. The Church had announced that its Bicentennial sermon would be about "Present Threats to Priceless Freedoms." We queers would be mentioned as one of the threats. DAR performed guerilla theater in front of a gathering crowd. The characters were The Patriarchies, The Church, The State and The Lesbians. While planning the action a week or so before, we all volunteered for roles and I ended up being The State. We all contributed to creating the costumes, the makeup and the scenarios. I remember it was a tremendous amount of fun. After our play we read out the Declaration to the stunned crowd and left.

Next we went to our third target, an outdoor celebration at St. George's Episcopal Church in yet another extremely wealthy suburb of Philadelphia. There we split into three groups, surrounded the church, and walked in unison in slow motion to a central point. At 2 p.m., when the church bells began ringing to commemorate the signing of the Declaration of Independence 200 years before, we began our theater. When finished, we managed to read our Declaration aloud to the crowd before getting swept away by security and eventually the police. No one was arrested. We thought perhaps it was because they would not risk yet another run-in with us before their/our trial.

After these actions, along with the Declaration, DAR also published an article in *Hera* to explain the logic of the targets. It declared: "The suburbs must no longer be a haven for the rich to flee the poverty they have created. The church must no longer be the dictator of human morality, working hand in hand with the State.

The DAR supports the efforts of the July 4th coalition, a coalition of various groups protesting the Bicentennial in Philadelphia, in uniting oppressed people against the state."

After the three July 4th actions we just could not resist protesting the International Eucharistic Congress in early August. Without a permit, a mass demonstration would not be possible. So we decided on three smaller actions. For the first, we placed a book table in front of the Congress's official women's event, with copies of the Declaration for distribution, but also information about nuns' participation in the 1975 International Women's Year Conference held in Mexico and a number of posters with slogans such as "Who cooked the last supper?" and "The Church Condemns Witches in the Middle Ages and Condemns Lesbians Today."

During that first action I remember going inside the women's event, where a discussion was going on, raising my hand, being handed a microphone and asking, "What about lesbians?" The microphone was pulled from my hands, even as I kept repeating into it: "What about lesbians?" Finally, an elderly white woman came to help me retain the mike and also yelled: "Yes, what about the lesbians?" At that point we were both pulled out of the room. Outside, the elderly lesbian said to me: "You're young now, and you identify as a lesbian. Let's see if that will always be so. Only time will tell." I was shocked. I thought she was on my side. I wondered whether the comment was ageist, racist or just an unfortunate result of the battle fatigue experienced by the generations before me.

For our second action, we in DAR protested the public Mass being held to pray for the military by walking through the crowds with poster boards denouncing the Church's collusion with the State in war. One poster read: "Don't Pray for the Military, Pray for Its Victims." Our third action took place at the concluding Mass, hosted by President Ford. For that one, we stood on the sidewalk with posters reading "What happened to separation of Church and State?" in reference to both Ford's presence and the Church's increasing Wall Street investments in Lockheed, Boeing and other military-related stocks. We then issued a press release detailing all the actions and the logic behind them.

As I come to a close here, I would like to open something else up: The politics of representation. I was not elected by DYKETACTICS! to be our mouthpiece in these pages. We never held any elections. We came to full agreement, or to disagreement, through discussion. I spoke then and speak now only for myself. It

is not possible for any one person, least of all myself, to take full account of the myriad elements that constituted our collective lives,
practices and political actions. It is possible, even likely, that given
the heterogeneity of DYKETACTICS! and our allies, and given our
intensities, each one will remember the period somewhat differently. So much happened, and so quickly. We often had divergent
perspectives even then. Indeed, our differences constituted one of
our many strengths. My brief personal recollections here should
not be taken as the definitive word on DYKETACTICS! and our allies. We were much more than I have written. We experienced and
did much more than I alone can recollect.

I would like to note a definite gap between the existence
of DYKETACTICS! and other such political groups, and how the
period has come to be recorded in institutionalized feminist and
LGBTTIQ historiographies. In accounts about feminist and lesbian
analytics and practices of the period there is no trace of the existence of DYKETACTICS! or of our main allies in Philadelphia,
across the United States and elsewhere. In the mid-1970s there
were many political groups of lesbians of color and racially mixed
groups that took a myriad of forms. We in DYKETACTICS! were
directly connected with so many. We met through common struggles, conferences, political actions and music festivals. Today it is
often affirmed that lesbians of color, and issues of race, colonialism, capitalism and war, came later into feminism and LGBTTIQ
politics. This erroneous notion works, unfortunately, to position
some (dominant) subjects as forever in the forefront and (subal-
tern) others as forever in the background. It works to distort our
very struggles. The fact is that we have always existed, within and
prior to DYKETACTICS! We have always demanded not integration into hetero-normative, sexist, racist, class, neocolonial society,
but rather its demolition and the construction of something else.
The silencing of this history has definitely produced effects on subsequent generations.

As I write this, the United States is still an imperial nation at
war. It has tried to bury the spirit of our most radical, vital struggles for change while supporting homo integration. I now live in
a state, California, that is increasingly domesticating its queers. It
recently agreed that "homosexuals" can marry, and unfortunately
this seems to be quite enough for some queers. We need a wider
debate about divide and rule tactics and what it means for queers

to integrate into a profoundly queerphobic, sexist, racist, class and neocolonial nation-state.

We once fought on so many fronts at once. We once united across so many differences to struggle for a more just world. I dream of a new generation of queers of all sizes, shapes, colors, ages and sexual, racialized, class and geopolitical positionalities, who will understand the struggle for queer liberation as inseparable from the struggle against sexism, racism, class oppression, colonialism, war and the destruction of the environment.

Paola Bacchetta is Associate Professor in the Department of Gender and Women's Studies at UC Berkeley. She is the author of Gender in the Hindu Nation, *co-editor of* Right-Wing Women: From Conservatives to Extremists Around the World *and author of numerous journal articles and book chapters on transnational feminist, lesbian, queer, antiracist and postcolonial theories, practices and movements. Since the days of DYKETACTICS!, she has been an activist in pluralist lesbian, feminist, queer and antiracism movements, in the United States, France, India and Italy, and in movements against religious-political conflict in India.*

TWO POEMS

Barbara Ruth

Barbara Ruth continues to be an anarcha-lesbian-feminist with wide-ranging passions. Following the 2000 presidential theft by Bush and subsequent events, those passions include election integrity, the 9/11 Truth Movement, prisoners' rights here and abroad, and indictment of Bush/Cheney et al. As she is severely disabled, most of her activism now takes place from home. For over 20 years, creating disabled women's culture and increasing accessibility have engaged her mind and heart. She is currently the resident poet of Fabled Asp, a San Francisco Bay Area disabled lesbians' storytelling project. She hopes to continue and strengthen her continuing friendship with sister dyketacticians.

WE ARE WIMMIN WHO NAME OURSELVES
(1975)

We are wimmin who name ourselves.
We are wimmin who cut off our hair.
We are seekers of pleasure, tellers of stories,
    Seers of visions.

We are wimmin who bleed into sponges.
We are wimmin who cry out in rage.
We are wimmin who heal each other.
We are wimmin who name ourselves.

We are lovers of wimmin, fighters of battles,
    Avengers of wrong.

We are wimmin who name ourselves.

PIG

(1976)

Revolutionaries,
Vegetarians,
People who should certainly
Know better by now
Still use the word "pig"
When what they mean
Is a terrible human being.
When what they mean
Is warmonger.
When what they mean
Is rapist.

No pig
Ever called me chick
Threatened my life
Invaded another country
Or dropped an atom bomb.

No pig
Ever factory farmed
Another species
Sentencing them to a life of torture
And an agonizing death
Because he craved the taste of meat.

It is important to not only recognize your oppression
But also, to rightfully identify
Your oppressor.
And if you would free yourself
You must free the language
As well.

So don't use the word pig
When what you mean is
Man

The Baltic Street Collective

N. A. Diaman

In the early part of 1971, several of the men in my consciousness-raising group expressed an interest in collective living. However, after I found a house for us they chose a farm in the country instead. At the next Gay Liberation Front meeting I asked for men to join a collective in Brooklyn. Several responded and we met two or three times to discuss plans for the collective. We agreed to pool our money and share all our possessions except our toothbrushes. However, we spent little time getting to know each other before seven of us moved to the Baltic Street house owned by Byrne Fone, a university professor who subsequently published several gay studies books.

The Baltic Street Collective in Brooklyn was one of a half-dozen group living arrangements involving members of New York GLF. David, Don, Joe, Leslie, Peter, Richard and I were five white and two black gay men ranging in age from 18 to 34. David was a medical school dropout who lived in another collective before joining ours. Don was studying to be a social worker. Joe was Richard's partner. Leslie was eager to move away from his mother. Peter considered it cheap rent. Richard was totally engaged in all aspects of political activism and filled with boundless energy. I saw it as an opportunity to put political theory into practice, hoping to find a circle of loving companions in the process.

The Baltic Street house was rather ugly with mostly small, odd-shaped rooms and an unusual floor plan. It included a storefront at street level with boarded-up windows and a drab, windowless back room with a door that opened onto a cement patch outside. The front door was to the right and opened onto a long narrow flight of stairs to the main living quarters above.

The kitchen was the largest room on the middle level, which also included a bathroom with a tub and a toilet, a small space between the kitchen and the cramped living room at the front of the building, and another (even smaller) space off the living room we used as an office.

The top floor included a room near the back large enough to accommodate a double bed, an adjoining room with space for a single bed, and an area with a kitchen sink on one side facing a long pole for hanging clothes and built-in storage units below, the remainder being one large open space with two windows overlooking the street.

We rented a truck to move all our belongings from our various residences in Manhattan to the house in Brooklyn. Once we got everything inside, we took a break. No one was in a rush to unpack. One man undressed and lay down on a mattress. Another followed suit. Those two beckoned for others to do the same. One by one we each undressed and joined the pile of warm bodies. All of us laughed as we playfully rolled around on the mattress.

It was difficult to tell where one body began and another ended. It seemed like a wonderful beginning. The misgivings I had about the collective were forgotten for the moment. That spontaneous event seemed like a very positive omen. It demonstrated our capacity as gay men to come together in a mutually nurturing way. Perhaps I made the right decision after all. But I soon realized there were only six of us on the mattress. Peter was downstairs, oblivious to what was happening and how it developed. I wondered how he would react when he finally appeared. It was important that we all be involved so that none of us would feel left out.

He stood looking at us, his dark hair neatly in place, wearing horn-rimmed glasses, dressed in cut-off jeans. "Join us!" we called out to him. "Come on, Peter!" we urged. His body tightened. "No," he replied angrily, before quickly walking away. Suddenly the magic and intimacy I felt just moments before dissolved. One by one we disentangled from the pile and scattered, somewhat guiltily aware that we had failed to bring together everyone in the group.

The following day, a framed print of a Madonna and child appeared over the living room mantel. It reminded some of the stereotype of women in society and was deemed politically incorrect. Life in the collective was to conform to our belief system. Since the entire house was communal space, we needed to decide as a group what images would hang on the walls. Hoping to avoid a long meeting, we opted for a quick but totally unsatisfying solution. We brought all the art we wanted to display to the living room and held each piece up for a vote. Anything that elicited an objection was immediately put aside. What remained were the most inane images no one felt passionate about.

We all hated house meetings. Decisions were made as quickly as possible just to shorten the agony. Expediency tended to triumph over careful deliberation whenever difficult issues were discussed. Instead of experiencing the benefits and advantages of socialism and other ideals, we willingly succumbed to repressive measures providing easy solutions to difficult problems. We accepted proposed rules with little or no discussion.

As a result, decisions were made by individuals without consulting the group. One day, Richard bought a waterbed and came home with a dog he named Gay. Another day he redeemed the supermarket stamps we collected for an ugly kitchen wall clock.

Since there were seven of us, we each cooked dinner once a week and whoever did the cooking was also responsible for cleaning up. David and I were the best cooks, so the other five meals were generally disappointing. One meal I remember was Joe's initial preparation. He bought sliced ham, a can of pineapple rings, a jar of maraschino cherries and a loaf of white bread. Richard discouraged him from buying white bread again, suggesting whole grain instead.

We often had dinner guests and enjoyed socializing with whoever dropped by to visit. I didn't wear clothes in the house even if we had visitors. Other members of our household might be scantily dressed or entirely naked when it was warm, but I invariably sat down to eat dinner nude even when everyone else was fully clothed.

Openness was equated with freedom, the elimination of shame. Whatever we did with our bodies was natural and need not be hidden. Someone even suggested removing the bathroom door, but that never happened. We initially planned to tear down the remaining walls upstairs so that we would all sleep in one large open space but, within weeks, we each put up a tent to ensure some privacy.

I built a substantial structure in one corner of the upstairs space that incorporated a window overlooking the street so I had both natural light and a view of sorts. I constructed a redwood frame and hung maroon canvas walls on four sides and a tie-dyed sheet as a canopy above. A hanging lantern provided light and a shelf along the side of my mattress allowed me space to keep a few things such as my glasses, wallet, keys, tissues and lube. During the day I could either raise the canvas walls or tie them to the corner posts. It was cozy and aesthetically pleasing.

However, I could keep out neither the noise nor the light from my tent, so I was awakened by others coming or going while I tried to sleep. Even worse was the smell of smoke that penetrated my space early each morning as Peter lit his first cigarette of the day. I was nauseated by the smell. My only defense was pulling the covers over my head, but that seldom worked.

I shopped carefully and took good care of the clothes I had. Sharing my wardrobe didn't come easy, but I hung what I brought with me on the collective clothes rack initially. I knew that Joe, David and I all wore size small shirts and jackets; Peter, Richard and Don, size medium; and Leslie, large. I imagined I'd be sharing clothes only with Joe and David. But I soon discovered that knit shirts I contributed were stretched out and hung loosely around my torso. If that continued, there would only be medium and large shirts left.

Richard was fond of wearing skin-tight shirts to show off his muscular body. When I complained at a house meeting, he accused me of being into clothes. While it was true, that observation could apply to him as well. I got permission to de-collectivize a few of my shirts to prevent them from being resized.

A small window behind the sink in the dressing area looked into an airshaft, and another window looked into a house around the corner. Both windows were about chest height. The neighbors wasted no time complaining about the view of our naked torsos. They made loud remarks if one of us passed in front of the window. It seemed ridiculous since no one was forcing them to look at us. I ignored them, but others who were annoyed by the macho straights told them to shut up and mind their own business.

Some of the houses in the neighborhood had flags flying on Memorial Day. Richard hung a yard of blue cotton fabric with a Japanese print from the living room window. We went for a walk with the dog in early afternoon. When one neighbor asked, "What kind of fairy flag is that?" we just smiled and continued walking. Obviously they got the message. We were not supporting the mindless patriotism of war deaths, but calling to question traditional stereotypes of manhood.

Sex was a difficult issue within the collective. Richard and Joe had a different dynamic as a couple sharing intimacy while the two of them were together. The rest of us were single and on our own. I felt an emotional lack that compelled me to seek sexual satisfaction outside the house. I was sexually attracted to one of the other men in the collective and felt close to another but neither relationship developed. Cruising for sex eventually became a nightly routine for me.

I tried the local cruising spots, with little success. A few times I explored the potential of a park near downtown Brooklyn. I didn't meet anyone there. I did much better on the Promenade in Brooklyn Heights and liked the wonderful view of Manhattan across the river. I even walked along Prospect Park two or three times but didn't see much there. One night, I noticed a man across the street struggling to free himself from two men. I wondered what I could do to help him, but his assailants warned me to stay away and I wasn't willing to expose myself to danger. I wasn't sure if they were armed with knives or guns. I bought a whistle so I could at least make enough noise to scare away muggers or mobilize assistance in the future, but fortunately I never had to use it.

Walking along Christopher Street at night was enjoyable because I frequently ran into people I knew. I stopped to talk or sat on a stoop with friends. Some of the men were on their way to or coming from the trucks parked along the waterfront (where men had sex), but that scene seemed too scary for me. The best venue for me was Central Park West, where I cruised nightly. My dark beard and long hair were definitely assets during the early '70s. If I didn't meet anyone I left after an hour and a half of cruising.

One night I met an attractive husky man on Central Park West. He said he had worked that day for the phone company, which I knew was on strike, but I didn't question him. Riding back to Brooklyn on the subway I thought about my reluctance to have sex with men bigger than me because I feared being overwhelmed by them. It seemed an unnecessary concern. However, when we arrived back at the house, he told me, "I was going to rob you but you're such a nice guy. I just need 12 dollars to get to Boston."

I had ignored all the warning signs and ended up in a potentially dangerous situation. More than likely there were other collective members asleep upstairs, but I didn't want to endanger them as well. I remained calm. My primary objective was to see to it that he left the house with the minimum of damage. I told him I had to go upstairs to get the money, but he didn't trust me and followed close behind. When I opened the drawer where the collective funds were kept he demanded all the cash, a few dollars more than the 12 he requested earlier.

"Are you still interested in having sex?" he asked once we were back in the living room.

"No," I said, hiding my anger.

He warned me not to call the police when I unlocked the front door to let him out.

I went to bed without waking anyone. When I recounted what occurred in the morning, one or two of the others in the collective thought I should have called for help, but I was convinced I did the right thing.

Don was the first member to leave the Brooklyn Collective. He wisely kept secret a bank account containing sufficient funds for a trip to Europe and pursued a long career as a social worker. David was the second man to leave, returning to medical school to complete his degree before starting his residency in the field of psychiatry. Bruce joined the collective briefly, and Marc came later. Richard's new boyfriend Ron was an unofficial collective member, as was Ernest, another one of his boyfriends.

Joe sought solace in the music of his favorite singer, Diana Ross, after he and Richard broke up. He moved down to the room behind the storefront containing the waterbed that seemed too heavy, once the mattress was filled with water, to be safely installed upstairs.

I originally envisioned a collective dedicated to gay male peer counseling. It would include a 24-hour help line and opportunities for one-on-one and group peer counseling sessions. Fortunately no effort was put into making that a reality. Certainly the day-to-day situations we faced among ourselves were more than enough to deal with. If we took on the mental and emotional health of gay men in New York we would have been overwhelmed by the difficulties such an ambitious mission entailed.

Lacking a clear internal focus, some members of the collective proposed we start a coffeehouse in the storefront to provide gay men in Brooklyn with an alternative to the bars. I was indifferent to the project but was outnumbered.

Richard knew the owner of an electronics company who was willing to donate funds for the project and managed to collect chairs and tables from the landlord. I designed a leaflet to pass out to men cruising the Promenade. We were open two nights a week, I believe Sundays and Wednesdays. Several men from GLF came from Manhattan on a regular basis, but less than a handful from Brooklyn ventured to visit the place. I was glad when one of them ventured upstairs, because I didn't like going down to the storefront myself. But since we were the coffeehouse hosts, we were each obligated to spend time there.

Vito Russo inaugurated a weekly gay-themed film series at the Gay Activists Alliance firehouse in Soho. Richard arranged to borrow the films from Vito before they were returned to the distributors and each of them was shown again free of charge in our storefront during the Sunday coffeehouse nights.

I cofounded a gay video production group while I was living on Baltic Street. Ray, another cofounder, renamed it Queer Blue Light some months later. One of our first projects involved the Cockettes, who brought their show to New York in November. I called Link Cupp at the Chelsea Hotel to ask if we could videotape them there, and Ray, Jon and I spent an afternoon with Link, Scrumbly, Pam and her baby son, Ocean Moon. We got stoned and documented the improv routines, casual conversation and laughter before their disastrous New York premiere.

Several of us from the collective drove to Madison to celebrate Gay Thanksgiving. Most of those who attended were from either the East Coast or the Midwest. I had a vegetarian Thanksgiving on a farm. We stopped in Chicago on the way back to New York and stayed with a collective in Hyde Park.

I volunteered to cook a quiche for everyone and went to a nearby supermarket to shop, accompanied by Marc, the youngest collective member, and Deshawn, another man who was staying there. While the three of us were shopping I noticed Deshawn slip a small jar of pickled herring into his coat pocket but didn't say anything. I paid for everything in the shopping cart and was about to walk out of the store when the manager asked Deshawn what he had in his pocket.

"Oh, I forgot this," Deshawn said, offering to pay for the jar he pulled out.

But the manager was not about to let him get away with that. Instead, he ordered the three of us to the office upstairs and held us at gunpoint until the police arrived. The two officers who came didn't want to arrest the three of us, but the manager insisted. He wanted to make an example of us: Deshawn, a black man; me, a longhaired hippie; and Marc, a young juvenile.

We spent nearly 24 hours in jail, because if we were bailed out we would have had to return to Chicago at a later date. In the morning a police wagon transferred us to the holding cell of a juvenile court because Marc was a minor. We waited our turn among young men charged with murder, armed robbery and other serious crimes. They were amused to learn I was there for disorderly conduct. The charges against me were dropped after I told the judge I was coordinator of QBL Video. I cooked the quiche before we left Chicago later that day.

Valerie Solanas was brought to the house one morning after being released from prison at the completion of her sentence for the attempted murder of Andy Warhol. As she sat at our kitchen table I realized I saw her years earlier at Lefty O'Doul's in San Francisco where I sometimes ate lunch when I was working at Brentano's Books. She was thin, dark-haired and androgynous when I first noticed her. I wasn't quite sure if she was male or female then. In Brooklyn she seemed quite sane and nonthreatening despite having written the *S.C.U.M. Manifesto* and shooting Warhol. Richard suggested calling one of the lesbians we knew from GLF to provide a place for her to stay rather than agreeing to take her in. It was certainly a wise decision.

The Baltic Street Collective lasted about six months, but I remained in the house until the end of our one-year lease. We received notice the house was for sale and the lease would not be renewed, so I began looking for another place to live. Everyone else moved out, and I shared the Baltic Street house during the final month with Ray and Jon before moving to another place.

Despite the chaos and inconsistencies of the collective experience and the emotional discomfort I felt much of my time there, ultimately it provided excellent preparation for the future. I learned how easy it was to say and do things that fell far short of what I envisioned. All of us who joined the collective had good intentions, but none of us was perfect. I'm more aware of the pitfalls of group ventures and wary of situations demanding unquestioning loyalty and conformity. I remain an idealist committed to issues of social justice, as concerned with the means utilized as I am the goals proposed.

N. A. Diaman is the author of eight books published by Persona Press. His two newest titles are Following My Heart, *a memoir, and* The City, *his seventh novel. For more information go to www.nikosdiaman.com.*

Gay Pagans and Atheists Manifesto

Originally published in Gay Community News *January 10, 1976, it was written a year or two before that by Gay Pagans and Atheists, a Philadelphia group that believed that liberation for queers would only come with the abolition of religion.*
—Tommi Avicolli Mecca

The recently passed California bill legalizing gay sex has, of course, come under attack by fundamentalists organizing to oppose the bill in a referendum, next year. It seems likely they will at least succeed in getting the signatures they need to promote such an action. In other states, other cities, everywhere, wherever gay rights or anti-sodomy statutes have risen, so have the crazies—the religious fanatics with their bibles, self-righteousness and their tales of impending doom. It's all so confusing to me that in the midst of this, gay church people are still urging us to cling to Christianity. But to give them the benefit of the doubt, let me examine briefly the HIStory of the Christian church!

The Jewish nomads settled in the promised land, a land rife with patriarchy and father-right. Whatever remained of the former matriarchies had been washed away by the onslaught of the male deities Zeus, Jehova and Rama. Some matriarchal influence remained in the pagan cults which the Jews protected themselves from through such ordinances as the ban on homosexuality, on idolatry, etc., attempts to purge themselves from their neighbor's lifestyles.

The Jews were a small people, yet Christianity was born out of their patriarchal roots. Jesus, who we're not even sure existed (read *The Pagan Christ*), established a new order. His was to be a church of love, yet his teachings speak only of "brotherhood" and of men, not of women. His only dealings with women seem to be the forgiving of a prostitute. What did he do with her afterwards? Was it for his own "convenience" that he forgave her?

Christianity was strongly misogynistic from the start. St. Paul denies the right of women to teach; he further asserts that Adam was innocent of the first sin. Writings of the early church fathers also try and deny maternity, but in theological terms, of course! Corinthians 11:8–9 said, "The man is not of the woman, but the woman is of the man." It's not much different than the attempt in Genesis to deny maternity by depicting Eve's creation from Adam's rib. Clement in the second century AD said: "Every woman should be overwhelmed with shame at the thought that she is a woman" (Elizabeth Gould Davis, *The First Sex*, p. 231). Thus echoing an earlier Jewish prayer and completing a full circle.

Later, Christians sought out the witches, females who revived earlier totemic practices, and together with the faggots, burned them on the altars of male supremacy. A woman could be persecuted for the most obvious "crimes": lesbianism, refusal to have sex with a priest, and/or even striking back a husband who had just beaten her. Heresy was a catch-all charge, loaded and convenient for the medieval patriarchs to use against any attempt on the part of women or faggots to break the chains of their oppression.

Modern Christians try to whitewash this tradition, apologizing for Paul and Clement, for the persecutions of the 9 million women and countless faggots! Even the gay church apologists strive to make right the wrong of Christianity.

Christianity is based upon the belief that men are superior to women; witness Genesis. Witness the absence of any strong female deity. Mary is an impotent fertility figure probably robbed from the Egyptians. The main deities of the Christian faith are male. The basic creation myth of the Christians concerns a male god creating life, an impossible situation since only women biologically can give birth. Christianity is a good psychological study of *womb envy* on the part of the male sex, the envy to procreate.

Christianity punishes women for the first sin. Eve is told to bear children in pain as punishment and to be subservient to her husband. In medieval times, women were denied use of the painkiller belladonna during childbirth, because the church felt it was against God's will. After all, they said, women were meant to suffer in childbirth.

Christianity clearly declares gay love sick. The bible cannot be changed. Nowhere does it give us the freedom to love. All those vague passages about everything are of no use to any free-thinking gay person.

244

From a Gay Pagans & Atheists demonstration at St. Patrick's Cathedral in New York City, about 1974

© Gabriel Imhof

Christianity is a bigoted way of life. It segregates one person from others of different faiths, declaring them heretics and sinners; it promotes prejudice and male supremacy. In other times, Christians waged holy wars against pagans and murdered millions of us. Today, it wages these same wars in other ways, through political manipulations and economic control. Witness the defeat of (New York's) Intro 554 (a gay rights measure) at the hands of the Catholic church.

It has never been accurately determined how much wealth the Vatican has. Millions (if not all) of the poor could be fed on what the Catholic church owns. Yet the Pope chooses to live like an aristocrat and to appease the poor with phony encyclicals and ridiculous pomp and circumstance.

The poor have been deluded by centuries of queer-baiting and sex role reenforcement done at the expense of their freedom to love and to be adequately fed and housed. The church helped the feudal lords oppress the masses, helped capitalism, and did nothing to stop Hitler in the '30s. The silence of the church during times of oppression only reenforces my own concept of it as concerned with its own continued patriarchal existence.

Christianity has most of all created a network of cooptation that can incorporate any current trend back into itself. A few years ago the church complained of dwindling members; now recently it's rejoicing at its growing numbers. A clever propaganda campaign? Probably not. Economic recession sends people back to their security blankets, and Christianity is an easy crutch to lean on.

Christianity can even absorb gay liberation. It can pretend to be accepting and loving to us while all the time greedy to snatch our cooperation. What will the church of the future be like? Will gays be worshipping a male deity, marrying and establishing nuclear family units (2.8 adopted kids) and supporting holy wars in new Vietnams? Will we be feeding the new popes and patriarchs? NO!

Christianity has attempted to coopt feminism by setting up a token commission to study the status of women and in some churches by ordaining women. Yet if it were truly feminist, it would burn the cathedrals and feed the poor, abolish male deities, obliterate the nuclear family and allow us to love and live in total freedom. I don't understand why gays find it necessary to apologize for their homosexuality by asserting that God loves them, too. The Christian's patriarchal God doesn't love dykes and faggots and queens. He's all of our fathers, the strict disciplinarians who for years told us to be women and men in the finest tradition of the sex-role system. Little ladies and gentlemen, pooh!

We are queers in the eyes of this male god. We are perverted. But we shouldn't be ashamed of this fact. We should realize that in this fact we are most free. Free to challenge the millions of years of oppression and persecution against gays and women for their violation of a sexist and male supremacist theology, a theology based upon the twisted logic of man creating life through *womb envy*. Man has never created life; his HIStory is one of wars, violence and persecution.

This male god is my enemy. I do not ask any acceptance from him. I rejoice in my queerness. He is not my god, nor my savior. I await his destruction as I await the destruction of all homophobes.

There is no salvation in Christianity: only a continuation of our oppression as queers and as women. As free entities. As androgynes. As pagans and atheists. As goddess worshippers. As earth lovers, as matriarchy seekers. The goddess lives. Paganism now!

1972 Gay Pride march in Philadelphia.

40 YEARS AFTER
STONEWALL

Looking Back from the Mexico-U.S. Border

Roberto Camp

The 1970 Revolutionary People's Constitutional Convention in Philadelphia was a lost opportunity to coalesce GLF energies with the Black Panthers and the Young Lords, and move forward to a Rainbow Coalition long before that terminology was coined.

That gathering of 15,000 multicultural people, organized by the Black Panthers and held at Temple University in North Philadelphia, a traditional poor and working-class Black neighborhood, marked the first time that Gay men and Lesbians were openly recognized by the Black community. The event was filled with the awe-inspiring presence of Panther leaders Huey P. Newton and Bobby Seale, and boxing legend Muhammad Ali, strutting up the street leading a contingent of young Blacks from Philly and waxing social justice in poetic form.

To this day I wonder what might have been if Gays had fostered and nurtured that sense of comradeship that the Black Panthers and Young Lords (a Puerto Rican organization) offered us, instead of moving in diverse directions and compartmentalizing ourselves into ghetto communities and pushing our own agendas.

From that time on, GLF wandered into the propagation of issues that separated us from the Black and Hispanic communities and included strong stances that ran counter to the values of those communities, such as attacks on monogamy, the family unit and religion.

On a brighter side, that original Black Panther and Young Lords outreach stimulated a broader mosaic of Gay and Lesbian Blacks, Hispanics, Asians, Arabs and other peoples who banded together to assert their rights from coast to coast and around the globe in Third World communities.

My own contemporary reference points are mainly with Hispanic milestones: Thanks to President José Luis Rodríguez Zapatero of Spain, Gay marriage is now an integral part of that country's legal code. In 2006, Sevilla Mayor Alfredo Sánchez Monteserín made history by marrying two male soldiers.

Marcelo Ebrard, Governor of the Federal District of Mexico, formulated and enacted the 2006 initiation of civil unions in that vast metropolitan area, and in 2007, President Tabaré Vásquez of Uruguay carried out a similar proclamation.

There is an active Gay Pride organization in Yucatán, where I was presented as a GLF veteran in Mérida's 2006 Gay Pride March.

On June 29, 2008, I joined 1,500 others in a vibrant *Orgullo* (pride) Gay march in my hometown, Ciudad Juárez, Chihuahua, where we marched on the main street of 16 de Septiembre, a revered symbol of Mexican Independence.

We moved past applauding neighbors on the corner of the street where I live, which itself was a border crossing area for goods and munitions for Pancho Villa during the Mexican Revolution.

Buenos Aires is another bright spot in contemporary Gay Liberation. During the '70s and '80s, that city was the scene of horrendous repression, torture and assassination of mass numbers of political activists, who like GLF members, were outgrowths of the liberation movements of the '60s.

Politically and culturally, Buenos Aires is now a fulcrum of New Millennium social, political and economic advancement, and the city where one of GLF's founders, Néstor Latrónico, has been a proactive component of that progress.

During 2008, Cuba has been at the front of Gay Liberation, thanks in large part to the feisty and influential efforts of Mariela Castro, who in reflection of the revolutionary fervor of her mother Vilma Espín and father Raúl Castro, and that of her uncle Fidel, has been a tireless supporter of Gay and Lesbian rights as director of CENESEX, that country's National Center for Sex Education.

Forty years after Stonewall and GLF, the Web continues to carry off base attacks on the supposed chauvinism and anti-Gay attitudes of the Black Panthers.

Very little is found on the positive vibes of the Young Lords with the NYC Gay and Lesbian communities, nor, for that matter, on the dramatic openness of Puerto Ricans in general to our community.

Time-warped Old Fart déjà vu criticism of 1970 Cuba continues to dominate Gay and straight media, which overlooks the fact that Cuba has approved sex change benefits as part of its public health system, and is openly discussing gay marriage.

But much worse than that, very little is found to reinforce

the fact that it was precisely Third World trannies like Sylvia Rivera, Marsha Johnson and Nova, and not upper-middle-class White Boys, but working class Whites like Bob Kohler, and benchmark Lesbian journalists like Lois Hart and Marsha Shelley, who had the *cojones* to take on New York and the world to forge contemporary Gay and Lesbian Liberation.

Hopefully, this anthology will help bring attention to some of these issues.

Roberto Camp of Ciudad Juárez, Chihuahua, Mexico, is a binational and bicultural business journalist. He was a 1969–71 member of NYC GLF and the Come-Out! Collective.

A Letter from Huey Newton to the Revolutionary Brothers and Sisters about the Women's Liberation and Gay Liberation Movements, 1970

During the past few years, strong movements have developed among women and among homosexuals seeking their liberation. There has been some uncertainty about how to relate to these movements.

Whatever your personal opinions and your insecurities about homosexuality and the various liberation movements among homosexuals and women (and I speak of the homosexuals and women as oppressed groups), we should try to unite with them in a revolutionary fashion. I say " whatever your insecurities are" because as we very well know, sometimes our first instinct is to want to hit a homosexual in the mouth, and want a woman to be quiet. We want to hit a homosexual in the mouth because we are afraid that we might be homosexual; and we want to hit the woman or shut her up because we are afraid that she might castrate us, or take the nuts that we might not have to start with.

We must gain security in ourselves and therefore have respect and feelings for all oppressed people. We must not use the racist attitude that the White racists use against our people because they are Black and poor. Many times the poorest White person is the most racist because he is afraid that he might lose something, or discover something that he does not have. So you're some kind of a threat to him. This kind of psychology is in operation when we view oppressed people and we are angry with them because of their particular kind of behavior, or their particular kind of deviation from the established norm.

Remember, we have not established a revolutionary value system; we are only in the process of establishing it. I do not remember our ever constituting any value that said that a revolutionary must say offensive things towards homosexuals, or that a revolutionary should make sure that women do not speak out about their own particular kind of oppression. As a matter of fact, it is just the opposite: we say that we recognize the women's right to be free. We have not said much about the homosexual at all, but we must relate to the homosexual movement because it is a real thing. And I know through reading, and through my life experience and observations that homosexuals are not given freedom and liberty by anyone in the society. They might be the most opprosed people in the society.

And what made them homosexual? Perhaps it's a phenomenon that I don't understand entirely. Some people say that it is the decadence of capitalism. I don't know if that is the case; I rather doubt it. But whatever the case is, we know that homosexuality is a fact that exists, and we must understand it in its purest form: that is, a person should have the freedom to use his body in whatever way he wants.

That is not endorsing things in homosexuality that we wouldn't view as revolutionary. But there is nothing to say that a homosexual cannot also be a revolutionary. And maybe I'm now injecting some of my prejudice by saying that "even a homosexual can be a revolutionary." Quite the contrary, maybe a homosexual could be the most revolutionary.

When we have revolutionary conferences, rallies, and demonstrations, there should be full participation of the gay liberation movement and the women's liberation movement. Some groups might be more revolutionary than others. We should not use the actions of a few to say that they are all reactionary or counter-revolutionary, because they are not.

We should deal with the factions just as we deal with any other group or party that claims to be revolutionary. We should try to judge, somehow, whether they are operating in a sincere revolutionary fashion and from a really oppressed situation. (And we will grant that if they are women they are probably oppressed.) If they do things that are unrevolutionary or counterrevolutionary, then criticize that action. If we feel that the group in spirit means to be revolutionary in practice, but they make mistakes in interpretation of the revolutionary philosophy, or they do not understand the dialectics of the social forces in operation, we should criticize that and not criticize them because they are women trying to be free. And the same is true for homosexuals. We should never say a whole movement is dishonest when in fact they are trying to be honest. They are just making honest mistakes. Friends are allowed to make mistakes. The enemy is not allowed to make mistakes because his whole existence is a mistake, and we suffer from it. But the women's liberation front and gay liberation front are our friends, they are our potential allies, and we need as many allies as possible.

We should be willing to discuss the insecurities that many people have about homosexuality. When I say "insecurities," I mean the fear that they are some kind of threat to our manhood. I can understand this fear. Because of the long conditioning process which builds insecurity in the American male, homosexuality might produce certain hang-ups in us. I have hang-ups myself about male homosexuality. But on the other hand, I have no hang-up about female homosexuality. And that is a phenomenon in itself. I think it is probably because male homosexuality is a threat to me and female homosexuality is not.

We should be careful about using those terms that might turn our friends off. The terms "faggot" and "punk" should be deleted from our vocabulary, and especially we should not attach names normally designed for homosexuals to men who are enemies of the people, such as Nixon or Mitchell. Homosexuals are not enemies of the people.

We should try to form a working coalition with the gay liberation and women's liberation groups. We must always handle social forces in the most appropriate manner and this is really a significant part of the population—both women and the growing number of homosexuals that we have to deal with.

All power to the people!

Huey P. Newton
Leader/Chief Theoretician for The Black Panther Party

"A Letter from Huey Newton to the Revolutionary Brothers and Sisters about the Women's Liberation and Gay Liberation Movements," from *To Die For the People* (City Lights, 2009), reprinted by perission of the Huey Newton Fondation.

Making History

Sidney Brinkley

This article was originally published in Blacklight, *vol. 4, #4, in 1983. The first issue of* Blacklight *was published in Washington, D.C., in August 1979 under founding editor Sidney Brinkley. It was the first black gay publication in the nation's capital.* Blacklight *published from 1979 to 1986. In those years it chronicled the birth of the black gay political movement and witnessed the havoc that was the dawn of AIDS.*

The 1970s were exciting years for the Gay movement. In the decade following the 1969 Stonewall riot, Lesbians and Gay men were organizing in increasing numbers, demanding freedom and equal rights, culminating in the first national Gay March on Washington in October 1979. For much of that time the public face of the Gay movement was White. Whites comprised the overwhelming majority in the political and activist organizations of the day. "Gay" was synonymous with "White" and White Gays became the de facto spokespersons for Lesbians and Gay men of all colors.

However, in the background a number of African American Gay men and Lesbians across the country (as well as Gays of other colors) were also coming out in the midst of this politically charged atmosphere, blending the new Gay political thought with their Black identity, forging a unique Black Gay consciousness. Washington, D.C., for all the obvious reasons, was becoming increasingly important as the legal battle for Gay rights gathered momentum. Billy Jones was keenly interested in the Gay/Lesbian civil rights movement and felt he couldn't be the only Black Gay who had an interest, but the groups were predominantly White.

"At the time very few African Americans were affiliated with Gay political groups," he said, "and I wanted to bring together Gay, Bi, Lesbian and Transpersons who had a strong desire to become politically involved in the Gay/Lesbian civil rights movement. It was an attempt to go beyond the agenda of the Black Gay Social

Clubs of the day and address the issue of homophobia in Black communities and organizations."

Mr. Jones began by placing ads in the D.C. Gay papers. Meanwhile, in Baltimore, Maryland, Louis Hughes had been involved with a group named the Baltimore Gay Alliance since 1975. In 1977 he saw an ad that Jones had placed in the Washington *Blade* and invited him to come to Baltimore to speak about Black Gays.

"Billy lit the fuse for organizing," Mr. Hughes said. "From 1977 going into 1978 I remember Billy going around lighting fires, saying we should have a Black Gay organization. Delores Berry came out at that time. And we began organizing the DC/Baltimore Coalition."

In April of 1978 Mr. Jones—who lived with his wife and three children in Columbia, Maryland—held the early meetings of the Baltimore-Washington Coalition in the basement of the Washington, D.C., Youth Service Agency he worked for at the time.

"About six months after the Coalition was formed, there was an agreement to split the organization into two groups," Mr. Jones said. "We formed the Baltimore Coalition of Black Gay Men and Women and the D.C. Coalition of Black Gay Men and Women."

In 1978 Gil Gerald was a frustrated would-be Gay political activist. Excited by what was going on around him in the city, and wanting to be a part of it, he was put off by a predominantly White movement—in a city with a majority Black population.

"In early 1978 D.C. was going through the process of determining who was going to succeed Walter Washington as Mayor," Mr. Gerald says. "From the sidelines, I read in the newspapers how Marion Barry was getting the support of the Gay community. However, the way I read it 'Gay' really meant 'White Gay.' It really was code for a community that I did not feel included in. The visible organizations were mostly White and I knew they didn't represent the broader Gay community in D.C. Then I saw an announcement in 'Out' that spoke of the meeting of a new group called the D.C. Coalition. I went to the meeting and saw Billy Jones, who seemed to be chief organizer. I saw him as a charismatic individual, even romantic in the radical sixties mode."

In a few short months there was a core group who would eventually serve as officers at various times. In addition to Mr. Jones and Mr. Gerald—who would become the first male executive director—the group included Darlene Garner, Louis Hughes,

Renee McCoy, Jon Gee and Delores Berry. (Garner, McCoy and Berry would eventually become ordained ministers in the Metropolitan Community Church.) "We soon realized that we had [the potential] for a national, rather than a regional, organization in place." Mr. Jones said. "We became the National Coalition of Black Gays (NCBG)."

However, Mr. Gerald, who says he has a "bias for structure and process," had his concerns about the expanding organization. "I was excited by the growth but privately concerned that organizational skills or experience were not always prevalent in the group," he said. Years later, his concern would prove well founded. But at the moment, NCBG's emergence on the scene as a voice for Black Gays was perfectly timed, and in 1979, during events leading up to and following the March on Washington, they would get the opportunity to test their growing clout.

In the weeks leading up to the March a horde of GLBT activists descended upon the city to help set up logistics. Nothing like this had ever been attempted and NCBG made its presence known.

"We made sure the organizers of the March on Washington took into account racial balance," Louis Hughes said. "This was not going to be a White Gay event. There were mandates to have space for Third World Gays in D.C."

That stand led to an accomplishment that all the founding members say was one of the high points in the life of the organization: The first National Conference of Third World Lesbians and Gays. Asian, Native American, Latino/a and Black Lesbians and Gays gathered at the Harambee House—a new Black-owned hotel adjacent to Howard University—for two days of workshops, entertainment and networking. Audre Lorde delivered the keynote address, and on the day of the Gay March, GLBTs of color marched down Georgia Avenue, which runs through the heart of the Black community, to join the main March to the Mall.

"That was a thrill to see Third World Gays get together in 1979 and see the spin-off groups," Mr. Hughes said. "An Asian group formed; an Hispanic group formed; everybody went back and formed groups with a new spirit that we had a Third World bond and our own agenda that was not under White Gay male authority. It was like planting a seed and watching rain forests grow everywhere." However, it was an event that happened shortly after the March that would display the new clout and independence of the group. The National Gay Task Force Task (now NGLTF) parlayed the March on Washington into a meeting with White House officials to discuss Gay Rights but didn't invite NCBG.

"I was angry at the National Gay Task Force," Mr. Jones said, "And at the time I was young enough, and naïve enough, to believe that one could just pick up a pen, write a letter and ask for a meeting, and that's what I did. I wrote a few letters, made a few calls, and finally got an invitation to meet with White House officials. My guess is that our presence and leadership at the March on Washington and the Third World Conference gave us some credibility; it certainly gave us media coverage, that we otherwise did not have."

Mr. Jones says NCBG was careful not to repeat the mistake of the Task Force and actively sought to include other Gays of color in the meeting. "NCBG was the only non-White national organization at the time, but we had done an extensive and successful outreach to other organizations, communities and persons of color. So it was not hard to expand our network."

To Mr. Jones that meeting 25 years ago stands out as a particularly proud moment.

"I wore a white suit to go to the White House and meet with the White folks! Perhaps this doesn't sound like much now, but to the founders, all of whom were in that room, it was a high point of our activism."

The following year, in October 1980, NCBG met in Philadelphia to formally incorporate a national organization out of a growing but still "loose affiliation" of groups in seven cities.

"The coming about of NCBG was to establish a national presence of Black Lesbian/Gay leadership and to assure that Black voices were heard when Lesbian/Gay civil rights issues were addressed," Mr. Jones said.

Official chapters were in Philadelphia; New York City; Norfolk, VA; Minneapolis; New Orleans; Atlanta; Chicago; Portland; St. Louis; San Francisco; and Boston. In 1984 NCBG changed its name to the National Coalition of Black Lesbians and Gays (NCBLG). But behind the scenes there were problems. Despite the enthusiasm of the early years the organizers were discovering that managing a national organization, maintaining membership and recruiting new leadership was no easy task. And Gil Gerald's early concerns about organizational skills would become reality.

"We had great visions for solving some of the problems of

the world. Ending every form of oppression you can think of and networking with local groups all over the nation," Mr. Jones said. "But for the most part, we lacked the know-how and skills to generate the resources needed to sustain the organization. And while mainstream White Gay and Lesbian organizations wanted our involvement, few offered support in what we needed most: Fund development and organizational development."

Mr. Jones also faults the group's failed efforts to find new leadership as a key factor in the stalling of NCBLG—a situation he says had more to do with the times than NCBLG's ability to groom new leadership.

"In the era in which NCBG/NCBLG operated, it was difficult to find any person who would be willing to head up a Black Gay/Lesbian civil rights organization," Mr. Jones said. "This was a period when it was still risky in terms of one's employment, family relationships and community presence to be 'out' and 'vocal' about Gay rights."

As a result Mr. Jones says NCBLG had to rely on the same small pool of people who were worked to the point of burnout with little or no remuneration.

"NCBLG never had a strong funding base. We burned out our leaders by poorly paying, and sometimes not paying them at all. We expected them to do the impossible with little or nothing. Gil Gerald did the best job of bringing money in from foundations, grants and contracts but our attempts to sustain ourselves through chapter and individual membership fees were failures."

The organization limped along and by the time NCBLG reached its 10th year, on its face it looked to be a strong organization. The board of directors included a number of high profile, experienced activists including Audre Lorde, Carl Bean, Barbara Smith and Joseph Beam. It listed a string of chapters that stretched coast to coast and said organizing efforts were under way in 14 new cities. But behind the façade was an organization in disarray. Gil Gerald left the organization in 1986. Then, on the heels of the 10th anniversary celebration, executive director Renee McCoy announced she was resigning her position and returning to her native Detroit. According to Mr. Jones, the remaining board members were in deep denial about the continued viability of the organization.

"When Renee McCoy left NCBLG as executive director and returned to Detroit we should have closed the organization then," he said. "Some board members just refused to acknowledge that it was time to say good-bye. Instead the board stayed in place, with no executive director, and tried to continue to function with Angela Bowen of Boston as board chair."

The organization hobbled along in that state for a short while till, in stark contrast to the excitement and explosive energy that accompanied its founding and early development . . . NCBLG just ceased to exist.

"There was never an announcement that informed folks that NCBLG had officially closed its doors," Mr. Jones says. "We just faded away. Some board members refused to acknowledge that it was time to say good-bye, but folks just burned out and faded away."

Presently there are no national Black Lesbian and Gay groups in the manner of NCBLG. The Black Gay and Lesbian Leadership Forum (BGLLF), which emerged on the national scene in 1987, shut its doors last year. Occasionally one hears talk of some group or other, on one coast or the other, talking about starting "a new national organization," as if it were as easily done as said. But national organizations require a tremendous amount of effort and money to start, run and maintain, and so far it's come to nothing more than wishful thinking.

But, funding aside, Jones feels the Black GLBT organizations of the future won't have to face one major impediment that plagued NCBLG, a lack of suitable candidates for leadership roles.

"Because there have been organizations like NCBLG and BGLLF, because of the expanded agendas of local Black Lesbian and Gay organizations, because of the presence of more Blacks in mainstream GLBT organizations, because there are more support systems for Lesbian and Gay youth as well as adults, identifying Black Lesbian and Gay leadership is much easier than it was in 1978."

He had one final piece of advice for all the leaders to come: Take time to learn from the mistakes of those who did it all before you.

"I would hope, at some point, the new leadership will convene a meeting with the founders of NCBLG for a 'lessons learned' retreat," he said. "I think they could learn something from their now grey-headed elders."

Sidney Brinkley is the founding editor of Blacklight, *the first black gay publication in Washington, D.C., published from 1979 through 1986. It chronicled the social, cultural and political life of black lesbians and gay men. The* Blacklight *archive is online at www.blacklightonline.com/archive.html*

Marsha P. Johnson: New York City Legend

Tommi Avicolli Mecca

Marsha P. Johnson, cofounder with Sylvia Rivera of Street Transvestite Action Revolutionaries (STAR) and the STAR house for homeless street queens, is a New York City legend for her giving spirit and strong sense of self.

She was there at the Stonewall Inn on the night of the infamous riot that kicked off the gay liberation movement. According to one account, she threw the first shoe that triggered the violence.

Transgender Warhol superstar Holly Woodlawn, in an interview in September 2008 in *Metro Weekly*, recalled that night in late June 1969 when she first ran into Marsha. "'I was walking toward Sheridan Square where the Stonewall Inn was, and I saw all these people,' said Woodlawn. 'There was this black queen, Miss Marsha, and she was running around screaming and yelling. I said, 'What the hell is going on?' And she said, 'Oh, the girls, they got the cops in there!'"

Marsha became a champion for "the girls." At the 1973 gay pride march in New York, Marsha and Sylvia rushed onto the stage and grabbed the mic, urging the crowd to march past the city's detention center to support transgender prostitutes who had been arrested the night before on 42nd Street. A struggle ensued and they were tossed offstage. A short while later, a young singer who started her career at the gay baths took to that same stage and urged the crowd to stop fighting. With that now famous New York Jewish accent, Bette Midler launched into her trademark "Ya gotta have friends—"

Marsha, who was born in Elizabeth, New Jersey, devoted her life to helping homeless and poor queers on the streets. She spent a lot of time panhandling, hustling and living on those same streets. She earned the nickname St. Marsha for her kindness to strangers. A story has it that one day she had finished working the streets for change when she ran into a queen who had only managed to make $1.50. Marsha poured her change into the queen's cup and went back out to collect more for herself.

In the early '70s, in addition to her political activism, Marsha was part of the flamboyant New York counter cultural theater troupe Hot Peaches, which attained national attention with such hits as *The Watergate Scandals of '73*. She was also photographed by Andy Warhol in 1974 as part of his series on drag queens.

She was never afraid to be herself. A friend recounts riding the train into New York from Hoboken with her. Marsha, he said, would start out dressed as a man and gradually transform herself into a queen by the time they got to the Village. Guys on the train nicknamed her "the transformer."

Bob Kohler, a lifelong civil rights, queer and AIDS activist, recalled once that when he arrived to bail Marsha out of jail one night, the judge asked her, "Marsha P. Johnson. What's the 'P' stand for?" She snapped her fingers and replied, "Pay it no mind." The judge replied, "That's exactly what I'm gonna do. Get outta here."

Marsha was found dead in the Hudson River off the West Village piers in July 1992. Police said that it was a suicide, but community activists asked for an investigation, claiming that she had been harassed in that spot earlier in the day. No investigation ever took place.

Hundreds came to her funeral, far more than the church could hold. As Kohler described it, people wanted to march in the streets down to the river where she died, but the group only had a permit to walk on the sidewalks. Kohler spoke with one of the cops outside the church to ask if they could take over the street with the big crowd. The cop insisted that they couldn't use the street. But the head officer had known Marsha, and told the first cop to let the crowd march. Police proceeded to close down Seventh Avenue for the funeral-goers.

"It was that kind of effect that Marsha would have," Kohler said. "People wouldn't expect that the chief of police would suddenly close down Seventh Avenue because Marsha Johnson was going to be carried down to the river, but he did."

Such is the stuff that legends are made of.

Lessons from the ENDA Mess

Doug Ireland

PERSPECTIVE

Regardless of whether or not Congress, in the days ahead, passes an Employment Non-Discrimination Act (ENDA) that protects all LGBT people, there are lessons to be drawn from the controversy that has been roiling our community for weeks now.

Let's briefly recall the facts. Late this summer (2007), the Human Rights Campaign cut a back-room deal with the Democratic House leadership to strip from the original ENDA bill introduced in April any protection of the transgendered or of those who present their gender identity differently from the heterosexual norm—like butch lesbians or effeminate gay men.

But HRC did not inform the rest of the community of the deal for a truncated ENDA, and the rest of us only found out about it some three weeks ago.

Disgust and revulsion at this betrayal of the most vulnerable among us swiftly became widespread—and within days, a broad coalition of national, state and local LGBT organizations, called ENDA United, had sprung up to oppose the version of ENDA that failed to protect gender identity and expression and the transgendered—because if a shorn bill passes, the transgender community is so politically weak and unpopular Congress will never grant them protection separately.

As of now, more than 300 organizations have joined the ENDA United alliance, leaving HRC all alone in failing to oppose passage of the stripped-down bill.

Thus was revealed a deep fault line in our communities, one that can be traced back to the death of gay liberation and its replacement by what Jeffrey Escoffier, in his seminal 1998 book *American Homo: Community and Perversity*, called "the gay citizenship movement."

How did we get to where we are?

When Sylvia Rivera and other transgendered and gender

rebels launched the fight-back against a brutal police raid at New York's Stonewall Inn 38 years ago, that signaled the birth of a radical rebellion—against the State, which made us criminals; against the medical and psychiatric professions, which declared us sick; and against the culture of heterotyranny which made us the targets of disdain, ridicule, opprobrium, hate, and violence.

Born in the wake of the Stonewall rebellion, the gay liberation movement insisted—to borrow from the title of an early film by the gay German cineaste Rosa von Praunheim—that "it is not the homosexual who is perverse, but the society in which he lives."

Drawing from feminist critiques of the tyrannies of patriarchy and the family, gay liberation rejected the white, middle-class culture's patriarchal rigidities, hierarchies and rituals; homophobia and misogyny were seen as two sides of the same coin.

Gay liberation insisted on the right to plural desires and opposed "any prescription for how consenting adults may or must make love," as the historian and gay activist Martin Duberman then put it. Gay liberation was, he wrote, "a rite of passage—not into manhood or womanhood as those states have been traditionally defined; not sanctioned by supernatural doctrine; not blueprinted by centuries of ritualized behavior; not greeted by kinship rejoicing and social acceptance; not marked by the extension of fellowship into the established adult community," but rather to placing "ourselves in the forefront of the newest and most far-reaching revolution: the re-characterization of sexuality."

In the early '70s, when I came out, gay liberation saw itself as "a paradigm of resistance" to the stultifying political culture of the Nixon years, and was infused with a sense of commitment to unleashing the collective energies of a hitherto invisible people as part of the much larger effort to maximize social justice and human liberation for all.

Since official liberalism rejected gay liberation as a "pathetic" celebration of "perversion," we felt it was doubly subversive, and were proud of that.

The accomplishments of the gay liberation movement were many. It shattered forever the silence that had imprisoned same-sexers in untenable solitude and alienation; its raucous, media-savvy confrontations changed the nature of public discourse on homosexuality—symbolized by the insistence on the word "gay," a code word for same-sex love for more than a century, instead of the clinical, one-dimensional "homosexual."

The most significant victory was the successful fight to have the American Psychiatric Association drop same-sex attraction from its catalog of "disorders" in 1973. And, of course, gay liberation made coming out—the most radical act in a homophobic society—not only the basis of mental and emotional health for gay people, but the imperative for creating the political movement that could carry through the fight for civil rights.

As more and more people began to come out, thanks to the liberationists' clamorous visibility, the out gay community increasingly began to reflect the demographic, political and cultural make-up of the society as a whole. And thus the gay liberation movement became the gay rights movement.

Gay liberation considered innate homosexuality as much a challenge to a suffocating an unjust social order as the political radicalism that many of its proponents, including myself, embraced. But it was transformed in a relatively short time into a more limited quest for gay citizenship.

Or, as Escoffier wrote, the liberation movement "celebrated the otherness, the differentness, and the marginality of the homosexual; whereas the gay politics of citizenship acknowledges the satisfaction of conforming, passing, belonging, and being accepted."

The deradicalization of the gay movement was accelerated by a number of factors. For one thing, gay liberation was largely the work of people who had been participants in or influenced by the '60s movements for black civil rights and against the war in Vietnam, or by labor struggles. As the first generation of activists began to burn out, the movement was populated with younger people with little or no previous history of political protest.

Simultaneously, the fulgurant rise of the commercial gay ghetto and the emergence of the gay market contributed to the rapid growth of an out gay middle class, which saw itself as having more of a stake in the dominant culture than did the young marginals and intellectuals who made up the movement's first wave.

Finally, the backlash against visible homosexuality and against the demand for full gay citizenship drove the movement to seek political advances through a more traditional form of interest-group politics. The need to appeal to the non-gay electorate helped water down and eventually extinguish the radical liberationist discourse; in this, the gay movement did not escape the similar fate of other initially radical social protest movements.

And then came AIDS.

From 1981, when it was first identified as a "gay cancer," until well into the '90s, AIDS was used to stigmatize homosexuals, especially gay males, by the political homophobes of the right.

And whatever shards of liberationist thinking and attitudes that remained in the gay community were effectively snuffed out.

First, the epidemic and the social opprobrium it brought with it forced the gay community to turn back in upon itself in a struggle to survive.

Government was entirely absent from the fight against AIDS in the Reagan years, so the burden of prevention, education and even care for the sick fell upon gay people themselves.

AIDS consumed an enormous amount of the gay community's money and energies, as we took day-to-day responsibility for our afflicted "extended families" of friends and lovers.

Worst of all, this grimmest of reapers also took away forever thousands of gay liberation's most original and tireless activists, a loss unparalleled in the history of any other U.S. social movement. I always think of my late, dear friend Vito Russo as symbolizing the enormity of this lethal hemorrhage of irreplaceable talent.

Finally, any radicalism that still existed in the gay community was increasingly channeled into the fight against AIDS with the founding of ACT UP. The struggle for simple survival took primacy over the larger issues of social and sexual transformation.

By the end of the '90s, the institutionalization of the gay movement was complete. Human Rights Campaign (HRC), the wealthiest national gay organization with the largest staff, some 114 people now—to which today's corporate media invariably turn for the "gay view" on issues—adopted a top-down, corporate structure that demands little more of its members than writing a check, attending a black-tie dinner or occasionally writing a letter, or more likely sending an email, to a public official.

In their endless search for corporate sponsorships for gay events and activities, in their insistence on presenting a homogenized and false image of gay people, the gay institutions like HRC and their access-obsessed gaycrats are committing serious strategic and tactical errors—like acquiescing in an exclusionary version of ENDA—that play into the hands of our heavily funded and organizationally sophisticated enemies on the right.

Yes, the political center of gravity in this country has moved significantly to the right in the decades since Stonewall—and with it the political center of gravity of the out gay community. But I detect something enormously hopeful in the unprecedented mobilization we've seen in these last weeks against the exclusion of the transgendered and gender nonconformists from ENDA.

Since the ENDA controversy erupted, I've heard more real, heartfelt debate about what values a gay movement should hold dear and immutable than I've heard in years. There's also genuine anger at the lack of accountability by the top-down institutions like HRC, whose unelected leadership elites claim to speak for all of us.

Moreover, now that three and a half decades of struggle has created an ever enlarging cultural and political space for LGBT people, I'm sensing a hunger for a return to some of the earlier principles of sexual liberation for all with which our movement began, not just here at home but abroad—and that includes a growing demand for our gay institutions to abandon their navel-gazing isolationism and embrace international LGBT solidarity.

In the long term, developing new strategies of resistance and liberation will require the gay movement, which has become so embourgeoised, to begin a serious and radical rethinking of homosexualities and gender identities so as to understand at a deeper level why the fear and loathing of same-sex love and gender variants are so deeply engrained in society and culture not only here in the United States, but around the world.

This also means breaking the forms of social control implicit in the gay market ideology. And reconnecting to other movements for social justice who should be our natural allies—all the while remembering the dictum of a great black civil rights organizer who also was gay, Bayard Rustin, who taught us that "all successful coalitions are based on mutual self-interest," which means embracing the struggles of others as we ask them to embrace ours.

But, as important as the demands of the gay citizenship movement are, ultimately one cannot change minds and hearts simply by legislation alone. Only a fundamental redefinition of human freedom that includes a recharacterization of human sexuality in all its glorious varieties—the original project of gay liberation—can do that.

This article originally appeared in *Gay City News* in 2008.

Doug Ireland, a veteran radical journalist, has been a columnist for the Village Voice, *the* New York Observer, *the Paris daily* Libération, New York *magazine, and other publications on both sides of the Atlantic. He is currently the U.S. correspondent and a columnist for the French investigative-political weekly* Bakchich.

Happy to Be Childless

Allen Young

Much has appeared lately in the media (gay and straight), about lesbian moms and gay dads. Initially, I enjoyed these articles and television pieces, but I am beginning to have some second thoughts about this media trend. There are many circumstances under which gay men and lesbians become parents—and often they are excellent parents—but what is often forgotten is the simple fact that the majority of gay men and lesbians are childless, whether by choice or circumstance.

More of us now have the choice of having children because of changing societal factors and the liberation movements we have worked very hard to create and expand. This is a good thing, but the key word here is "choice." In the gay community, there should never be an obligation to have children or an obligation to get married (should that become a legal possibility).

We all know there are countless numbers of lesbians and gay men who became spouses and then parents in heterosexual marriages because of societal pressure, not by choice. Such liaisons often (though not always) result in much pain and sorrow.

Will there now be societal pressures on uncloseted gay men and lesbians such that they too feel they MUST or SHOULD be parents? I think this is already beginning to happen. Publicity about celebrities who are gay parents, such as Melissa Etheridge and Rosie O'Donnell, suggest they are role models. There needs to be more awareness, even explicit warnings, that many people, whether heterosexual or homosexual, are not cut out to be parents.

There are many good reasons for caring human beings, gay and straight, to refrain from having children, and the status of childless should be celebrated, not denegrated.

On the first celebration of Earth Day, April 22, 1970, an irreverent leaflet written and distributed by the New York Gay Liberation Front, part outrageous humor and part serious politics, had the following text:

EARTH DAY LEAFLET
"Homosexuality is the only answer to the problem of
over-population."—Pope John XXIII

EARTH DAY announces with great pride . . . a citation
for exemplary and meritorious conduct, awarded by the
United Nations, Red China and The Margaret Sanger
Clinic [a sister organization of the Daughters of Bili-
tis]. This citation is being accepted by the Planned Non-
Parenthood cell of the GAY LIBERATION FRONT in the
name of all those homosexual women and men through
history who in couples and small groups turned for
warmth, sex and friendship to members of their own
gender thereby providing the human race with an affir-
mative and joyous alternative to the problem of population explosion. These fortunate women and men are
the vanguard of the revolution-forging life-styles that
liberate energies and love for the formation of the NEW
HUMANITY and the salvation of Planet Earth.

HOMOSEXUAL MEN AND WOMEN, WE SALUTE YOU!!!!!!
BE GAY!
GIVE EARTH A CHANCE.

While the language in the leaflet is "over the top," politically
incorrect by today's standards, and simply wrong in its assumption
that homosexuals are nonparents, there is a great deal of merit in
this early expression of gay liberation's linkup with the equally
embryonic environmental movement.

I reflect with pride on the fact that some members of New
York's Gay Liberation Front attended the first Earth Day with their
message, one that should be taken seriously today.

Is there an overpopulation problem on the planet Earth today?
You bet there is, a grave problem which is often ignored, largely
due to the influence of the same Roman Catholic Church that op-
presses gay men and lesbians.

The respected organization the Population Connection, formerly Zero Population Growth, explains the issue in stark, simple
terms: "We entered the 20th century with a [global] population
of less than two billion people. We started the 21st century with
more than six billion. We are now adding one billion people every

14 years. At this rate of growth, world population will double in just over 50 years.

"Human impacts can damage the environment. Increasing population growth puts enormous pressure on the environment. Every day, we use more resources, damage more of the earth, and generate more waste. This makes it increasingly difficult to meet people's needs and improve our quality of life."

There is no support in our culture for the purposefully childless, and in fact, straight friends I know who have decided not to have children have told me that friends and relatives hurl the word "selfish" at them. It's a harsh word that I have heard myself, as a childless gay man, to describe my attitude toward life.

I by no means consider myself selfish. As a taxpayer, I certainly contribute to operating the public schools in my community as well as to all other government functions. As a gay man, I know that my gay and lesbian peers play an inordinately large role in the helping professions (education, health care and all other social services).

Am I glad that I don't have to spend my hard-earned money on child-rearing? Yes, I am, and I don't feel it is anything to be ashamed of. The fact that I can direct my resources toward other things that give me pleasure (my home, garden, travel, dinners out, charitable contributions, early retirement and more) is something that I can live with quite comfortably. I imagine childless straight people have some of the same positive feelings about how they can utilize their limited resources. Such straight people have to suffer the indignity of would-be grandparents and others invading a very personal and private aspect of their lives, namely, the question of reproduction. I have long felt a special bond with my cousins and friends who are childless for this very reason, and out of politeness, I never ask straight people about their plans regarding children.

Are gay men and lesbians who want children doing the right thing by adopting them or having them through artificial insemination and other means? Of course they are doing the right thing, if they truly understand what's involved in raising children—emotionally, physically and financially. We all know that many gay parents love their children deeply and are creating wonderful families. These aware and dedicated parents are to be congratulated. However, the picture is not always as pretty as the media make it out to be.

Gay parents are not doing the right thing if they are having children just because they think it'll make their blood relatives happy, or just because they've read an article somewhere or seen a TV show about gay parenting and it sounded rewarding or beautiful. We are not doing the right thing if we have children primarily because we think heterosexuals will understand us and like us better. Yes, lesbians and gay men with children do have the possibility of positively impacting the straight parents they interact with. Yes, they can be excellent parents. But gay parents, like straight ones, can easily underestimate how tough it is to be a good parent, can experience heartbreak and can be bad parents.

I agree with the early gay liberationists who attended that first Earth Day. Let's celebrate those people, gay and straight, who don't bear children by choice and thus help alleviate the population explosion. Let's celebrate childless gay men and lesbians and recognize that each of us has the capability of being a good human being in our own right, as an individual, whether we are single or in a relationship, whether we have children or not.

Allen Young, who holds a master's degree from the Columbia University Graduate School of Journalism, left a reporter's position at the Washington Post *in 1967 at age 26 to become involved in the antiwar "underground press." In early 1970, he became active in the New York Gay Liberation Front, where he met lesbian writer Karla Jay. The duo edited three anthologies, including the groundbreaking* Out of the Closets: Voices of Gay Liberation *(still in print), and wrote* The Gay Report *based on a survey of thousands of gay men and women. He is also the author of the* Gay Sunshine Interview *with Allen Ginsberg and* Gays Under the Cuban Revolution. *Since 1973, he has lived at Butterworth Farm, a gay-centered community in Royalston, Mass., where he continues his work as a writer, editor, publisher and activist. He and his partner have been in a committed relationship for 29 years.*

The Gay Community in Crisis

Don Kilhefner

> Community is first of all a quality of the heart. It grows from
> the spiritual knowledge that we are alive not for ourselves
> but for one another. Community is the fruit of our capacity to
> make the interests of others more important than our own.
> The question, therefore, is not "How can we make commu-
> nity?" but "How can we develop and nurture giving hearts?"
> —Henri Nouwen, *Bread for the Journey*

In October 1979, after I had returned from the first "Spiritual Gathering for Radical Faeries," which Harry Hay and I had organized in
the beautiful Sonora desert of Southern Arizona east of Tucson, I
was contacted by Christopher St. West, the organization that sponsors Los Angeles's Gay Pride Parade and Carnival every June, to
write an article for the slick, glossy program it prints each year. After spending a week in the desert with nearly 200 Radical Faeries
from all over North America, I was on fire with gay spirit—flames
shooting out the tips of my fingers and every orifice of my body.
Of course, I would gladly write an article for Gay Pride on what
I thought was the most important issue facing us as gay people
at the time—*gay assimilation vs. gay enspiritment.* Thirty years later,
it still is. You cannot have both at the same time. It's an impossibility. It's either one or the other. Just as today we cannot have
American democracy and American imperialism at the same time.
It's an impossibility.

The *Crossroads* article 30 years ago was based largely on workshops I had been doing with gay men since 1975 at the Gay and
Lesbian Community Services Center in Los Angeles (now the Gay
and Lesbian Center—"Community" and "Services" having been
erased from its name by assimilationists in the early 1990s) named
Gay Voices and Visions: The Enspiritment of Gay Politics/The Politics of Gay Enspiritment. I had gathered together all the gay visionary literature I could get my faggoty hands on, beginning with Walt

Whitman and including Edward Carpenter, Gerald Heard (writing under the pseudonym D. B. Vest in homophile publications), Harry Hay et al.; culled the evolutionary biology and sociobiology literature about us at the time; and also rounded up the other usual suspects. Between 1975 and 1979—week after week, workshop after workshop—gay men read this literature together in Los Angeles. And the literature soon began reading them. Like a white dove coming from the invisible world, pecking on their hearts, cooing in their ears, asking them to remember—something was brought alive in them. They experienced that gay consciousness was real. It was intellectually and spiritually exciting, and a new type of gay consciousness-raising group was being birthed.

Shortly after submitting the article in late 1979 I received a phone call from Christopher St. West (CSW) telling me that they had decided not to print the article. CSW was angry with me. They felt the article was fantasy on my part and gay people simply would not be able to understand what I was saying. The sad irony of this, of course, was that I had played a central role in organizing the first two Gay Pride marches in Los Angeles in 1970 and 1971. It was felt, however, that the article really did not have much to do with celebrating Gay Pride and really was not about gay people and the gay community—and, if it was, it was much too radical to print.

By 1979 largely middle-class gay assimilationists were beginning to take over the community that had been created by the radical gay liberation movement during the past decade, and often they were embarrassed by their radical roots. By then, Gay Pride *marches* had become *parades*; gay *demonstrations* against oppression were becoming *carnivals*; a *marketplace of ideas* was turning into *a marketing niche*. Increasingly, with startling speed, gay men could not remember anymore. It was as if Tinker Bell had flown over the United States sprinkling fairy dust and saying that gay people should not think or remember who they are and from where they came. Increasingly, there was little awareness by the organizers of or the attendees at these Pride events that they were paying respect to those who had gone before them and honoring a social and political revolution of major global proportions that had been fought on their behalf. (Recently, on returning to me a copy of the first documentary ever done on the Gay Liberation movement in 1970—Ken Robinson's *Some Of Your Best Friends*—a young gay man angrily said to me: "Why hasn't anyone ever told me about this history! This is something I can be proud of!") Gay Pride events became just another party with marketing opportunities. It was not too long thereafter that some Radical Faeries, alas, I am sad to say, minus the word *radical*, turned into *common fairies*—lots of glitter, little substance. In my last conversation with Harry Hay before he died, he deeply lamented the deteriorating state of affairs. Gay assimilationist triviality was raising its shallow head.

Shortly thereafter my friend Mark Thompson asked if he could use the *Crossroads* article and the readings I had assembled for the Gay Voices and Visions workshops for a book he was beginning to edit, which became *Gay Spirit: Myth and Meaning* (White Crane), an important and groundbreaking statement about enspiritment by gay men.

Since 1979 the pace of gay assimilation has picked up tremendous speed and with the advent of the extreme right-wing Reagan Revolution it has become the dominant political and social ideology of the gay community. Community building, grassroots activism and the exploration of gay identity became dirty words; now individual financial achievement, checkbook activism and gay *bourgeois* conformity reigns. I draw your attention to an important article by nationally syndicated columnist Gregory Rodriguez on the op-ed page of the *Los Angeles Times* titled "Gay—the new straight" (November 5, 2007) and my op-ed response to Rodriguez in the *Times* (December 5, 2007). Let me hasten to add that I have no interest in demonizing gay assimilationists per se. I am interested, however, in commenting on the phenomenology of gay assimilation and how it is impacting our community—extremely negatively, I suggest.

Hey! What's Happening?

What has been the price we have had to pay for mindlessly allowing, and maybe even participating in, gay assimilation? **One price is that very little is happening in the gay community today except for endless parties and fundraisers.** Assimilationists will say we are basically just like heterosexuals except for our choice of sex partners. (Harry would say to me: "We're just like hets when it comes to sex, and in most other ways we are different.") Assimilationists act as if we already have an identity (homosexual), and with cybersex and hookups who needs a community or even an intellectual life? A gay leader in Los Angeles recently thought that Chief Joseph was a Supreme Court judge. Evolutionary biologists inform us that the basic function of heterosexuals is the reproductive survival of our species. The most essential question for us at present is: *What is the evolutionary function of gay people? What are gay people for?* To mimic heterosexuals? I don't think so. Otherwise, evolutionarily speaking, we would have gone down the drainpipe of history long ago.

Inherent in gay assimilation theory and practice is the disappearance of the gay community and gay identity, and it is happening all across the country. In a front-page article in the *New York Times* (September 30, 2007) titled "Gay Enclaves Face Prospect of Being Passé," the reporter writes about "a waning sense of belonging that is also being felt in gay enclaves across the nation, from Key West, Fla., to West Hollywood, as they struggle to maintain cultural relevance in the face of gentrification." The *Times* says you are no longer a community but an "enclave." They get it wrong when they say the problem is "gentrification." The problem is gay assimilation.

It saddens me tremendously today when energized young gay men want to know where they can go to become actively and constructively involved in the community. For the first time since the 1980s I have no place toward which to point them. It tears me apart when intelligent young gay men tell me they have to "dumb it down" to be part of the gay community. I have a hunch this is true in your community as well.

Now You See It, Now You Don't

Another price we are paying for gay assimilation is that we are becoming invisible again. Please, hold off on the *Will and Grace* argument. *Will and Grace* had about as much relationship to gay people's lives as Liberace had to do with heterosexuality. (To his everlasting glory, he won a libel case in England when a journalist accused him of being a "homosexual"—now that's *real* chutzpah.) Gay artist and filmmaker Bruce LaBruce, observing what's happening with our portrayal in the media, recently fumed about contemporary assimilationists "who seem to have no problem being represented in such Stepin Fetchit shows as *Will and Grace* and *Queer Eye for the Straight Guy* as bourgeois, shallow, materialistic and vain, obsessed with appearance and conspicuous consumption" (*And the Bland Played On*, Nerve.com). We have become entertainment for the dominant corporate/entertainment/consumer culture. With the exception of the assimilationists' same-sex marriage agenda, we are not making hard news in any significant ways.

In the all-night dialogues I used to have with Harry Hay when we lived together during the early Radical Faery years (he would stay up all night reading, listening to music or writing; would go to bed when the sun came up and sleep until the midafternoon), he often reminded me that political winds can change very quickly, and what was bestowed on a minority group one year with media access and media portrayals can be taken away quickly the next by the dominant culture. History is replete with examples. Weimar Jews, of course, immediately come to mind.

Let me give you a current example of increased *gay invisibility* in Los Angeles. News of the gay community here has virtually disappeared from the pages of the *Los Angeles Times* with the exception a few and far between same-sex marriage updates when they cannot be avoided. I also read the *New York Times,* and it appears the same is true for the East Coast. The recent California ruling giving constitutional "equal protection" status to gay marriages naturally increased media attention briefly but died off quickly.

I arranged a lunch recently with a city editor of the *Los Angeles Times* to ask why we had become invisible again—I was curious. In 1970 I played an important role in the Los Angeles Gay Liberation Front's project to take over sparsely populated Alpine County in Northern California and establish the first openly gay government in history there. Then governor Ronald Reagan called a news conference threatening to call out the California National Guard to stop us, and the *Los Angeles Times, Time Magazine, NBC Nightly News*, etc. were forced to cover Gay Liberation as a political movement—which was our intention—instead of treating us as a medical issue and sending its medical reporter to our news conferences like the *Los Angeles Times* had before. When I asked the *Times* city editor why we were invisible again, he replied that he simply did not *need* to cover the gay community anymore, and in any case he felt nothing newsworthy seemed to be happening there, just endless social events of one type or another—nothing of substance.

Hey Brother, Can You Spare Ten Thousand Bucks?

Another place we pay a high price for gay assimilation is the weakening of our gay political power and integrity as a community.

Let me ask you a question: Could you imagine the Jewish community (or any other politically and socially aware minority group for that matter) holding a special dinner honoring and praising President Bill Clinton after he had issued a presidential order stating that no Jews can reveal they are Jews and they must act as if they are gentiles in the U.S. military? If their Jewishness is uncovered, they will be discharged (12,000 gay men and women so far). And, furthermore, only gentiles can be married as dictated by the Defense of Marriage Act, for which Clinton actively lobbied and which he signed into law? Do you think Jews would honor Clinton? I don't think so. They would have protested this injustice loudly, vehemently and intelligently. But the gay assimilationists threw a "thank you" dinner for Clinton. They are so hungry for political acceptance by heterosexuals—rather than self-acceptance—they will sell their souls to the highest bidder. And that is exactly what the gay assimilationist political claque has become—the cash cow of two political parties, neither one of which really wants us otherwise. Gay Republicans still need to use the back door of the GOP when their bagmen deliver the loot. Ask McCain and Obama about their positions on same-sex marriage. McCain says "no!" with the loudspeaker turned to high volume. Obama sounds like a theologian, not a constitutional law professor, with his nuanced and convoluted elocution. Are their positions any different from Clinton's 15 years ago?

Coors Whore Award—Who's Next?

We pay a high price for gay assimilation with the eroding of the grassroots support for and the integrity of our community institutions. Here in Los Angeles not too long ago, right-of-center assimilationists clandestinely got the West Hollywood City Council to honor the Coors Brewing Co. for its hiring policies regarding gay people (as a marketing ploy on Coors's behalf). Coors then gave $15,000, chump change, to Outfest: The Gay and Lesbian Film Festival in Los Angeles, trumpeting the City Council resolution and plastering West Hollywood with banners crowing that Outfest was sponsored by Coors (trying to give the impression the Coors's Boycott—the most successful in gay history—was over, which it was not). The Coors Boycott Committee raised holy hell. It is a well-documented fact that stocks and profits from the Coors Brewing Co., a family-owned business, are being funneled into Coors's

Castle Rock Foundation, which funds extreme right-wing homophobic organizations. These organizations constitute the gay-hate coalition in this country, and they are out to destroy every advance gay people have made since 1969.

The Gay Tavern Guild here responded by restating its support for the boycott—since 1978 not a single gay bar in Los Angeles sells Coors. After exhaustive research and public hearings on the subject (plus two debates between Coors employee Mary Cheney and me before the Stonewall Democratic Club and the ACLU) both the Stonewall Democratic Club and the City Council of West Hollywood endorsed the Coors Boycott, asking gay people not to feed the hand that bites them. After Morris Kight and I provided Outfest with the facts of the matter, its leadership agreed not to accept Coors's money in the future. In every case, when gay people have the full story on Coors funding, not just the Coors public relations/marketing spin, they endorse the Coors Boycott. Yet even today gay community newspapers carry very lucrative, sophisticated, full-page color ads for the Coors Brewing Co., and the Gay and Lesbian Association Against Defamation (GLAAD), of all organizations, for Christ's sake, not so long ago accepted money from Coors as one of the sponsors of its banquet in New York City. Hello, GLAAD. Hello, New York City. The lights are on. Is anyone at home? Is anyone tending the store?

Several years ago the Coors Boycott Committee met with the GLAAD Board of Directors to discuss the problem. As *Hashem* is my witness, their gay assimilationist Board just did not get that GLAAD should not accept money from one of the primary oppressors of gay people and did all kinds of transparent intellectual acrobatics to justify taking Coors's money. I was stunned. It was like talking to fourth graders caught with their hands in the cookie jar. They refused to even discuss the antigay funding of Coors's Castle Rock Foundation. To them, all money was good money. GLAAD was being coached by the Wittek and Combs public relations firm, run by two assimilationist gay men in Washington, D.C., who were on the Coors payroll at the time. At the end of the discussion, seeing that GLAAD would not return Coors's money, I presented its president with the "Coors Whore Award"—a beautiful full-color, poster-size framed drawing showing a golden cockroach with a bottle of Coors in one hand and with his dick in the other hand pissing on a rainbow flag. GLAAD is not the exception; it is the rule among major gay organizations. **Gay assimilation is having a corrupting and** corroding effect on the integrity and accountability to gay people by our major community organizations.

In his Pali discourses, Gautama Buddha taught that there are times when anger is in the *dharma*—exactly what the situation naturally calls for (like the uprising led by Buddhist monks in Myanmar recently). Moses, Jesus and Mohammed spoke and acted likewise. What has happened to gay men? Why are they not angry with what is happening to them and their community? Why are gay men silent? As Martin Luther King Jr. warned us: "Our lives begin to end the day we become 'silent' about things that matter" (*Eternal Vigilance*, 1967).

Take It to the Center of the City

I was communicating with Toby Johnson recently, sharing with him that there is a line in *The Odyssey* that has always caught my attention. *The Odyssey* is the great archetypal story in Western literature about the father-son mysteries of the soul. At its beginning, Telemachus was lamenting not having a father. His father, Odysseus, departed when he was a baby to fight the Trojan War and had been gone 20 years. On his departure Odysseus, however, had placed Telemachus under the tutelage of Mentor, through whom Athena speaks. Mentor was consoling Telemachus and telling him that in his father hunger lamentations he was finding his voice as a man. And then Mentor/Athena says to him: **"And when you have found your voice you must take it into the center of the city."** I respectfully suggest, beloved brothers, that is the task that is staring us in the face right now vis-à-vis gay assimilation. For all of you who have been laboring in the vineyards of gay spirit and gay consciousness at the edge of the village—it is now time to take your voice to the center of the city. You have been slowly finding your voice, sometimes in terrible isolation and lack of brotherly succor. I hear the voice you have found in the books, articles, poems, Web sites and blogs you are writing and the gatherings you have been organizing at the edge of the city. And the center of our gay cities and villages are hungry for the food of gay spirit and consciousness after decades of gay assimilationist pretentiousness, self-alienation and empty calories. **"And when you have found your voice you must take it to the center of the city."** The edge of the village must stop talking *only* to the edge of the village. The edge of the village, where so many dimensions of gay soul are gestated and midwived, must take its newly found voice to the center of the city. Gay soul making and the communal and political evolution of our people demands it.

There is a critical need to create a *new frontier of gay consciousness* as we move past the present wreckage of the gay assimilationists (remembering always that they are also our brothers and we must truly be our brother's keeper). A frontier is a growing or expanding edge. Individuals, if they are psychospiritually and psychophysically alive, will have a growing edge. And communities and nations also have a growing edge. It is where the new, the challenging, the disturbing, the dangerous, the impossible is being constellated. It is the place where our lives, often unwillingly, move forward into the great unknown. The frontier is the most exciting and frightening place to be.

And as my fingers press the last keys of this commentary, the last notes of a J. S. Bach cantata are playing synchronistically on Los Angeles's KUSC. It's name: **"I go and seek with longing."**

This article first appeared in the Fall 2008 issue of *White Crane*.

Don Kilhefner, Ph.D., played a pioneering role in the creation of the gay liberation movement. He is also a founder of Los Angeles's Gay and Lesbian Center, Van Ness Recovery House, Gay Men's Medicine Circle and numerous other seminal organizations in the gay community including (with Harry Hay) the Radical Faeries, an international gay spirituality and consciousness movement. He is a Jungian psychologist and shamanic practitioner. Don can be reached at donkilhefner@sbcglobal.net.

Stonewall Was a Riot—Now We Need a Revolution

Merle Woo

August 2008

To my dear friend Anh,

Last spring, as you were about to graduate from high school, you asked me about the significance of the Stonewall Rebellion in New York. You had just come out and you were so curious about so many things. I'm glad you asked, because Stonewall was key to our liberation as queers of color.

Since next year will be the 40th anniversary of that rebellion, it's a good time to reflect on what it was all about, the kind of movement it engendered, and what Stonewall can tell us about organizing a militant, unified movement today.

At the Stonewall Inn

On Friday night, June 27, 1969, during a routine police raid, cops began their usual brutalizing of customers at a rundown gay bar in Greenwich Village called the Stonewall Inn. Both the Mafia and the NYPD were getting kickbacks from the bar's management, but the patrons were undesirables in an undesirable dump, quite unlike the neighborhood's chic heterosexual bars and respectable gay bars for Ivy League types. Stonewall's customers were mostly Black and Puerto Rican, young teenage street queens, dykes and effeminate gays. They were tired of police brutality, filled with righteous anger, and had nothing to lose.

And this time, they did not go quietly, peacefully or in shame. They started a riot.

They yelled and screamed and called for people to join them. The cops brought in paddy wagons and tried to round up the enraged queens. But as soon as one group of queens was herded into a paddy wagon, they'd pop back out and return to the melee. They formed chorus lines and kicked their heels high like the Rockettes at the Radio City Music Hall, singing,

We are the Stonewall Girls.
We wear our hair in curls
We wear no underwear
We show our pubic hair
We wear our dungarees
Above our nelly knees!

One cross-dressed dyke was arrested for not wearing at least three items of clothing "appropriate to one's gender" (a New York law). She was loaded onto a wagon but promptly got back out and started rocking the paddy wagon on its side.

When the crowd saw the cops brutalizing the patrons, they started to boo and throw coins and garbage. The cops locked themselves inside the Stonewall Inn for protection, but the windows were broken out and lighter fluid and burning matches were tossed inside. The crowd grew larger and larger, threatening, chanting and yelling. Tactical police squads were brought in, but the riot continued on.

This was the night that drag queens, transgendered folks, lesbians and gays said *NO!* No more to gay oppression, police brutality, societal contempt. The homophobia that had oppressed so many for so many years would no longer be tolerated.

Did they say "No" to racism because they were Black and Puerto Rican?

Or "No" because of their gender or sexual orientation?

Was it "No" because they were poor and working class?

It was *all* of those things.

That night turned loose all the anger. The undesirables fought back for being outsiders, for being treated like dogs. They challenged sex-role stereotyping, racism and class bigotry. They challenged the dysfunctional monogamous nuclear family, its patriarchal values, oppression of women and children, and sermons that sex is for procreation only.

Capitalist Patriarchal Amerikkka got it in the face: from drag queens who wanted to dress like women and effeminate males; from perverts outrageous enough to behave like women—those slaves of slaves, the weaker and subordinate sex; from diesel dykes who committed the biggest crime of all—daring to assume the male role in this patriarchal capitalist society.

For three consecutive nights, gays, lesbians, transvestites and their supporters clashed with roving tactical squads. There was no going back. The subsequent ad hoc organizing within the gay community laid the basis for today's Queer movement, infused with the vigor of youth and armed with revolutionary ideas, strategies and tactics. Almost overnight, militancy replaced the moderate homophile movement. What a time to be alive—at the awakening!

Post-Stonewall: the 1970s

Before Stonewall, there were gay and lesbian organizations like the Mattachine Society and the Daughters of Bilitis (whose leaders, Del Martin and Phyllis Lyon, married for the second time in San Francisco in 2008—a meaningful celebration of over 50 years of their political activism in the Queer Movement).

The Daughters of Bilitis (DOB), like the men's organizations, focused on educating people that gays and lesbians were just like everyone else. They urged respectable *fitting in* and trying to change institutions without fundamentally questioning them. It was courageous, nonetheless, because the DOB was started in the 1950s at the height of McCarthyism's witch hunts. Despite the legal perils, lesbians needed to find each other, to fight isolation and invisibility, and to establish community.

They had to fight not only homophobia but also entrenched sexism, which are inextricably connected. Lorraine Hansberry, Black radical playwright and award-winning author of *A Raisin in the Sun*, said it best in an anonymous letter to *The Ladder*, DOB's publication: "homosexual persecution and condemnation has at its roots, not only social ignorance, but a philosophically active anti-feminist dogma. . ." (from Jonathan Katz's *Gay American History*. Thomas Crowell, 1976.)

In *Gay Resistance: The Hidden History* (Red Letter Press, 1997), authors Sam Deaderick and Tamara Turner aptly describe what came immediately after Stonewall:

An unprecedented upsurge of gay protest ensued, sparked by the Stonewall riots but drawing inspiration, courage and expertise from the Black struggle, feminism, and the antiwar movement. Borrowing their rhetoric, political ideas, and organizational precepts largely from the New Left, chapters of the vociferous Gay Liberation Front sprang up nationwide.

The GLFs were often explicitly socialist and multi-issue; there were diversity caucuses, a promise of a revolutionary rainbow coalition.

A GLF activist spoke at a Black Panther rally in New Haven (May Day, 1970), and while wholly supporting Black liberation, he publicly admonished the Panthers for homophobia: "The very oppression that had made so many gay people identify with the Panthers was being reproduced within the Panther movement" (Martin Duberman in *Stonewall*, Penguin, 1993). Three months later, Huey Newton published "A Letter from Huey to the Revolutionary Brothers and Sisters About the Women's Liberation and Gay Liberation Movements." He wrote,

> Homosexuals are not given freedom and liberty by anyone in the society. Maybe they might be the most oppressed people in the society. . . .
>
> But there's nothing to say that a homosexual cannot also be a revolutionary. . . . maybe a homosexual could be the most revolutionary.

It was incredibly significant that a nationally known Black leader recognized not only the depth of gay and lesbian oppression but also our potential for radical leadership!

Although the GLFs strongly inclined toward a movement allied with women, people of color and radicals, they generally lacked organizational structure and hence were dominated by charismatic personalities. Many prominent gay male leaders imitated the male chauvinism, lack of organizational structure and leadership of the New Left.

Women's leadership, especially, was never respected or encouraged in the early GLFs. Lesbian rights were considered peripheral to "general," i.e., male, gay liberation. Inspired by feminism, lesbian activists criticized, threatened, warned, and finally, amid bitter political fights, stormed out of GLFs nationwide.

Unfortunately, at that time the more privileged sectors of the feminist movement cowered from the charge that feminism equaled lesbianism. They distanced themselves from lesbians and ostracized them. Rejected, many lesbians turned to lesbian separatism and the fantasy of a women-only paradise somewhere in the woods. Separatism was a dead end, especially for lesbians of color. They could not afford to abandon their ethnic communities in which they fought together against the racism outside—and the simultaneous battle against sexism and homophobia *within* their communities. We queers of color live these multi-issue contradictions on a daily basis, and many of us figured out that the logic of multi-issueism leads to anticapitalism.

The bottom line is this: single-issue reform politics *or* multi-issue, anticapitalist, revolutionary politics.

Single-issueism isn't about focusing on one issue; it's about raising that issue above all others. Capitalism can absorb a single-issue movement by watering it down and diverting it into moderate reformist politics. It's the perfect divide-and-conquer strategy. For example, the New York GLF disintegrated when one faction championed single-issue, exclusively gay, reform politics, ignoring links between gay liberation and the women's movement, racial equality struggles and working-class solidarity. From the GLF split came the Gay Activists Alliance, which soon drifted toward that same single-issue strategy and out of existence.

Despite their subsequent adulteration and demise, the explosive force of the leftist GLFs broke political ground for many successful gay rights campaigns. From 1969 until the mid-'70s, the movement grew powerful enough to overturn sodomy statutes in several states and to codify protections against discrimination in many municipal ordinances.

However, after substantial reforms had been won, a new layer of rich, professional gay males crept out of their closets and quickly rose to public prominence by selling out the needs of the community's less affluent and less respectable layers—you guessed it: working class lesbians, transgenders and people of color.

Liberalism and the Democratic Party

Careerists like David Goodstein, the wealthy owner of *The Advocate*, a tabloid for gay males, began to mold a tasteful, moderate image of gays that would be acceptable to non-gay sympathizers within the Democratic Party (the *other* Party of Corporatism). These professional queers advocated the notion that lesbian and gay rights must be approached slowly in cautious little stages. Radicals and militants must be denounced and discredited.

However, the momentum of Anita Bryant's rabid antigay crusade in the mid-'70s—and the militant response of lesbians and gays—caught gay liberals off guard. During Gay Pride Week in

June 1977, the largest gay demonstrations in history were staged. More than 250,000 people marched in San Francisco, and 100,000 people in New York. Marches occurred throughout the United States and around the world.

Gay moderates had tried to counter the hysteria of Bryant's crusade with public information campaigns that emphasized privacy rights, downplayed or didn't even mention homosexuality, and ignored the far right's ongoing mobilization against *all* civil rights gains. These timid reformists scorned alliances with other oppressed groups and insisted that outspoken opposition to anti-gay initiative campaigns would spark a backlash. They betrayed gay rights, as they have betrayed people of color, workers and women—*as if there are no gays among these groups.*

In the mid-'80s, one gay San Francisco Supervisor refused to fight for immigrant rights while he campaigned for gay rights legislation, saying, "I don't want to hitch my wagon to a losing star." *As if there are no queer immigrants.* Last year, the Human Rights Commission refused to add transgender rights ("gender identity") to the Employment Non-Discrimination Act (ENDA) because we're supposed to accept liberation in stages!

For utter opportunism and conservatism—the standard *modus operandi* of the Democratic Party—the examples above are excruciatingly typical.

It was during the Clinton years in the 1990s when gay careerists tried to bury the gay movement in the Democratic Party. Only the onslaught of the AIDS crisis kept the movement alive and militant. President Clinton's "Don't Ask, Don't Tell" policy drastically worsened the status of lesbians and gays in the military. DADT is actually a draconian employment law that *requires* the firing (dishonorable discharge) of armed services personnel because of their sexual orientation!

Further, Clinton's "Defense of Marriage Act" clearly states that the federal government does not recognize same-sex marriage as a legal union. In 2004, Democratic Party leaders—gay and straight—tried to hush up the same-sex marriage issue before election time. Afterwards, they blamed Bush's presidential victory on the "spectacle" of thousands of queer couples, in cities nationwide, lining the sidewalks waiting for marriage licenses. But it was precisely these same displays of matrimonial civil disobedience—in defiance of state law and the party line—that set the stage for the 2008 California court victory for same-sex marriage rights!

And don't forget that voters put the Democrats in charge of Congress in 2006, because they believed Dems who said they would get us out of the illegal war in Iraq. Well, it's August 2008, and we are still there.

Now the same Democratic Party fakers urge us to vote for Barack Obama, who (like John McCain) refuses to support gay marriage. On the campaign trail, Obama vows to rescind "Don't Ask, Don't Tell," but I think he'll stall on that one.

On the Left

Many queers, radicalized by Stonewall and fed up with reformist single-issue politics, gravitated to the Left in the 1970s, but they didn't always find the welcome mat out. If you want to understand how radical parties and organizations have responded to the lesbian/gay uprising in the United States, it's crucial to know their history, political analyses and the resulting programs that guide them.

To begin with, lots of the earliest gay pioneers were socialists inspired by the October 1917 Russian Revolution, which granted many new freedoms for women and gays in the Soviet Union. The domination of the monogamous nuclear family was weakened—an institution so aptly described by Frederick Engels as one in which men had been the "bourgeoisie" and women were the "proletariat." Homosexuality was decriminalized, abortion was legalized, and women could easily obtain a divorce.

However, abject poverty, technological backwardness—and immediate imperialist invasions by nearly 20 countries—left the new government in dire need of a way to organize and distribute what little food and other goods existed. In these circumstances, a bureaucracy arose under Joseph Stalin, the man put in charge of distribution. Stalin and his cronies skimmed goods from the top, traded favors for favors and engineered what was really a counter-revolution. As his power and self-serving support grew, Stalin brought back the oppressive nuclear family structure with its bourgeois morality—he called it the "revolutionary fighting family"—and revised the Soviet constitution to strip women and gays of their newfound rights. Leon Trotsky, a co-leader of the Russian Revolution, became Stalin's fiercest critic and the leader of the opposition. Trotsky maintained the necessity of leadership by the most oppressed, in direct contradiction to that of a privileged bureaucracy. He was exiled in 1929 and eventually murdered by a

Stalinist assassin in Mexico in 1940. To this day, Stalinism's adherents revile sexual minorities.

Maoism, a variant of Stalinism, was well represented in the United States by the Revolutionary Union in this statement from the late 1970s:

> Gay liberation is anti-working class and counter revolutionary. Its attacks on the family would rob poor and working class people of the most viable social unit for their survival and the revolutionary struggle. . . . The only real liberation . . . for homosexuals—like all people caught in the mire and muck of bourgeois decadence—is to eliminate the reactionary, rotting system that drives them to homosexuality.
> (from Yolanda Alaniz and Megan Cornish's *Viva la Raza: A History of Chicano Identity and Resistance*. Red Letter Press, 2008)

Parties that emerged from the Trotskyist movement had a more progressive view, but nonetheless, most saw gay and women's rights as secondary issues, separate from "classical Marxism." They conveniently ignored the analysis put forth by Frederick Engels in *The Origin of the Family, Private Property and the State*, which describes patriarchy as a fundamental building block of the system of private property upon which capitalism is founded.

The Socialist Workers Party (SWP), the dominant Trotskyist party during the 1970s, recruited a large number of committed queer activists during its brief period of gay activism but later shed both its gay rights platform and its Trotskyist ideas, concluding that too close an association with gay liberation would give the SWP an "exotic image" and alienate it from the masses.

The militancy of today's queer movement has forced the Left to sit up and take notice. But the same theoretical shortcomings that led to the SWP's opportunism—a failure to understand the revolutionary potential of feminism, of which gay liberation is an integral part—still plagues many left groups.

A case in point is the International Socialist Organization (ISO). After decades of ignoring the LGBT movement, ISO hopped on the bandwagon in search of recruits when thousands of queers hit the streets in defense of same-sex marriage. At the same time, however, the ISO teaches its members that the autonomous gay and feminist movements are fundamentally "bourgeois" in nature and "divisive" to the working class struggle. They fail to see that what divides the U.S. working class is racism, sexism, homophobia and xenophobia!

Four decades of activism as a working-class mother, Asian American lesbian and daughter of immigrants has taught me that it is precisely us—the workers—who face double and triple forms of oppression, and it is our several civil rights movements that have rekindled the labor movement. And it is *we* who will be the catalysts for revolutionary change.

Lesbians and Gays of Color

In the fall of 1969, because of the Third World Student Strikes the year before, I got my first teaching job in the Educational Opportunity Program at San Francisco State University. Because we found ourselves teaching students of color who never dreamed they would find themselves on a college campus, our orientation was toward race liberation first. My environment overflowed with Maoism and "Marxist-Leninism"—sexist and homophobic—which was part of the legacy from the Student Strikes.

I came out as a lesbian in the early 1960s. But I didn't claim that identity openly—or within myself as a vital part of who I was—because I feared ostracism from my family, my community, the Catholic Church and society at large. (Thankfully, my daughter didn't have to come out as I did, moving toward wholeness bit by bit.) So being a proud Asian American came first. Then, in the early 1970s, came feminism. I ran into the Freedom Socialist Party and Radical Women, two Trotskyist feminist organizations (founded in 1967). There I found a revolutionary program that saw the most oppressed—people of color, women and gays—as central to the coming revolution. They said lesbians and gays of color were going to lead the revolution! And this was before Stonewall! Actually, it was they who pointed out the international significance of the Stonewall Rebellion to me.

It was also in the mid-1970s that the writings of Audre Lorde and the Combahee River Collective gave me a sense of what it meant to be different, an outlaw. And to take extraordinary pride in being all things at once: a lesbian of color, a multi-issue anticapitalist and an advocate for revolution that had to be feminist and antiracist.

For many lesbians and gays of color, autonomous organizing, as a temporary tactic, helped them to build their identities, define their issues and become confident of their leadership. For example, besides the Black lesbian feminist Combahee River Collective (Boston), there were the National Coalition of Black Gays (NCBG), Unidos (in California), and the Gay Latino Alliance in San Francisco—organizations that drew inspiration from lesbian/gay organizations around the Latino world.

In October 1979, the NCBG organized the first National Third World Lesbian and Gay Conference in Washington, D.C. More than 450 lesbians and gays of color convened and called for a mobilization to "end all social, economic, judicial and legal oppression against us." They then led the 100,000-strong National Lesbian and Gay March on Washington, imparting to it the vibrancy of internationalism and militancy.

Unlike moderate gay leaders, lesbians and gays of color understand that more than sexual orientation is at stake in their struggle. Reproductive rights, employment equality, police violence and the right to boycott, organize unions and strike, are gay issues, just as gay freedom is a working-class issue. Lesbians/writers/activists of color like Pat Parker, Audre Lorde, Barbara Smith, Cherríe Moraga, Gloria Anzaldúa, Chrystos, Kitty Tsui and Willyce Kim began publishing works that made us proud, and they gave young lesbians of color affirmations of themselves and their responsibilities. As Audre said, "We are not responsible for our oppression. We *are* responsible for our liberation!"

In 1979, a sisterhood developed with the coming together of the anthology *This Bridge Called My Back: Writings by Radical Women of Color*, edited by Cherríe and Gloria. The majority of contributors were lesbians or transgenders. And we *were* radicals, although from a diverse spectrum; we demanded root change based on our triple oppressions. That was a beautiful and inspiring time to get the support to write as women of color who were silenced until that moment.

I joined Radical Women and the Freedom Socialist Party just before comrades went to the March on Washington in 1979. In 1981, I spoke at the San Francisco Lesbian and Gay Pride Celebration, whose theme that year was "On the Front Line of Freedom."

That summer I was secretly demoted at UC Berkeley, and a year later I was fired because I was out as a radical lesbian and a staunch supporter of student democracy. Through the help of my organizations, we built a multi-issue defense committee, and because I had the full support of my union, the American Federation of Teachers, I was able to beat UC three times: in 1983, 1984 and 1989. We charged UC with violations of my free speech rights and discrimination based on race, sex, sexuality and political ideology. In 1984, UC offered an out-of-court settlement because a faculty member was willing to testify that my boss had said, "It is inappropriate for a lesbian to represent Asian American Studies."

I was fired for the same reasons in 1997 from Women Studies (back at San Francisco State again) because a few of us wanted to maintain community involvement, student democracy, and lesbian-focused undergraduate classes. Del Martin and Phyllis Lyon publicly went to bat for me. Gays and lesbians, transgendered folks and transvestites have always been the most supportive of me.

Back to the Future

The 1980s initiated the years of the AIDS epidemic, Reagan's "Family Protection Act," and the destruction of social and health services funding. The AIDS crisis galvanized the gay movement because at the time, AIDS was a death sentence and there was nothing to lose. ACT UP (AIDS Coalition to Unleash Power) became a nationally known organization committed to direct action.

My own experience in ACT UP showed me that although its militancy helped the coalition gain respect, there was no political program to bolster ongoing action. ACT UP's attitude toward leadership came directly from the New Left: If you attended the most meetings and spoke out, you were a leader. Such leadership was generally antiradical, and they made decisions based on consensus—the tyranny of the minority. But I loved the passion and even heroism of it. ACT UP's achievement was to educate the general public about AIDS as a *medical* condition—instead of a condemnation by god for being gay—and they succeeded in demands for funding for research and medical services.

ACT UP's opposite were the single-issue civil rights activists who held candlelight vigils for AIDS victims instead of militant protests.

Today, although we have made huge progress, the Queer movement is fragmented. We are at an urgent period similar to that which preceded Stonewall in 1969. But where 1969 called for a riot, 2008 calls for revolution. Where 1960s discrimination based on race, sex, sexuality and class became so oppressive that rebellion was the only answer, today's climate demands much, much more. Now, it's life or death for the majority of people. We are living in a deepening, worldwide, capitalist political and economic crisis: runaway oil prices and inflation; soaring unemployment and poverty; cuts in health care, pensions and social services; the debacle of the Iraq and Afghanistan wars; the brutal occupation of Palestine; and a growing environmental catastrophe. How must the future look to you—queers on youth's side of life's spectrum?

No doubt, there are some great things happening: dykes in the service industries are organizing LGBT caucuses in the unions, lesbians and gays of color are leading the fight against AIDS in their communities, and young gender-benders are defending gay/straight alliances in their schools, joining immigrant rights marches and blockading arms shipments to stop the war.

California and Massachusetts have legalized gay marriage (only 48 more states to go!). And as long as there are murders of trans youths of color, like teens Gwen Araujo (2002) and Lawrence King (2008), we are far from free. Transgenders are the most reviled in the Queer movement; they are openly ridiculed and murdered. It is they, then, who have the greatest potential to lead the movement for radical social change. We must have a broader, more encompassing agenda.

We need to build an explicitly Queer Socialist Movement that is antiracist, feminist, and international. We can no longer afford to have our militancy, anger, and commitment to freedom absorbed into the Democratic Party, nonprofits, or organizations focused on social and professional networking.

Queers are key to socialism. The persecution of lesbians and gays is an extension and intensification of the oppression of all women in a class society, and that is why Queer liberation is integral to the struggle for socialist revolution. We're not fighting for just sexual freedom alone, but to end the economic, political and social oppression that characterizes our lives in capitalist society.

Forty years of gay resistance since Stonewall teaches us some very important lessons:

1. The growth of gay resistance since 1969 has always coincided with movements of women, workers and radicals. And whenever the gay movement was weakened, so were the other movements—and by a right-wing and state apparatus that was multi-issue;

2. Attacks on the movements always intensify under economic chaos and right-wing reaction. These are the times in which we now live;

3. Queers of color demand more than gay rights or gay marriage. Their agenda is much broader and more inclusive;

4. Women's right to an abortion and queer rights are the focus of right-wing attacks because they represent, on the most fundamental level, people's right to control their bodies and sexuality;

5. When we can see the real interpenetration of sexual oppression with class exploitation, then we will be able to intervene in the Queer movement and lead it to revolutionary action;

6. Gay liberation cannot fully be won short of international socialism, and international socialism will not be won without the liberation of queers. Our goal is to create an egalitarian socialist democracy and a truly human culture.

The Stonewall Rebellion put us on a trajectory that was radical, fully inclusive of all who make up the Queer movement, and it was led by the most disenfranchised among us. Now it is up to you and other queer youth to carry that rebellion into freedom.

My dear Anh, there will be no revolution without you. And when the reality of the conditions of your lives is understood in the context of the necessity for change at the very root of the problem, you will fight for yourself and in the process, fight for everybody. I will be there for sure, standing shoulder to shoulder with you. I look forward to your response!

Peace and solidarity,
Merle

Merle Woo is the lesbian daughter of a Chinese immigrant father and an orphaned Korean mother. She is a retired lecturer (after 34 years) in Women and Asian American Studies, fired from both UC Berkeley and San Francisco State University because she is a socialist feminist lesbian and staunch supporter of student democracy. Merle is a longtime leader in the Freedom Socialist Party and Radical Women, a published writer and poet, a breast cancer survivor and the mother of two great adults, Emily and Paul; she has two grandboys and two grandcats.

GAY LIBERATION MEDIA

Like all social change movements in the early '70s, gay liberation spread its message by publishing its own newsletters, newspapers and magazines. The mainstream press didn't cover news of
the LGBT community, except for bar raids. (They actually ran the
names and address of the men arrested.) To break the silence that
surrounded our lives and to offer a different perspective from the
one presented in the pre-Stonewall homophile publications, such
as *The Ladder* (a lesbian magazine) and *One* (gay male), gay liberation groups created their own media. Hundreds of publications
sprang up in those early years of gay liberation.

ComeOut!

ComeOut! was the newspaper of New York's Gay Liberation Front.
According to Martha Shelley, a member of GLF, the first issue was
dated November 1969 and the last appeared in winter of 1972.
Members of the newspaper collective wrote the copy, took the
photographs, typeset, did pasteup and layout, and distributed
the paper in the streets of New York. Although only eight issues
were published, they included lively art that reflected the intensity
of the time; coverage of demonstrations, conferences and other
newsworthy events; and some of the movement's groundbreaking theoretical articles. The paper's radical politics were laid out in
the first issue: "We will not be gay bourgeoisie, searching for the
sterile 'American dream' of the ivy-covered cottage and the good
corporation job, but neither will we tolerate the exclusion of homosexuals from any area of American life."

Gay Sunshine

Started by the Berkeley GLF in August 1970, *Gay Sunshine* was
later published by GLF member Winston Leyland until 1981. As
Leyland writes in his introduction to *Orgasms of Light: The Gay*

Sunshine Anthology, "The title of the paper reflects in part the fact that 'sunshine' was a counter culture slang word for acid (LSD), as well as the general implications of light: a new gay dawn." The first few issues of the publication were mainly geared toward the Bay Area's gay liberation movement. After Leyland assumed the role of publisher, *Gay Sunshine* started to feature more literary content, including interviews with many literary giants of the day, among them Allen Ginsberg, Tennessee Williams, Gore Vidal, Jean Genet, William Burroughs, Christopher Isherwood and John Giorno. It also ran poetry from the famous and not-so-famous alike, including Harold Norse, Federico García Lorca, John Wieners, Pier Paolo Pasolini and Xavier Villaurrutia. It published translated works from Italy, Chile, Mexico, Peru, Israel, Japan and the Soviet Union as well as Arab poets from the medieval classical period.

Fag Rag

This Boston-based newspaper was once denounced by Manchester New Hampshire *Union* Publisher William Loeb as "one of the most loathsome publications in the English language." We guess he wasn't impressed with some of *Fag Rag*'s front-page articles like "Cocksucking as an act of revolution" by Charlie Shively, one of the founders of the publication. The collective that ran the publication remained staunchly gay liberationist, even as the gay movement of the mid to late '70s became more Reformist. In its June/July 1976 double issue, the collective penned its "Second five-year plan," intended to keep alive the "butterflies of '69" also known as "that spirit of rage, revolt and resistance that began on Christopher Street." The plan denounced religion ("more than an opiate, it is an absolute poison"), psychiatry ("no one has ever shown that a person can not help him or herself just as well without psycho-psychiatric intervention"), academia ("a bastion of middle-class values"), law reform and electoral politics ("dead-end streets"), breeding ("people are valuable in themselves for themselves, and not because they contain semen or eggs"), and wanting a piece of the pie ("the pie is rotten"). It folded in the 1980s.

Body Politic

Referred to by the Toronto media as "child-rapers," this gay liberation publication started in 1971 and published its last issue in 1987.

It was produced by a collective that eventually formed its own publishing house, Pink Triangle Press. *Body Politic* often ran provocative material that got it in trouble with the law. A May 1975 issue with a cartoon of two men having oral sex became the target of the Morality Squad of the Toronto Police Department, which ordered it taken off the newsstands. On December 30, 1977, the offices of *Body Politic* were raided and the collective charged with distributing obscene material because of an article called "Men Loving Boys Loving Men." The paper was acquitted after a five-year battle. In 1982, the collective was charged with publishing obscene material for an article on "fistfucking." Again, the collective was deemed not guilty as charged. The Body Politic folded in 1987.

Boston Gay Community News (GCN)

The country's first radical gay weekly, *GCN* was founded in 1973 in Boston and published regularly until 1992, then off and on until about 1999. For many years, *GCN* was the voice of the queer radical left. It also had strong lesbian/feminist content. Former editor Amy Hoffman, in *An Army of Ex-Lovers: My Life at the Gay Community News*, described the paper's goals as political: "*GCN*'s mission was explicitly activist—we wanted to encourage readers to come out of the closet and become involved in the movement and also to provide a forum where ideas and actions could be proposed and debated. . . . We supported the most radical expressions of the gay liberation movement. We believed in upsetting the social order and in creating alternatives to traditional gender roles, definitions of sexuality, and hierarchical power structures of all kinds."

The Radical Queen

One of the country's first transgender magazines, *The Radical Queen* promoted the freedom to choose one's gender and not be bound by society's strict masculine/feminine dichotomy. Published by the Radicalqueen collective in Philadelphia, the magazine featured writings by collective members as well as a pagan column and the castration block (reserved for particularly piggy male chauvinists such as the actor who once said his wife was his best possession). It started in 1973 and folded in 1976.

Sinister Wisdom

The country's oldest surviving lesbian literary and art journal, it began publishing in 1976 and continues through the present. It describes itself as a "multicultural, multi-class, female-born lesbian space." Its former editors have included renowned writers Adrienne Rich (81–83), Melanie Kaye/Kantrowitz (83–87), Elana Dykewomon (87–94) and Akiba Onada-Sikwoia (95–97). It describes its mission as publishing "work that reflects the diversity of our experiences: as Lesbians of color, ethnic Lesbians, Jewish, Arab, old, young, working class, poverty class, disabled, and fat Lesbians."

Off Our Backs

A radical national women's newspaper that features strong lesbian content, *Off Our Backs* has been publishing since 1970. In its first issue, it described its purpose: "We must strive to get off our backs, and with the help of our sisters to oppose and destroy that system which fortifies the supremacy of men while exploiting the mass for the profit of the few." In the early years, *Off Our Backs* reprinted the CLIT (Collective Lesbian International Terrorist) papers, a collection of radical commentaries on lesbian oppression by several activists, including Argentina-born Maricla Moyano; a long investigative piece on women in Cuba; and communiqués from the Weather Underground, a radical antiwar group. After one of the latter communiqués was published, *Off Our Backs* found its offices broken into and files ransacked. No money was taken. It was a sign of the times. Despite a few hard times in the past four decades when the paper seemed doomed to extinction, it continues publishing today.

GLOSSARY OF TERMS

Note from the editor: We recognize that this glossary isn't complete in its list of terms or even in some of its definitions. We hope it serves as an aid for those new to the vocabulary of gay liberation.

Angels of Light: Hippie gay drag theater troupe; split-off from the Cockettes.

APA: American Psychiatric Association, which, as a result of gay activist pressure, in 1973 dropped homosexuality from its list of diseases.

Aversion Therapy: A "cure" for homosexuality that involved attaching electrodes to a man's genitals and zapping him with electricity when he became aroused by images of male nudity, with the idea that this would lead to behavior modification (i.e., making him straight). Practiced by psychiatrists until the mid to late '70s.

BAGL (pronounced "bagel"): Bay Area Gay Liberation, a group formed in San Francisco in 1975.

Blacklight: Black lesbian and gay periodical, published in Washington, D.C., 1979–86. Continues to publish online.

Black Panthers: Radical African American group that promoted self-empowerment for blacks. It was formed in 1966 in Oakland, California.

Body Politic: Canadian gay liberation newspaper, 1971–87.

Butch and femme: Masculine and feminine roles played in a gay or lesbian relationship. These were popular in the days before Stonewall and were rejected by gay liberation, which saw them as an imitation of heterosexual couplings.

Closeted (or "in the closet"): Not public about one's homosexuality; hiding the fact that one is queer from family, friends, coworkers.

Cockettes: A troupe of outrageous hippie drag queens who did Busby Berkeley–style musicals in San Francisco from 1969 to 1972.

Come out (v.): Act of being public about being queer

ComeOut! **(magazine)**: Gay Liberation Front newspaper published in New York 1969–72.

Compton's Cafeteria: San Francisco site of a pre-Stonewall riot between drag queens and police.

Consciousness-raising: A process of opening one's mind to new ideas or of broadening one's knowledge on a certain topic, usually involving discussion groups and the relating of personal experiences to understand a societal practice. Used by gay liberation organizations to help those new to their groups explore topics such as sex roles, cruising, class, racism, sexism and so on. First used by women's groups.

Cruising; to cruise; cruisy: Related to the act of checking out potential partners in order to pick them up for sex. Often done in parks, in bars, on certain streets or at sections of the beach.

DOB: Daughters of Bilitis, a pre-Stonewall national lesbian organization that started in the '50s and lasted until the early '70s.

Drag: Wearing clothing other than what is considered appropriate for one's gender. Various forms of drag were identified in the gay liberation movement, including radical drag, genderfuck and traditional drag. Some in the movement felt that all clothing was drag, i.e., a costume that we wear to show our gender or position in life (businessman, construction worker, housewife and so on).

Drag queen: A man who enjoys dressing in what are usually considered traditional women's clothes.

DYKETACTICS!: A Philadelphia-based lesbian/feminist separatist organization.

Effeminists: Gay men who supported the women's movement and saw male chauvinism and male domination as the roots of gay male oppression.

Fag Rag: Gay male newspaper published in Boston from 1971 to 1987.

Gay Raiders: A radical Philadelphia group that conducted zaps against media outlets for their refusal to cover gay news stories. See "zaps."

Fop: Archaic derogatory word (17th century) for a man who is overly concerned with clothing and appearance, also often an effeminate man.

Gay Sunshine: Literary gay male newspaper published in Berkeley, then San Francisco 1970–1982.

GCN; Gay Community News: a national LGBT weekly that covered news and events from a progressive queer perspective. Published in Boston.

Genderfuck: Dressing in a combination of the clothing of both sexes in order to make a political statement, e.g., a man in beard and evening gown, army boots and makeup.

GLF: Gay Liberation Front, the first gay liberation group formed in New York (and later many other cities) after the Stonewall Riots.

HAL: Homophile Action League, a pre-Stonewall group that included men and women.

Harry Hay: Founder in 1949 of the Mattachine Society, the first gay male organization in the United States.

Homophile: Word used by pre-Stonewall gay groups to replace homosexual.

LSD: Popular hallucinogenic drug of the counterculture.

Del Martin and Phyllis Lyon: Pioneering lesbian activists of the '50s and '60s who founded the Daughters of Bilitis.

Neshineau: Rough guy, usually straight, who picks up gay men or drag queens and beats them up or threatens them. A term primarily used on the East Coast, probably originating in Philadelphia.

Off Our Backs: A radical women's newspaper from Washington, D.C., that has been published since 1970.

Out of the closet: Publicly affirming one's identity as an LGBT person.

Radical drag: See Genderfuck.

Radicalesbians: A split-off of GLF that became a radical organization for lesbians in New York and Philadelphia in 1970.

Radicalqueens: A radical organization for transvestites, transsexuals, drag queens and others, formed in Philadelphia in 1972.

Revolutionary People's Convention: Gathering organized by the Black Panthers in November 1970 for the purpose of writing "a new constitution that will guarantee and deliver to every American citizen the inviolable human right to life, liberty, and the pursuit of happiness!"

SDS: Students for a Democratic Society, student-led antiwar organization that started in 1962 and officially folded in 1969, though campus chapters continued for a couple more years.

Separatist: A lesbian who believed in living apart from all men, even gay men, and concentrating her time and energy building women's community and culture.

Sinister Wisdom: The country's oldest lesbian literary and arts journal.

ACKNOWLEDGMENTS

Grateful acknowledgment is made to the publications in which these works have previously appeared:

Excerpt from "Where Will You Be?" from *Movement in Black* by Pat Parker, published by Crossing Press, 1978

"A Letter from Huey Newton to the Revolutionary Brothers and Sisters about the Women's Liberation and Gay Liberation Movements" from *To Die for the People* (City Lights, 2009) reprinted by permission of the Huey Newton Foundation.

"Lessons from the ENDA Mess" by Doug Ireland originally appeared in *Gay City News* in 2008.

"Militant Foreshadowings" from *Transgender History* by Susan Stryker, reprinted by permission of Seal Press, a member of Perseus Book Group.

"Making History" by Sidney Brinkley was originally published in *Blacklight*, vol. 4, #4, in 1983.

"The Gay Community in Crisis" by Doug Kilhefner was originally published in the Fall 2008 issue of *White Crane* and can be found online at www.gaywisdom.org.

STAR: Street Transvestite Action Revolutionaries, a group formed in 1969 in New York by Stonewall veterans Sylvia Rivera and Marsha Johnson to help poor and homeless queens on the streets of New York.

Stonewall Inn: Name of the West Village bar where a riot erupted in June 1969 between police and patrons that sparked the gay liberation movement.

Third World Gay Revolution: Organization founded by Latinos and Blacks as a result of racism inside the early gay liberation movement.

Wimmin, womyn, womin: Variations of spelling of "woman" to take the "man" and "men" out of the word. Used by lesbians and feminists in the early '70s.

Young Lords: A Puerto Rican activist organization (similar to the Black Panthers) started in 1968 in Chicago and spreading out to several other cities, including New York and Philadelphia.

Zap: Sudden picket, protest or invasion of any space (including offices, newsrooms and public spaces), without permission or forewarning. The purpose was to catch the target off guard and get attention for the movement's cause.

gender is the caste system by which male— DOMINATED $OCIETY designates Women & effeminates as inferior!

You are a tr tacky rabb

than Y

The back cover of the second Radical Queen magazine, 1974.